Celebrity, Inc.

Celebrity, Inc.

How Famous People Make Money

Jo Piazza

OPEN ROAD

INTEGRATED MEDIA

NEW YORK

To
John & Tracey
and
George & Joanna

Contents

Foreword by Bonnie Fuller — PAGE 9

Introduction — PAGE 13

1

#babies Shiloh Jolie-Pitt: The Magazine Market and
the Bull Run for Celebrity Baby Pictures
A blind auction can exploit supply shifts in a rapidly changing industry.
PAGE 21

2

#realityTV Spencer Pratt: When Fame-Whoring Became a Business
*As the reality TV business model matured, savvy upstarts learned how to forge multiple
income streams while navigating the vagaries of supply and fickle consumer demand.*
PAGE 43

3

#diets Valerie Bertinelli: Turning Pounds into Dollars
*Celebrity endorsers of weight-loss companies and products enjoy
the externalities of the marketplace for fat.*
PAGE 60

4

#littlegoldmen Oscar: What's an Academy Award Worth?
In Hollywood, investing in an Oscar win is high risk, high reward.
PAGE 71

5

#scandals Kim Kardashian Versus Paris Hilton:
Innovation in the Celebutante Market
*Executed with care and overseen by the right management team,
the second-mover advantage can be worth many millions.*
PAGE 91

6

#perfume Tim McGraw: Using Fragrance to Maximize
Customer Lifetime Value (CLV)
*To maximize CLV, a celebrity needs the right distribution channels
and forward-looking customer analysis for licensing deals.*
PAGE 109

7

#feuds 50 Cent: The Evolution of the Hip-Hop Beef

Competition, real or manufactured, can benefit both entrepreneurs and parent companies.
But a new generation of consumers makes friendlier alternatives more profitable.

PAGE 122

8

#tweets Ashton Kutcher: The Evolution of the Digital Celebrity

Consumer products companies were skeptical of online advertising until celebrity muscle
made social networks safe for brands and the Internet profitable for Hollywood.

PAGE 141

9

#singingsolo Taylor Hicks: Building a Career After *American Idol*

Sometimes a company's desire to cull unprofitable assets
is just what that unprofitable asset needs.

PAGE 160

10

#bleedinghearts David Arquette and Celebrity–Charity Synergy:
Fame Will Feed the Poor

Celebrities bolster a charity's visibility. Charities lend celebrities
a reputation for empathy. Win-win?

PAGE 176

11

#consistency Lindsay Lohan and Charlie Sheen:
The Importance of Brand Consistency

Brand consistency in the face of a crisis is essential for maintaining
customer loyalty and industry support.

PAGE 192

12

#beingdead Michael Jackson and Elvis Presley: The Afterlife of Fame

The postmortem monetization of celebrity images is a perfect example
of entrepreneurial endeavor changing laws and industry practice—
and generating millions—within one generation.

PAGE 210

Foreword by Bonnie Fuller

In the past ten years I have helmed both *Us Weekly* and *Star* magazines as they transitioned into leaders in the celebrity news market. Today I am the editor in chief and president of the celebrity news website HollywoodLife.com, trying to pioneer how celebrities are covered on the constantly changing landscape of the Internet.

The dirty little secret I have learned over the course of my career is that everyone, no matter how educated, rich, or cultured, wants to know something about the lives of famous people. I could enter almost any dinner party in the world and someone will ask me what's going on with Lindsay Lohan, Kim Kardashian, Britney Spears, Mel Gibson, or whichever celebrity is currently squirming under the spotlight. Why? Because celebrities are a shared experience. They're the universal water cooler topic. No one is entirely immune to their charms, and if anyone says they are, they're hiding a *People* magazine in their briefcase.

If there were an MBA that specialized in celebrity, this book would be its CliffsNotes. The business behind being famous is a genuinely fun game. Once you know the rules, you won't be able to read Ashton Kutcher's tweets the same way ever again.

In my time covering the sometimes weird and yet wonderful world of celebrity culture, I have watched as the market for celebrities has exploded in a myriad of ways. There are so many more celebrities today than there were when I first took over as the editor in chief of *Us Weekly* in 2002. There are still actors and actresses and musical artists and sports stars. But today there are oodles of reality stars, mistresses, friends of mistresses, socialites, and fashion designers. Even politicians have become celebrities in their own right: Is Sarah Palin a celebrity or a politician? Most days I'd say both.

There is also more of a market for the buying and selling of celebrities today. These days the real money is made through endorsement, licensing, and partnership deals.

And finally, the media marketplace that covers the rich and famous has grown by leaps and bounds. Where there used to be just *People* and *Entertainment Tonight*, there are now half a dozen celebrity newsweeklies, ten different entertainment news shows, and thousands of celebrity websites.

Celebrity was always big business, but now it's grown into a conglomerate that has its hands in nearly all aspects of consumer culture. Celebrities are the most powerful lobbying group in America today. Celebrities today are supersized—they're bigger, faster, and louder. They have to be to compete with the hundreds of celebs-in-training waiting in the wings.

Jo Piazza once asked me why I thought the average American found celebrities so compelling. I think it's because we start to relate to them like they're our friends. I think we look up to them and look down on them and occasionally judge them, but at the end of the day we feel we know them. After spending years as a gossip columnist and an entertainment journalist, Jo has become fascinated with them and with our own fascination with them. She has consistently dug deeper, to try to figure out why they behave the way they do and what the consequences of their behavior will be. An economist at heart, Jo has accomplished this by breaking down the industrialization of fame in the age of celebrity.

That's the point of this book. It puts celebrities in context, but it also puts the consumer of those celebrities in context.

A lot of books written about the entertainment industry and celebrity culture make us feel bad or feel stupid for enjoying celebrities as much as we do. This book doesn't do that. Jo has been a careful and at times critical watcher and chronicler of celebrities for the past ten years, yet she remains just as captivated by them as the average reader of *Star* magazine or HollywoodLife.com. No one should feel bad about enjoying pop culture, but they should understand how and why it is being marketed to them. *Celebrity, Inc.* gives the reader the tools to do exactly that.

— Bonnie Fuller

Introduction

In the summer of 2008, I bet a friend who worked in finance that Britney Spears, the pop star then teetering on the brink of insanity, would make a comeback within a year. My friend laughed. He told me that Lehman Brothers, the global financial firm then on the verge of bankruptcy, had a better chance of clawing its way back from the brink. Lehman, my friend argued, was too big to fail, and Britney Spears had nowhere to go but down.

We all know how this story goes. By the end of the year, Lehman had experienced the biggest collapse the banking industry had ever seen, and Ms. Spears had reinvigorated her brand. It was Britney Spears who was too big to fail. Admittedly, as an entertainment journalist and gossip columnist I had insider information. That didn't make me feel bad about taking his hundred dollars.

I was intimately acquainted with the Spears meltdowns of 2007 and 2008. It had been a busy twelve months of pantyless paparazzi photos, puking on her entourage, and bad parenting. Things really started heating up in early January 2008, when Spears locked herself in her Hollywood Hills home, holding her two young sons hostage.

While Britney was locked in her walk-in closet, I was flying back from Des Moines, Iowa, where I had been sent to report on the Iowa caucus, and where the biggest star had been Chuck Norris, karate-chopping for a scrum of Republican donors at a diner in west Des Moines. When I landed to catch my connection in Chicago, I had no fewer than four desperate voice mails from my editors at the *New York Daily News*. "Britney is trying to kill herself!" "Britney might kill the kids!" "Why aren't you calling us back?"

"We need you to get to L.A.," my editor barked at me after I was safely allowed to boot up my cell phone.

"What do you want me to do out there?"

"You'll figure it out. Just go."

Thus began my own up-close-and-personal involvement with Spears, and a continual dance over that fine line between journalist and paparazzo to find new ways to invade her privacy. It was six months of ups and downs, of rehab and hospitalizations, of court hearings and conservatorships.

But by the fall, something miraculous had happened. Somehow Spears had ceased to be crazy, and industry insiders began flipping her script. Britney was releasing a new single, Britney had lost weight, Britney had a new album, Britney was no longer a train wreck. She was making a comeback. She had brand value again. And that's what inspired this book.

Months later, I found myself back in New York at Britney's birthday party at Tenjune nightclub. It was an over-the-top, circus-themed bash at one of those venues that charge eight hundred dollars for the right to consume a forty-dollar bottle of vodka while seated at a table. The party was not a celebration for Britney. The woman couldn't have looked more miserable, propped up in a corner, sipping something nonalcoholic and inoffensive.

The celebration was for the team of managers, agents, publicists, and record producers who had crafted a strategy to rebuild the Spears brand, salvage her tarnished image, and start making money from Spears again. They high-fived one another a lot throughout the evening.

That's when I really started asking questions about branding, value, and wealth creation in Hollywood. I soon came to realize this was an industry just like any other, except that instead of making cars, they manufacture bottle-blonde pop stars. Britney Spears was just a product.

One of *Us Weekly* magazine's most popular sections is a photo spread entitled "Celebrities: They're Just Like Us." In it, famous people are featured doing quotidian tasks: grocery shopping, taking their kids to the park, eating a burger, or working out.

The rest of the entertainment magazine is devoted to telling us that celebrities are, in fact, nothing like us. They're much better looking, thinner, more expensively attired, and of course, richer. There is even a high likelihood that they have been paid for the pictures in which they appear to be behaving just like you or me.

When it comes to making money, celebrities are deeply abnormal. Their enormous salaries make them outliers in the American economy, on a pay grade above most chief executive officers, surgeons, and lawyers— the professions that typically come to mind when we think of the wealthy.

Some celebrities have day jobs. They act, they sing, they throw a ball. Sometimes cameras just follow them around and film them going to clubs and fighting with their boyfriends, but today even that is considered a job. Those activities earn them a paycheck. But in addition to that income stream, celebrities can make money from numerous other things that regular people typically *spend* money on, be it having babies or supporting a charity, tweeting or losing weight. The lucky ones even cash in on the afterlife. Plenty of celebrities will make more dead than you will ever make alive.

How much money celebrities are able to negotiate for these activities depends on the consumer. Make no mistake: Celebrities are commodities bought and sold by their fans. Sometimes the celebrity is the direct object of consumption, as in the case of a concert ticket purchase. Sometimes a celebrity creates the object of consumption, such as an album or a movie. Sometimes celebrities just lend their names to an item of consumption, like a fragrance or a clothing line.

As with any commodity, a celebrity's value is determined in the marketplace by the consumer. This is what I mean when I say *brand value* later on in these pages. A brand is all of that intangible stuff that makes consumers want a commodity. A celebrity's price depends on how the consumer views their brand.

After a decade spent working as a celebrity journalist and gossip columnist, I began to ask questions about the business behind celebrity. Why *do* they get paid so much more than regular people to do a job that doesn't look very difficult and seems to afford them the same amount of leisure time as most retirees? In this book I refer to the players in the fame game as the Hollywood Industrial Complex—an interconnected web of businesses, all working to maximize the value of the industry as a whole. It includes agents, managers, and publicists, each in their own way creating new business models and revenue streams for the complex's front line— the celebrities themselves. These individuals are constantly working to monetize everything in a celebrity's life.

Take the question of whether Celebrity X should marry Celebrity Y. That question triggers a series of negotiations between X's and Y's respective teams. How can the value of a marriage be maximized? Will it help or hurt X and Y?

The same holds true for these questions: Should X adopt a baby from Africa or Asia? Which market buys more movie tickets/music downloads? Should Y create a celebrity fragrance? Should X cheat on Y with Z? What is Z's brand value? It's the algebra of agent speak. The correct answer is always the one that maximizes a celebrity's brand value.

The market for fame, like the stock market, is rational over time, killing off brands that don't translate into long-term profitability. There is a reason Lindsay Lohan hasn't made a movie in years. There is a reason that George Clooney, Tom Cruise, and Meryl Streep are consistently rewarded with high salaries. But, again like the stock market, the celebrity market is irrational in the short term, offering great gains to individuals who have little talent to back up a sudden surge in popularity. That explains the market for reality stars.

Never in the course of human history has the market for celebrities been as saturated as it is today. Have you ever wondered why Paris Hilton is famous? Or instead of Paris Hilton, insert the reality star of the moment: Kim Kardashian, Kate Gosselin, Spencer Pratt, Heidi Montag, the entire casts of *Jersey Shore* and *Teen Mom*. The short answer is that the market had to create these celebrities from all of the leftover stuff in Hollywood—all of the stuff that didn't have real talent, that didn't have a real job with a movie studio, a recording company, a sports team, or on television—just to meet the insatiable consumer demand.

It is hard to overestimate the role of the Internet and the 24/7 news cycle that emerged in the last decade, or the intense expansion of celebrity media, first in the form of glossy weekly magazines and then celebrity websites. A new species of celebrity evolved: the person who is famous for being famous. Suddenly the life cycle of fame went from fifteen minutes to fifteen seconds, and the main barrier to entry to the once-exclusive club of the "famous"—extraordinary talent, looks, or blue blood—all but evaporated.

The Hollywood Industrial Complex, more so than many other industries, is constantly evolving and innovating, looking for the next best (read: most lucrative) thing. Any celebrities who think they can coast on past achievements are deluded. Celebrities who were big on MySpace were usurped by those who were big on Twitter. Sarah Ferguson pioneered the business model for getting paid to lose weight, but Valerie Bertinelli did it better. Elvis Presley was the gold standard for making money as a dead celebrity for years, then along came Michael Jackson to extract even more value from death. Frantic demand for newness causes reality stars to be replaced on a near daily basis.

In the following pages, celebrities are dissected in the way a case study would dissect any consumer brand or public company. Their value is analyzed, their branding strategies broken down, and their management models put under a microscope.

No celebrity operates in a bubble. When the actors Brad Pitt and Angelina Jolie consummated their relationship, they created what many celebrity watchers refer to as "the perfect celebrity news story," and they generated value for the entire entertainment industry. The celebrity news magazine industry has profited off the backs of Pitt and Jolie since 2005. A cover story about Brad and Angelina outsells one featuring nearly every other celebrity by at least 25 percent. Their first movie together, *Mr. &*

Mrs. Smith, generated nearly half a billion dollars at the box office. The effect of an affair on movie sales hadn't been so pronounced since 1963, when audiences flocked to see Richard Burton and Elizabeth Taylor in *Cleopatra*. Back in 1963, Liz and Dick were an anomaly, a scandalous couple that was able to turn headlines into millions of dollars. Today Pitt and Jolie are just one celebrity pair out of hundreds who have gotten wise to the fact that coupling properly translates into brand equity.

The process of fame hunting has never been as pervasive as it is now. There is a subset of people willing to do anything to be famous. For instance, of the sixteen mistresses alleged to have been involved in the downfall of professional golfer Tiger Woods in 2010, four appeared in *Vanity Fair* magazine, three competed on Howard Stern's radio show for the crown of Miss Mistress and a prize of $100,000, one wrote a tell-all book, one starred in a pornographic movie parodying her time with the golfer, and one became a correspondent for the entertainment news show *Extra*. Their investment was just their dignity, and the payoff was substantial.

The entire entertainment industry is undergoing its biggest revolution in the modern age. This book aims to pull the curtain away from the celebrity machine. Celebrities tell us what to wear, how to smell, how to lose weight, what to listen to, what movies to watch, and how to vote. In doing this, a lot of people, from the celebs themselves to the wizards of the Hollywood Industrial Complex—the publicists, agents, managers, licensing agents, and lawyers—all make a lot of money. This book tries to follow that money.

With the rebirth of the entertainment industry in a digital age, the celebrity market has no choice but to evolve. There are more opportunities than ever for an individual to create value in this fast-paced marketplace. There is money to be made on Twitter and in viral videos, from the sale of baby pictures and by losing weight, through fragrance sales and sex tapes. The folks who adapt to this brave new world are the ones who will survive.

The real fun of this book comes when you, the reader, bring your own expertise to the table. As consumers and watchers of celebrity, you have as good a perspective as anyone on how the Hollywood Industrial Complex works.

Here is where the armchair economist and the backseat paparazzo go out for a cocktail and agree to disagree. After a few martinis they may even decide to adopt an African baby together.

1

Shiloh Jolie-Pitt:
The Magazine Market and the Bull Run
for Celebrity Baby Pictures

Very little is precious in Hollywood. Even less is immune from the machinations of moneymaking. As the tabloid magazine market reached a tipping point and Internet gossip began to gain legs, the tiniest stars in Hollywood—celebrity babies—became the focus of multimillion-dollar bidding wars. Celebrity spawn became hot commodities, leading to the most expensive baby picture sale of all time.

Editors of celebrity weekly magazines would later say it was a little like a drug deal—the day they were led into a dark office and shown the first pictures of Shiloh Jolie-Pitt, premiere biological spawn of movie stars Brad Pitt and Angelina Jolie, and asked to place bids. The question posed to the editors was deceptively simple and impossible to answer with any confidence: How much were these photos worth?

It was the spring of 2006, but the perfect tabloid storm had begun twelve months earlier. Brad Pitt, two-time winner of *People* magazine's Sexiest Man Alive award, ditched wife Jennifer Aniston, America's sweetheart, for the sultry and slightly off-key Angelina Jolie. The daughter of actor Jon Voight and model Marcheline Bertrand, Jolie was the anti-Aniston. She had attended her first wedding, to British actor Jonny Lee Miller, in black rubber boots and a white T-shirt decorated with the groom's name written in her blood, while thousands of women across the United States were asking their hairdressers to give them layers like their favorite *Friend*'s. Jolie and Pitt met while filming *Mr. & Mrs. Smith*, and rumors of their on-set affair proved true when Aniston filed for divorce from Pitt in March of 2005. One month later, *Us Weekly* reportedly paid $500,000 for paparazzi pictures of Pitt and Jolie frolicking on a beach in Kenya with Jolie's young son Maddox.[1] In January 2006, Jolie announced that she was pregnant with Pitt's child, and everyone in the industry knew what that meant. The paychecks for pictures would only get bigger.

This was by far the most intriguing story of the modern celebrity journalist's career. It was the Liz Taylor, Eddie Fisher, and Debbie Reynolds love triangle of our time. Peter Grossman looked at his editor in chief, Janice Min, the moment the pregnancy was announced.

"This is it, we should just quit," he said.

Their counterparts at the newly launched American edition of British tabloid *OK!* magazine and at longtime celebrity stalwart *People* had similar thoughts. The birth of one of the most genetically advantaged children of all time was manna from heaven for celebrity magazines battling to stay relevant in a crowded magazine marketplace amid outside competition from the 24/7 cycle of television and Internet news.

That threat was real. Magazines' share of total ad spend was projected to decline to 10.7 percent by 2012, down from 14 percent in 2011. Their online ad spend was growing but not sufficiently to continue supporting international editorial staffs and outrageous photo budgets.[2] Online they had to compete with low-overhead, high-risk blogs like PerezHilton.com (launched in 2004) that titillated readers with nasty commentary, and also with online news organizations like TMZ.com that broke celebrity news around the clock with a team of seasoned journalists and sources ranging from paparazzi to police officers. Where Perez brought the bitchy, TMZ brought a sense of journalistic integrity to celebrity exploitation on the web. The magazines had no online niche.

While access to the biggest stars in Hollywood traditionally helped celebrity outlets maintain their bottom line, the battle in the war for twenty-first-century relevance was about to be fought over access to the littlest stars in Tinseltown—and it was fought with a checkbook. Celebrity babies were about to be worth millions. Shiloh Nouvel Jolie-Pitt was born via scheduled Caesarian section on May 27, 2006, heralding the start of a bull market in celebrity baby pictures, at the ideal time for her ambitious parents to capitalize on unprecedented competition in the tabloid journalism market.

A Brief History of the Celebrity Magazine Market

Since its founding in 1974 as a spin-off of the "People" pages of *Time* magazine, *People* magazine has been *the* household name in celebrity and entertainment news. Its editors have never been averse to paying to get the pictures they want. The magazine's founding editor, Dick Stolley, once bought Abraham Zapruder's film of the Kennedy assassination for Time, Inc. for $150,000. But as a magazine that covered Hollywood happenings, *People* built its name on cooperation with celebrities. It did not trade in gossip. Its stories were never salacious or mean. Perhaps it was too nice. *People* was so kind to celebrities it became a punch line. In the 1983 movie *The Big Chill*, actor Jeff Goldblum's character's vacuity is underscored by his job with the magazine.

People could laugh all the way to the bank, because for years it had a monopoly on the celebrity news market in glossy print. Every once in a while some ambitious magazine editor would get it into their head to launch a competitor, but he or she would eventually be dissuaded by the hefty entry fee—approximately $100 million in sunk costs—from trying to compete at *People*'s level.

That level meant an upstart magazine would need between sixty and a hundred people on editorial staff and stringers absolutely everywhere to report a story on a moment's notice. The office space alone would take up a floor of a building occupying an entire city block. It would cost between ten and fifteen million dollars for the newsstand real estate to live next to *People* magazine at checkout counters, and an additional fifty million dollars in market research and new hires.[3]

But *People*'s singular time in the marketplace would come to an end in 2000, when Wenner Media's *Us* magazine transformed from a movie industry trade rag into a celebrity weekly. According to former Wenner Media executive Kent Brownridge, the idea to go weekly was first floated at a boozy lunch meeting at tony Manhattan restaurant Le Bernardin between Brownridge and the magazine's advertisers.

"The client said, 'Have you guys ever thought about going weekly?' And I said, 'You guys are fucking nuts! We're losing two million dollars a year and you think we should go weekly?'" Brownridge told me. "But on the way to the office I thought maybe it could work. It was the timeliness factor of celebrity news that really mattered, and ten years ago you couldn't be much more timely than a weekly."

Brownridge says he suggested the idea to the magazine's publisher, Jann Wenner, who agreed that it was indeed nuts to try to enter *People* magazine's market. But before Brownridge could make it back to his office, Wenner phoned him to say that going weekly might be the last thing that could save *Us* from going under. Trouble with the plan began right away, when they couldn't find an investor. "Everyone thought we were fucking crazy," Brownridge said.

Initial evidence suggested they were. They appointed Terry McDonell, who would later become a successful editor in chief of *Sports Illustrated*, to the mag's helm.

McDonell's wheelhouse was more touchdowns and RBIs than red carpets and celebrity weddings. McDonell, Brownridge, and Wenner were three men in their fifties and sixties writing for women in their twenties and thirties. The product just wasn't right, and the consumer wasn't buying it. Wenner lost about $50 million in the magazine's first year. Then in February of 2002, they found their golden ticket in the form of *Glamour* magazine editor Bonnie Fuller, a Canadian-born magazine veteran who was a bit of an outsider and who knew what Americans outside the tristate bubble wanted to read. Despite Wenner and Brownridge's early misgivings, she was exactly what the magazine needed.

"With just three issues she blew the doors off," Brownridge said.

The paparazzi photo took on a new meaning under Fuller's reign. She turned the magazine into a celebrity photo album with titillating headlines meant to entice and engage the reader. *Us Weekly* differentiated itself from *People* by removing the fawning obsequiousness and providing intimate details of celebrities' lives as if they were personal friends. Late July of 2002 marked Fuller's first big success, when *Us Weekly* scooped other gossip outlets with Angelina Jolie's exclusive confession of "Why I Left Billy Bob." That issue sold more than 800,000 copies. During the second half of 2002, newsstand sales rose 55 percent, averaging 505,002 copies an issue. By the end of the year, Wenner had raised *Us Weekly*'s ad rate base from 800,000 to 1,050,000, and the magazine's finances were in the black.[4]

"What was the reward we got?" Brownridge recalled. "We got three new competitors."

That competition was *Star* magazine, *In Touch*, and *Life & Style*. *Star* was originally launched by media mogul Rupert Murdoch in 1974 as a paper-thin supermarket tabloid competing with the *National Enquirer* for Wolf-Man and Alien-Baby headlines. In 1990, Murdoch sold the magazine to the *Enquirer*'s parent company, American Media, and in order to differentiate this new acquisition from the *Enquirer*, American Media converted *Star* to the glossy *Us Weekly* format in 2004, upgrading its paper quality and staffing the magazine with *People* and *Us Weekly* refugees—and in the ultimate confirmation of their quest to emulate *Us Weekly*'s success, wooing Fuller away from Wenner Media and installing her as their editorial director.

The American celebrity market appeared so wide open that foreign publishing houses raised capital to get in on the market too. *In Touch Weekly* and *Life & Style Weekly* were both launched by German publisher Bauer and landed on American shores in 2002 and 2005 respectively. And the competition would only get fiercer. *OK!* magazine, the largest circulation celebrity magazine outside the United States, with editions published in the United Kingdom and Australia, launched in the United States in 2005.

The pressure was on *People* to maintain its premiere position. The chosen weapon was not price or poaching top editors, but photographs. Early on in their war with *Us Weekly*, *People* spent a reported $75,000 to buy pictures of Jennifer Lopez reading *Us Weekly*, just so that the competition couldn't buy and publish them to enjoy the publicity. *Us Weekly* editor in chief Janice Min saw that sale as a watershed moment in outrageous photo pricing.

"I had never seen anything like it. But they saw a competitor come along, and responded. It was a business move, and probably a smart one," Min said.[5]

The moment also portended that things were about to get ugly in celebrity media. "I think it's one of the most competitive, nasty areas to work in," former *OK!* editor in chief Sarah Ivens told me. The stately blonde with a big personality and bigger Rolodex was offered the top job at the American edition of the magazine after spending only eight months at the British version of *OK!*. She was twenty-nine years old, had spent nine years working in British media at the *Daily Mail*, the *Daily Mirror*, *Tatler*, and *Marie Claire*, and was given only two weeks to decide whether to uproot her busy life in London and move to America. Once she arrived, she realized just how different the American press was from the British. "In London there's a sense of camaraderie among journalists and publications. They're journalists and they love other journalists. Here in America everyone was just out to get each other."

By 2006 the six players in the celebrity magazine market brought in a combined ad revenue of more than $2.6 billion and sold more than 9.8 million issues yearly.

Exhibit A: Celebrity Magazine Ad Revenues 2005-2009

Figures courtesy of the Publishers Information Bureau of the Association of Magazine Media

	2005	2006	2007	2008	2009
People	$850,407,667	$872,662,782	$899,401,498	$979,760,812	$933,135,770
Us Weekly	$200,957,580	$276,238,077	$309,921,951	$308,831,664	$310,685,632
Star	$127,600,613	$153,842,519	$195,111,994	$169,274,582	$161,887,182
In Touch	$60,379,886	$106,533,489	$140,189,330	$136,093,942	$92,279,779
Life & Style	$13,294,014	$27,447,989	$45,997,004	$32,518,815	$19,377,548
OK!	N/A	$21,421,750	$45,179,623	$61,241,950	$73,704,094

Exhibit B: Celebrity Magazine Total Yearly Ad Pages 2005-2009

Figures courtesy of the Publishers Information Bureau of the Association of Magazine Media

	2005	2006	2007	2008	2009
People	3,852.97	3,741.18	3,889.30	3,422.23	3,367.20
Us Weekly	1,803.19	1,931.18	1,949.21	1,794.45	1,712.41
Star	966.03	1,010.34	1,260.46	1,173.24	1,131.40
In Touch	652.67	886.43	1,065.12	1,094.19	854.90
Life & Style	402.33	473.00	660.78	510.97	383.82
OK!	N/A	422.93	608.85	903.82	748.74

Exhibit C: Celebrity Magazine Total Paid and Verified Circulation Figures 2005-2009*

Figures courtesy of the Audit Bureau of Circulations

	2005**	2006	2007	2008	2009
People	3,691,167	3,750,548	3,691,819	3,618,718	3,613,902
Us Weekly	1,662,003	1,751,709	1,928,852	1,902,964	1,902,355
Star	1,430,373	1,542,218	1,365,753	1,225,521	1,035,713
In Touch	1,178,015	1,268,579	1,271,354	898,911	790,395
Life & Style	553,675	752,926	681,723	472,158	470,487
OK!	N/A	757,538	935,375	909,884	753,886

* Preliminary, unaudited figures
** Total Paid Circulation

America's appetite for celebrity gossip seemed insatiable. Circulation at celebrity magazines soared in the first half of 2005, at the same time more serious-minded magazines like *Time* and *Newsweek* were struggling.

The Economics of the Celebrity Magazine Market

Magazines command two major streams of revenue: revenue from the sale of the actual magazines (be it at the newsstand or through subscriptions) and revenue from the sale of advertising within the magazines.

For most magazines, the marginal profit on the advertising side is high, and low on the issue sales side. But the two revenue streams play off each other. By increasing circulation, a magazine can sell more ads, because it can honestly claim that it's reaching a bigger audience. Increasing circulation and acquiring new subscribers and newsstand purchasers costs money. Back in the day, magazine subscribers tended to be loyal consumers, but the rise of the Internet swelled the ranks of consumers who realized that they did not need to buy the magazine, as they could just as easily get their celebrity fix of Jennifer Aniston walking her dog on the beach in Malibu and "Who Wore it Best?" showdowns online. Magazine editors resorted to tricks like getting "must-see" photos before the competition, to get the public's attention and then, with any luck at all, turn that attention into affection, and with that, have a shot at consumer loyalty.

Every new cover presented a challenge. The magazine industry on the whole has high fixed costs due to high editorial costs (the purchase of photographs among them), high manufacturing costs, and the high cost of outreach to new subscribers. In its entirety, a typical issue of a celebrity weekly costs between $200,000 and $400,000 to produce. Of that amount, 40 percent is editorial and 60 percent pays staff salaries and overhead. Of the $80,000 to $160,000 in single-issue editorial costs, 75 percent will pay for pictures. On average, the marginal cost to produce a single copy of a magazine is around 78¢. Distributing that single copy costs another 35–45¢.

Once the magazines arrive at their point of sale, they need a place to live. That residence is composed of racks near cash registers in supermarkets and stores like Walmart and Target. Magazines are an impulse buy and publishers know it, so they're willing to pay for prime last-minute-before-checkout placement—right next to the chewing gum, breath mints, and batteries. Each rack represents a one-time cost of $100 to buy and $50 a year to "rent." While these are hardly huge sums in and of themselves, a magazine like *People* has 300,000 racks across the country. That translates to a fixed cost of $15 million a year in rack rentals alone. A set number of copies—typically ten per rack—is sent to stores week in, week out, regardless of whether those copies sell out or not. Once a copy is sold, the publisher gets 50 percent of the cover price.

Exhibit D: Celebrity Magazine Prices 2005-2009 (Single Copy/ One-year Subscription)

Figures courtesy of the Audit Bureau of Circulations

	2005	2006	2007	2008	2009
People	$3.55/$113.88	$3.55/$113.88	$3.84/$113.88	$4.09/$116.07	$4.12/$116.07
Us Weekly	$3.49/$75.00	$3.49/$99.00	$3.69/$99.00	$3.99/$99.00	$3.99/$125.00
Star	$3.49/$63.80	$3.49/$63.80	$3.49/$63.80	$3.99/$63.80	$3.99/$76.00
In Touch	$1.99/$139.99	$1.99/$139.00	$2.29/$139.00	$2.99/$100.00	$2.99/$100.00
Life & Style	$1.99/$139.00	$1.99/$139.00	$2.29/$139.00	$2.99/$139.00	$2.99/$139.00
OK!	N/A	$1.96/$102.00	$2.99/$102.00	$3.43/$102.00	$3.49/$102.00

With a cover price around $5.00, a magazine receives $2.50 in revenue from the newsstand distributor. With a cover price of $1.99, it will make only a dollar. But no matter the newsstand price, the marginal cost remains in that ballpark of 78¢ per issue, meaning a magazine needs to sell hundreds of thousands of copies at the newsstand to break even on a normal week, disregarding ad sales, which come in on more of an incremental basis. That's why a magazine has tremendous incentive to create a cover story that will trigger an impulse buy and leave the competition looking like a dowdy sister-wife by comparison.

The economics of online news are worth noting here, because they are so vastly different and they are what was scaring the well-cut pants off the magazine industry. A site like TMZ.com, AOL's entertainment property PopEater.com, or Yahoo!'s hugely popular omg! news website requires a staff of writers, editors, and designers, so these sites often paired with corporate partners like AOL or Yahoo!, which could pay for the $3 million–$8 million of overhead a year. That's still a bargain compared to the $35 million a year to run a magazine.

Gossip blogs like PerezHilton.com enjoy the economics of abundance: low overhead, few barriers to entry, bottomless advertising inventory, and enough revenue to support an endless array of new players in the category. A basic blog can be produced for free using a platform like Tumblr or WordPress. For less than five hundred dollars a domain name can be purchased from a company like Go Daddy in a package that comes with email addresses and enough server space for modest traffic. Once a site breaks fifty thousand unique visitors a day, it needs to lease a server. For a site as big as PerezHilton.com, which receives seventy-five thousand unique visitors a day, bandwidth can cost between $8,000 and $15,000 a month.

As of April 2010, PerezHilton.com averaged 280 million page views and 13.5 million unique readers per month. Eighty-eight percent of Hilton's readers were female, 59 percent aged between twenty-one and thirty-four (a demographic sweet spot).[6] Ad pages on PerezHilton.com cost between $2,400 to run on page three and beyond (sitting among old news) to $30,000 for an ad on the top right column of the front page.

Exhibit E: Celebrity Blog Ad Rates as of 2010

Rates from Blogads.com

	Price	Ad Views	Cost per Thousand Views
PerezHilton.com			
Bottom of the right column	$4,800	48,266,438	$0.10
Top of the right column	$30,000	47,945,086	$0.63
Middle of the right column	$12,000	47,577,287	$0.25
Standard back pages	$2,400	20,349,507	$0.12
JustJared.com			
Premium	$2,400	13,873,951	$0.17
Standard	$1,200	13,867,430	$0.09
The Superficial			
Premium	$6,000	8,474,615	$0.71
Standard	$1,200	3,416,798	$0.35
Dlisted			
Premium	$1,200	5,931,863	$0.20
Standard	$480	5,992,026	$0.08
Young, Black and Fabulous			
Standard	$360	4,438,166	$0.08

Based on Blogads ad rates, PerezHilton.com brings in between $120,000 and $200,000 a week in ad revenues, or between $6.2 million and $10.4

million a year. Because of selling costs, such as advertiser outreach and ad creation and maintenance, only 60 percent of those revenues belong to the site. Subtracting the selling costs decreases earnings to $3.7 million from $6.2 million. It's pretty easy money.

Still, magazines command higher ad rates than websites. *People*, on average, takes in $17 million per issue in ad revenue, while *Us Weekly* gets $5.9 million and *OK!* receives in the ballpark of $1.4 million per issue. A mature magazine will spend 11–15 percent of the ad revenue it generates for a single issue trying to secure those ad pages. Retaining advertisers depends on maintaining circulation as well as generating good content that advertisers like Proctor & Gamble and Pfizer wouldn't mind displaying their products next to. And what content could be more advertiser-friendly than photographs of healthy, beautiful babies in the arms of spectacularly famous, beautiful, adoring parents?

The Baby-Picture Bull Run

And so it happened that a first look at Pitt and Jolie's baby girl was considered the greatest possible "get" for one of the celebrity weekly magazines. But even this was no accident. Demand for the pictures rose exponentially due to a carefully orchestrated perception of scarcity.

Baby Jolie-Pitt in utero had been shielded from the press by the entire government of an African nation. To escape the media maelstrom, draw attention to their favorite humanitarian causes, and cast their illegitimate child in the sun-dappled haze of a global love-fest, Pitt and Jolie chose to deliver the baby in the southern African country of Namibia, where the government went to great lengths to protect the growing family. State officials arrested photographers, confiscated film, set up barricades on the beach, ringed the couple's hotel with heavy security, and threatened to deport any journalist trying to cover the birth without the parents' permission.

Namibian ambassador to the United States Hopelong Ipinge knew that his country had hit the jackpot with this pregnancy. The Namibian embassy in Washington, DC, was inundated with calls from the media and from individuals wanting to know more about the place. Scores of eager fans wanted to have their babies there too. Pitt and Jolie would bolster his country's tourism sector more than its tourism board could with a year's budget. "Never before have we had so much publicity," Ipinge said near the due date.[7]

Darryn Lyons, then-chairman of Big Pictures, the firm behind the celebrity photography website Mr Paparazzi.com, understood the rules of supply and demand. He knew the stars ginned up more attention and not less by taking up residence in a poor corner of Africa.

"I don't think they could have given the people more of an appetite to see the new creature," Lyons said. "It is the most anticipated baby since Jesus Christ."[8]

In the months prior to the birth, Jolie and Pitt struck a mutually beneficial deal with the photo agency Getty Images to broker a sale of the first photographs of their child. Getty would enjoy the publicity of being the organization that the high-profile couple trusted with their photos. At the same time, both the famous parents and the magazines could use Getty as a middleman to avoid the ugliness of a direct exchange of cash for personal photographs. It was the first major deal of its kind. If the birth had happened even a couple of years earlier, the photographs would have automatically gone to *People* without a fight. Even though *People* had already invested heavily in the story, assigning a staff reporter to be in near-constant contact with the Jolie-Pitt camp, the industry was changing, and *Us Weekly*, who had obtained those first paparazzi shots of Pitt and Jolie as a couple, was becoming a formidable competitor for breaking celebrity news, as was *Star*.

To top it off, Richard Desmond, the owner of *OK!* magazine in Britain, was also eager to play hardball. At *OK!*'s international magazines it was standard practice to pay for celebrity stories and photographs. Desmond had paid £1 million in 1999 for exclusive photographs of David and Victoria Beckham's wedding. Despite being a new entrant, the magazine had the infrastructure and the bank account to challenge *People* head-on. The problem for *OK!* was how to enter an already saturated market. The magazine thrived internationally, but in the United States it didn't offer anything new or different. Four years later, the magazine's founding editor, Ivens, would remember that moment in celebrity journalism as particularly trying. "If I had known what a challenge it would be launching a celebrity weekly in the American market, I would never go back and do it again. It was the boom of the celebrity magazine age, but we were the last ones invited to the party." She clung to the fact that Desmond was a legend in publishing and that every other editor in chief was a little afraid of him.

But when it came to assessing the worth of the Shiloh Jolie-Pitt pictures, *People* had no way of knowing about *OK!*'s low self-esteem, and *People* was nervous. The time was ripe for a serious bidding war.

A month after Shiloh's birth, Grossman and Min rode in the back of a black Lincoln Town Car to the Getty Images offices in midtown Manhattan. All they knew to expect was that they would enter the bleak office space and be shown the very first professional photos taken of baby Shiloh, and then be asked, along with editors from nearly a dozen other media outlets, to submit a blind bid for the rights to reproduce these pictures in their magazine and in abbreviated form on their website.

Upon arrival, Min and Grossman were quarantined in a little room containing only a conference table, chairs, and a snack machine. They were each given a glass of water. Ivens was also on the premises, a few doors down the hall in her own drab cell with her own tepid water. She never caught a glimpse of her rival bidders.

Separating editors from one another was imperative, because it forced each publication to formulate bids knowing little about how motivated the competition was. This was not the auction floor at Christie's or Sotheby's, and there would be no way to gauge the temperature of the room or hear or see the competing bidders' reactions. At some point they were informed that they would not even be seeing the entire portfolio of available photographs of Shiloh and her parents, but only a small introductory selection.

"It really is what I think a drug deal would be like," Rob Shuter, a former executive editor of *OK!* under Ivens said. "You are taken into a dark room and given a taste of what you can get before you decide what kind of money you are willing to spend. You are given the most vague details about what the pictures will look like and sometimes shown samples of pictures before you are herded out, back to your waiting black town cars, where you go back and figure out just how much you can break the bank for a particular baby."

Economist Tim Harford, author of the bestselling *Undercover Economist* series, doesn't know much about celebrity babies, but he knows a lot about auctions. When I asked him why the bids ended up so high, he referred me to the "winner's curse," a classic problem in game theory. The most obvious real-world example is when several oil companies bid for the right to drill for oil in a particular tract. They each hire geologists to figure out whether there's oil there, but in the end it's guesswork. Some will guess too high and some will guess too low. On average the guesses as to what the oil is actually worth are about right. But the auction doesn't select the average guess. It selects the highest bidder, which is also the company that made the most optimistic (read: highest) guess.

The same is true with baby pictures. When they bid for the rights to the pictures, no one really knows how much those pictures will add to the bottom line of a celebrity magazine. Some editors will guess too high, some will guess too low. The auction will systematically select the optimist.

After more than an hour of waiting, the rooms containing the magazine editors went dark. Getty had outfitted each dingy room with a slide projector and was now beaming the images of what many would later argue was the most beautiful newborn they had ever seen onto built-in screens. Shiloh was Pitt and Jolie times one hundred. Cuddling her were Pitt, embodying his Sexiest Man Alive status, and Jolie, no freakish tattoos in evidence or vials of blood around her neck. As for the baby, she was, to quote all of the dumbstruck editors who saw her that day, "impossibly gorgeous."

Grossman choked on his water. "Take the amount they were prepared to spend and double it," he thought.

Ivens was similarly impressed and suddenly extremely anxious. "I knew how important these would be for the *OK!* brand, and I had my phone with me. I was harassing my bosses in London, and there were frantic phone calls coming back in from them. At this point we didn't know how much the bid would be. We just knew it would be millions." At no point did Ivens imagine that the photos would make the magazine money in any immediate sense. She hoped the boost in PR and industry respect would make up for the dollar loss.

But no money changed hands right away. Everyone returned to their respective offices to mull over how much money they could cobble together. They were expected to submit their bids to Getty within twenty-four hours, after which the photo agency would award the pictures to the highest accepted bidder. The word *accepted* in all of the legal documents regarding the pictures was key to the contract and meant that even if a publication like, say, the *National Enquirer*, put in a bid for $100 million, it was at Brad and Angelina's discretion to dismiss them as unworthy of their photographs.

People magazine was the optimist. They outbid the competition and acquired the domestic rights to the first pictures of Shiloh Nouvel Jolie-Pitt for a reported $3.1 million. It was announced that proceeds from the sale would be donated to an undisclosed charity. The magazine's bump in sales for that single issue, released on newsstands on June 19, 2006, seemed to suggest they had named the right price. At the time, *People* was averaging sales of around 1.4 million copies per week. The Shiloh issue sold 2.1 million copies. Talk about a baby bump!

Exhibit F: Shiloh (Single Copies* of *People* Magazines Sold in 2006)

Figures courtesy of the Audit Bureau of Circulations

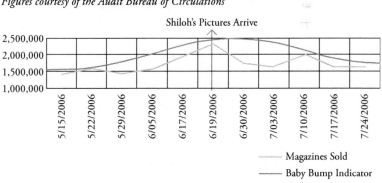

*This does not include subscriptions to People *magazine*

But magazines are cheap. *People* doesn't release cost figures, but it is possible to make some estimations. For a typical issue, the magazine would bring in a marginal revenue of $1.72 (the estimated gross revenue of $2.50 minus the 78¢ marginal cost). With the addition of these terrifically expensive photographs, the issue's marginal cost rose to $3.20. The loss for the print magazine on the Shiloh issue was approximately $1.47 million based on newsstand sales alone. *People*'s website, however, saw a boom in readers. The site set a new single-day traffic record of 26.5 million page views when photos of Shiloh Nouvel Jolie-Pitt were posted.

The repercussions did not end there. Because the bid for the Shiloh pictures had been so elaborate and fraught with tension, *People* now firmly believed that their competitors were out to conquer the celebrity market. They were especially concerned about *OK!*.

Word was out, and the baby-picture bull run had officially begun. It was now a matter of record that magazines were willing to pay millions for the right to put celebrity babies on their covers. Celebrities and the Hollywood Industrial Complex saw an opportunity to capitalize, to raise money and gain exposure at the same time. The phones at celebrity weeklies started ringing, and not every caller represented a star of Brad Pitt's stature.

Ivens was disgusted by some of the attempted negotiations. "The most hilarious has-beens that I had never heard of were trying to sell me pictures and getting quite upset if I said no. I said, 'We'll do a lovely spread and give you the pictures [to keep],' but it wasn't enough. It was really disturbing to witness these celebrities be more excited about money than the arrival of their child," she told me.

"Every C-list star was asking for money for their photos, and I ended up having to say no a lot. That's where the other magazines started coming into the picture," former *People* senior reporter Mark Dagostino recalled. "Our normal offer for a baby picture was a one-pager, no money. We ended up refusing to pay the Melissa Joan Hart–level celebrities, and we lost a lot of them, because they all thought they should be paid."

Some of them were.

In 2006, Nicole Richie was best known as an appendage to Paris Hilton. When Richie made tabloid headlines it was for getting into a cat-fight with Hilton or because her weight fluctuated. She was frequently chastised for being too thin, inevitably leading to speculation of drug use and eating disorders. The drug use rumors were confirmed in 2006, when Richie was arrested for driving while intoxicated. She had been going the wrong way on Burbank's Route 134 at 4:00 a.m.

Less than a year later, Richie completely changed her public persona by getting pregnant with rocker Joel Madden's child. All of a sudden she seemed less bratty, more benevolent. After Harlow Madden entered the world in 2008, Richie secured $1 million from *People* for the rights to the first photos of her baby daughter. It was around the same price paid for the Beckham wedding photos, and in 1999 the Beckhams were the biggest stars the UK had.

"It was probably Richie's only paycheck of 2008," *OK!* editor Rob Shuter said. Greater than the $1 million lump sum was the trickle-down effect of maternal goodwill. There were endless ancillary benefits to reap from being a new mommy, including negotiations to turn Richie's 2005 novel *The Truth About Diamonds* into a television series. She also debuted a jewelry line called House of Harlow and collaborated with maternity store A Pea in the Pod on a line of chic, starlet-friendly, new-mama clothes.

Having Harlow was a clinch move for the former party girl, but it marked a poor financial decision for *People*, which simply couldn't stop shelling out cash for baby pics. *People* next paid singer Christina Aguilera a reported $2 million for photos of baby boy Max in early 2008. Paying millions for the right to publish baby pictures was now common practice, and *People* was terrified to cede the territory to another publication.

In March, *People* beat out its previous all-time high bid for the Shiloh pictures when it offered singer Jennifer Lopez and her husband Marc Anthony a reported $6 million for the first photos of twins Max and Emme.[9] Lopez didn't offer as luridly fascinating a story as Jolie and Pitt, but she came close. The singer had had a series of well-publicized unsuccessful relationships, most notably with actor Ben Affleck and hip-hop mogul Sean Combs. Plus, Lopez was approaching forty by the time the twins were born, so she gelled with that advertiser-friendly demographic sweet spot of women keeping a nervous eye on their biological clocks.

The week of March 31, 2008, *People* published a twelve-page spread of Lopez and Anthony with the twins in their Long Island home. The photos were taken when the babies were only one month old. Why? Celebrity babies are like sushi. They're only good when they're fresh. Their value diminishes with time and after they've been exposed to the elements—and paparazzi—enough times. The parents also want to get the deal done quickly. God forbid they get snapped with the babe at Whole Foods or the gas station. They've just blown their exclusivity contract with the photo agency and a ton of cash . . . for the charities of course.

The average number of magazines *People* was selling each week had only increased a little bit when the magazine paid for the Shiloh pictures in 2006. They now averaged weekly sales of around 1.5 million copies. The 2008 issue featuring the Lopez-Anthony twins sold two million copies at the newsstands. A baby bump to be sure, but not as big as Shiloh's.

Exhibit G: J.Lo's Twins (Single Copies* of *People* Magazines Sold in 2008)

Figures courtesy of the Audit Bureau of Circulations

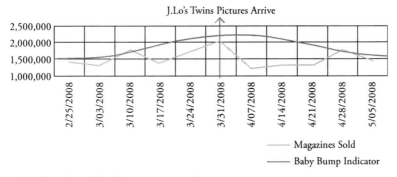

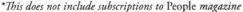

This does not include subscriptions to People *magazine*

Factoring in what *People* is reported to have paid, the marginal cost for the issue had rocketed from the usual 78¢ to $2.20, which would have led to a cash loss of around $5 million for the magazine.

Meanwhile, in the south of France, Angelina Jolie was expecting again. Not to be outdone by Lopez, Jolie, already the mother of four (Shiloh plus three adopted kids), was also expecting twins. Because of the precedent set by Shiloh and raised by Lopez, observers reasonably expected this payday to be huge.

"Shiloh was the teaser for the twins, you see," *OK!*'s Shuter explained to me. "The world had already sampled what a Pitt and Jolie baby would look like, and it made them hungry for more. Shiloh may have been the most beautiful baby in the world before the twins came along, but in the negotiations she was merely a coming attraction."

The Most Expensive Baby Pictures of All Time

If the Shiloh photos were like a street drug, Pitt and Jolie's twins were medicinal-grade heroin mixed with crack for magazine editors. Everyone in the business scrambled to figure out how badly they would have to blow the editorial budgets for the remaining issues of that year just to get hold of those pictures. At the end of the day, only *OK!* and *People* seemed to have enough cash to make formidable offers. Each publication had separate motivations. *OK!* was struggling to stay competitive in the American market, and *People* believed it was struggling to stay on top.

After more than a week of negotiations with Getty, which followed the same procurement process as for the Shiloh pictures, *People* won domestic rights for the pictures with a reported payment of $7 million. It was estimated that in total, including the sale of international rights, Pitt and Jolie received $14 million for the photographs introducing young Vivienne Marcheline and Knox Léon to the world. The proceeds were again promised to charitable causes. It was the most expensive celebrity photo buy of all time.

People had gotten smart to the economic truths surrounding baby photos. They knew they could charge a premium for the twin pictures, so they raised the cover price of the August 4, 2008, issue by a dollar. The special issue not only contained pictures of Pitt, Jolie, and their two perfect twins, but of the whole Jolie-Pitt brood—a multicultural, happy, and impeccably dressed family. The special issue sold a remarkable 2.7 million copies, at a time when the average for the preceding months was 1.5 million. *People* had finally nailed it.

Exhibit H: Brangelina's Twins (Single Copies* of *People* Magazines Sold in 2008)

Figures courtesy of the Audit Bureau of Circulations

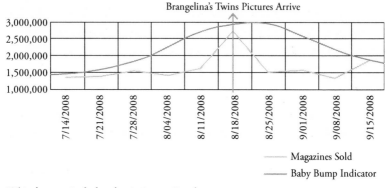

*This does not include subscriptions to People *magazine*

Conclusion

In hindsight, *People* magazine staffers believe they never would have lost the Jolie-Pitt baby pictures to another publication. The entire exercise had been a ploy by photo agencies and the celebrity machine to create an artificial bubble that inflated market values for the pictures. There was no way Jolie and Pitt were going to sell their images to a magazine that was constantly writing negative gossip about them. *People*'s policy of avoiding the extremes of salacious and negative coverage made them the only player major celebrities would want to deal with.

But the market wasn't sustainable. The frenzy for the Jolie-Pitt baby pictures was a perfect storm—the perfect story converging with magazines' fear of losing relevance and market share in a changing industry.

"The whole market for celebrity newsweeklies is smaller now, and it has shrunk primarily because of the Internet," said Bonnie Fuller, who helmed both *Star* and *Us Weekly* and now oversees her own celebrity website, HollywoodLife.com. Asking prices for celebrity baby pictures have also declined. "It's harder for a magazine to make up their expenditures in newsstand sales, and they don't have new entrants into the celebrity newsweekly market that will scare them into spending. No one is looking to spend to establish themselves anymore. Everything has shaken out."

People magazine used baby pictures as leverage to solidify its place atop a tumultuous market. Sales and ad rates began to decline across the board, as they did across the entire publishing sector, but the magazine remained on top. By 2009, *People* won 31 percent of all ad pages (up from 29 percent the year before) in the celeb sector, and accounted for 26.6 percent of all celeb magazines sold. Its market share did not suffer either. At 2009's end the magazine had grossed nearly half the category's roughly $3 billion in annual revenues.

Celebrity baby photos today still draw attention and traffic to the magazines' websites, which have devoted entire sections to the small stars. In 2008, *People* magazine got hip to that opportunity and acquired Celebrity Baby Blog, started in 2004 by Danielle Friedland. The month before *People* acquired it, Friedland's blog had attracted 6.9 million page views and 720,000 unique visitors. Fuller's HollywoodLife.com spun off a satellite site in 2010 called Hollybaby, which only chronicles celebrity children.

But as celebrity-baby traffic has been institutionalized and the lightning speed of the Internet makes yesterday's news seem like last century's, no one enjoys an exclusive on anything long enough to pay seven figures for it. After 2008, seven-figure deals for celebrity baby pictures became ancient history. By 2011, the Grammy-winning singer Mariah Carey and her actor husband Nick Cannon accepted just a six-figure deal from Bauer's *Life & Style* for three photo spreads—one of Carey pregnant and two first photos with her twins.

"It was an artificial bubble," *Us Weekly* photo editor Peter Grossman told me. "Not only was it inflated by the greatest celebrity story of all time, but it was a unique moment in the celebrity magazine industry, where magazines had money to spend but were insecure about their future."

Grossman, who represents the old guard of magazines, and Fuller, now working online, can agree on one thing. The bubble is unlikely to inflate again. That is unless Pitt and Jolie tell the world they are expecting triplets.

[1]   Miller, Lia. "So Many Paparazzi, So Few Coveted Shots." *The New York Times*, 9 May 2005.

[2]   *FIPP World Magazine Trends 2010–2011 Report.*

[3]   Petersen, Anne Helen. "The Gossip Industry: Producing and Distributing Star Images, Celebrity Gossip, and Entertainment News, 1910–2010." PhD dissertation, University of Texas, 2011.

[4]   Petersen.

[5]   Goldsmith, Jill. "People Who Need People." *Variety*, 9 July 2006.

[6]   According to Blogads.com, which sells PerezHilton.com ad space.

[7]   Silverman, Stephen M. "Brad & Angelina Boost Namibia Tourism." *People*, 28 April 2006.

[8]   "Namibia Shields Pitt and Jolie Birth." Associated Press, 26 May 2006.

[9]   Puente, Maria. "The High Cost of Celeb-Baby Fever." *USA Today*, 5 August 2008.

2

Spencer Pratt:
When Fame-Whoring Became a Business

Even after reality TV became a popular phenomenon in 2000, its stars remained the ugly stepchildren of the Hollywood Industrial Complex. Today, though still widely considered D-list celebrities, they are sought after for lucrative endorsement deals, can dictate their salaries, and often earn more per year than A-list movie stars. Chasing fame through reality TV became a viable career thanks to industry forerunners like Paris Hilton and Spencer Pratt of the MTV show The Hills, *who paved the way for the Kardashian family and the* Jersey Shore *cast to make millions. But Pratt also serves as a cautionary lesson about supply, fickle consumer demand, and the shelf life of faux fame.*

Rutgers University found itself an unlikely media target in March 2011, when Nicole "Snooki" Polizzi, a star of the MTV reality show *Jersey Shore*, was paid $32,000 to speak at two Q&A sessions at the school. This fee exceeded what Nobel Prize–winning novelist Toni Morrison would be paid to speak at the university's commencement months later.

The event had been arranged by the University Programming Association and the fee paid by PepsiCo, the main supplier of soda to the Rutgers campus. Some students were angry. Many others felt they got their money's worth.

"I think Snooki is really popular and prevalent in the media," Jill Weiss, a junior, told the student paper the *Daily Targum*. "It's great that Rutgers brought her. I don't watch the show, but my friends were so excited about coming and so am I. It's a very exciting event." Adham Abdel-Raouf, a freshman from Alabama, was even more supportive. "Honestly, I thought they would have paid her more," he told the *Star-Ledger* newspaper.

For Polizzi, it was just another Thursday, another five-figure payday.

Polizzi and the rest of the *Jersey Shore* cast had been on television for less than two years at the time of this controversy and were making approximately $5 million a year from starring on the program and the subsequent revenue streams associated with being popular on reality TV.

Less than five years earlier, reality stars were still seen as the bastard cousins of big Hollywood business, the lowest rung on the fame ladder, a dirty though poorly kept secret. By 2011, agents fought to acquire them as clients, and consumer product brands itched to sign them as endorsers. Reality TV can make a person very rich, very quickly, with little investment of time, talent, or money. Paris Hilton pioneered the business model for fame-whoring. It was perfected by the cast of MTV's *The Hills*, particularly *Hills* stars Spencer Pratt and Heidi Montag, who famously manipulated the press into making them millionaires by their mid-twenties. Pratt and Montag may have been successful entrepreneurs monetizing the public's fascination with their lives, but their story is also a cautionary tale about the shelf life of faux fame.

A Very Brief History of Reality Television

Reality television has been around since the 1940s, though back then "reality TV" mostly existed in the form of quiz shows, candid camera, and variety programs. Allen Funt's 1948 series *Candid Camera* is often credited as reality television's pioneer. What is less well known is that his broadcasting career actually started a year earlier on the radio, with a show appropriately called *Candid Microphone.*

Way ahead of its time with the documentary style of reality TV that we are familiar with today was the 1973 PBS series *An American Family,* which focused on an average American family called the Louds. Over the course of the show the Loud parents decided to divorce and their gay son came out of the closet—scandalous stuff for 1973. The anthropologist Margaret Mead noted at the time that the program was so significant that television needed to come up with a new name for this type of programming. *An American Family* received record ratings for PBS but was panned by critics for its exploitative nature. Its creator and director Craig Gilbert never worked in the industry again.

For reality television to become truly mainstream, it took two more decades, plus the technological advance of nonlinear editing systems. These digital systems, which allowed editors to access a single scene within several hours of footage without having to cut and edit all of the junk surrounding it, came on the market in 1989. Suddenly it was fast and efficient to comb through thousands of hours of content. Reality TV as we understand it today began in earnest during the 1990s with voyeuristic programs like *Big Brother* and *The Real World*, both of which staged an artificial environment for the "reality" to take place in.

Survivor, which began airing in 2000, is credited with launching the genre of competitive reality and spawning shows like *The Amazing Race*, *Project Runway*, *The Apprentice*, and *Top Chef*. That same year, the Fox network shocked America with *Who Wants to Marry a Multi-Millionaire?*, a reality competition–beauty pageant hybrid in which fifty women competed to be the bride of a multimillionaire named Rick Rockwell. Rockwell chose former emergency room nurse Darva Conger and married her on the spot. More than twenty-two million people viewed the series' final episode, and though questions soon arose as to whether Rockwell was actually a multimillionaire and Conger had the marriage annulled (and was subsequently paid six figures to pose for *Playboy*), the show quickly spawned imitators like *Joe Millionaire*, *Average Joe*, *The Littlest Groom*, and—most notably—the *Bachelor* franchise.

By 2003, executives from all four major networks saw reality shows win fifteen of eighteen half-hour time periods on Monday, Tuesday, and Wednesday nights. The success of the genre was so impressive that executives devised a radical restructuring of programming that would give reality precedence over scripted sitcoms and dramas. "The world as we knew it is over," said Leslie Moonves, the president of CBS Television. Gail Berman, the president of entertainment for the Fox network, added that "the 50-year-old economic model of this business is kind of history now."[1]

The early 2000s also saw an influx of celebrity reality shows, which gave celebrities in waning careers a platform for reinvention (or at least a swan song).

The year 2002 saw MTV's launch of *The Osbournes*, an updated version of *An American Family* starring aging rocker Ozzy Osbourne and his family. It was then the most-viewed MTV series of all time and aired through 2005.

"The television thing was a wild experiment that went out of control. It started because we did that thing for *MTV Cribs*, and it was one of the most requested reruns, so they suggested we do an extended version of that, and lo and behold, we invented a new effing form of television and everything is reality now," Ozzy Osbourne told me years after his show went off the air. "It went crazier than anyone expected it to, and it has dawned on me how much it must have fucked my kids up."

MTV had another hit on their hands in 2003 with *Newlyweds: Nick and Jessica*, which followed newly married celebrity pop stars Nick Lachey and Jessica Simpson during their first years of marriage. The show ran through 2005 and the couple divorced in 2006.

Then ordinary people got in on MTV's reality game. Soon soap opera–style reality shows like *Laguna Beach*, which debuted in 2004 and followed a group of teenagers navigating high school in the eponymous California seaside town, became wildly popular. *The Hills* debuted in 2006 as a spin-off of that show, following one of its main female characters, the design student Lauren Conrad, to Hollywood. It may not be a coincidence that by 2007, one in seven teenagers said they hoped to gain fame by appearing on reality TV.

The explosion of reality programming was partially due to the public's fascination, and partially due to the economic realities facing producers and broadcasters. Reality is cheap. Many reality shows have some sort of script (some of them are entirely scripted to provide a narrative structure for thirty minutes each week). But writers for reality television are on the lowest rung of the ladder of Hollywood scribes and don't receive union pay scale compensation, which significantly lowers production costs. In a competition-style show, contestants are only compensated on a per diem basis for their weekly appearances. On soap opera–style reality, the fees for cast members can start as low as $2,000 an episode. They have reached the astronomical rate of $100,000 an episode for the top stars in the genre, but that figure still pales in comparison to the $1 million an episode paid to each of the *Friends* cast members during that sitcom's heyday. A reality TV show without a high-profile cast can be produced for only $400,000 an episode, while production costs for a sitcom begin in the range of $5 million.

"Even television programmers see the genre as a kind of visual Hamburger Helper: cheap filler that saves them money they can use elsewhere for more worthy programming," said former VH1 exec Michael Hirschorn. "The money saved on *Extreme Makeover: Home Edition*, the logic goes, allows ABC to pay for additional gruesome medical emergencies and exploding ferries on *Grey's Anatomy*. NBC's crappy *Fear Factor* pays for the classy *Heroes*."[2]

Spencer Pratt: The Branding of a Reality Star

By 2011, *The Hills* reality star Spencer Pratt no longer wanted to be in front of the camera, but still loved to talk about making money from fame. Over the course of six months, I conducted a series of interviews with Pratt, the longest of which was during a three-hour breakfast in the Polo Lounge at the Beverly Hills Hotel. (The location was his choice.) Pratt told me that he was looking for a job behind the camera. He had applied to the talent agency N.S. Bienstock, Inc. to work as an agent for other reality TV stars. He said that he was in talks with Charlie Sheen's manager, Mark Burg, to produce the third installment of *Hot Shots!*, and that he had recently spent $70,000 of his own money to produce a reality series on the U.S. Marine Corps for the Military Channel. When we met for the final time, Pratt and his wife, Heidi Montag, had been lying low for six months, following the explosion and subsequent implosion of their brands during the three years—2006 to 2009—they spent on *The Hills*.

Pratt grew up the son of a dentist in Pacific Palisades. While his family was comfortably upper-middle-class, his circle of friends included the children of Southern California's elite. He got his first taste of fame in high school, when he snapped pictures of himself and his friends with the actress Mary-Kate Olsen at a party. Olsen was visibly drunk and Pratt negotiated with a photo agency to sell the pictures for $50,000, which to a kid in the Palisades seemed like millions. Pratt went to college at the University of Southern California, where he first studied business before switching to political science because he thought it would be easier. It wasn't, and he was miserable in school.

"I was like, 'This is awful. I have to get on a television show, because that is the easiest job in the world,'" Pratt said.

After watching shows like *Newlyweds* and *The Osbournes*, Pratt concluded that his friend Brody Jenner, the son of the Olympic medalist Bruce Jenner (stepfather to the Kardashian sisters), had a far crazier and more interesting family than anyone else on television. In 2005, Pratt bought a camera and started filming Jenner, his family, and himself. He edited a five-minute highlight reel and sold *The Princes of Malibu* to Fox. It aired for two episodes, when Jenner's mother—former Miss Tennessee Linda Thompson—announced her divorce from her husband David Foster. Fox cancelled the show on the premise that they hadn't bought a show about marital strife.

Pratt returned to school, but his interest in reality TV was again piqued when he watched MTV's newest reality soap opera, *The Hills*, and saw Montag, a girl he had hung out with a couple of times. His Machiavellian plan was to orchestrate a romance with Montag in order to get on television. He told Jenner that appearing on *The Hills* was an absolute must. At the time, Jenner was dating the reality starlet Nicole Richie, who egged the pair on. Pratt and Jenner started showing up at restaurants and clubs where *The Hills* was filming, in hopes of integrating themselves into the show. The plan worked, and Pratt and Montag began dating. Pratt then encouraged Jenner to break up with Richie so that he could date the show's star, Lauren Conrad, and the two couples could become a media-friendly foursome.

The start of both relationships was entirely masterminded by Pratt. Montag, meanwhile, was still relatively naive about fame. A Colorado native from a hometown of less than two thousand people, Montag had met Conrad at the Fashion Institute of Design & Merchandising before *The Hills* was in production. As the girl sidekick on the show, Montag made only $2,000 an episode when the show premiered in 2006. When Pratt and Montag became a serious couple on the show and in real life, Pratt also took on the role as their manager.

Conrad despised Pratt and his role as her bullying foil on the completely scripted "reality" program. Pratt relished it. At that point, celebrity magazines and gossip shows were not giving prominent placement to reality stars, but that was about to change. During the first week Pratt filmed with *The Hills*, he left such a bad taste in viewers' mouths that he landed on *Star* magazine's "Yuck-o-Meter." Pratt was thrilled. An advertisement the size of the Yuck-o-Meter copy would have cost about $40,000.

"I thought, 'Wow, being yucky just got me a $40,000 promotion. I'm cool with this,'" Pratt recalled. His mentality was, "We're not raping people, we're not killing people, we're not racist. It's better than going to work and being a jerk and not getting paid to be a jerk."

By the second season of *The Hills*, Conrad threatened to quit the show if Pratt stayed in it. The producers ignored her threats, and they all remained. Now Pratt and Montag were being referred to in the press by the single schmushed moniker "Speidi" and were able to command salaries of $25,000 per episode. Pratt formulated a scheme to make more money off their tabloid fame. He contacted the photo agency to whom he had sold his Mary-Kate Olsen pictures years earlier and worked out a deal to sell staged photos.

The staged photo is one of Hollywood's dirty little secrets and a revenue stream that even A-list celebrities take advantage of.

Here's how it works: Celebrities, or their representatives, strike a deal (typically a year-long contract) with a photo agency to broker the sales of staged photos to tabloid magazines, TV shows, and websites around the world. Profits from the sale are split down the middle, the celebrity and the agency each receiving 50 percent. The checks come in on a monthly basis. If an agent or publicist brokers the deal, they take a 10–15 percent cut off the top.

Pratt estimates that once he and Montag signed with an agency, they made a steady stream of $300,000 annually from selling pictures of themselves. "We were making more money doing that than doing the television show," Pratt said. "It was instant cash."

The bulk of the money was made internationally. What looks like a cheesy staged photograph in America sells for five times the price abroad, since the international audience doesn't begrudge celebrities who appear to enjoy their fame. Each photo had a different price, and they ranged from $300 to $30,000. When Montag revealed her breast implants for the first time, the picture was worth $10,000. Talking about her desire to remove them was worth another $30,000. A shot of Pratt and Montag frolicking on the beach could sell for $300, but the price would increase to $10,000 if they had a fight on *The Hills* the week before. "The magazines don't feel bad about it, because they're not writing their checks to us. It's going to the middleman and it's a standard deal," Pratt said. "That's when fame-whoring became a business for us."

Then there were the $25,000 appearance fees. Pratt and Montag originally did every appearance they were offered. They were approached by nightclubs in Las Vegas, Los Angeles, New York, and eventually venues in the middle of the country and finally around the world. "I was, like, I would go to this casino for free and stand in line—sure I'll let you pay me for this," Pratt said. "At that stage any dollar was winning." Then Pratt realized that their price went up if they did fewer appearances, so they cut back on their schedules. Their appearance asking price rose by 50 percent.

Other income streams included the secret endorsement. Big-time brands still felt it was dodgy to align themselves with reality TV stars, but they also wanted to capitalize on their exposure, so they struck unpublicized and "subtle" deals. Pratt claimed that if he or Montag were spotted wearing a T-shirt advertising a certain high-profile soft drink or sipping a can of said drink in 2007, that would translate into a "secret" check for $10,000.

Pratt played up his bad-boy image on and off the show, consistently picking fights with Conrad, calling her names, and starting a rumor that she had made a sex tape. At one point Pratt picked an unsolicited fight with *Today* show weatherman Al Roker, poking fun at his weight in interviews and on Twitter.

In May 2007, Montag and Pratt announced their engagement. Their eventual margarita-fueled elopement in Mexico in 2008 pissed off *Hills* producers because it undermined the integrity of their scripted narrative, and they demanded a second wedding, *Hills*-style. Speidi got married a second time on the show in 2009. The producers decided that the story line would have Pratt leaving Montag at the church and Montag and Conrad reuniting as friends. But the couple refused.

"They told me, 'It would be huge if you would walk away.' And I would have done it if the producers hadn't treated us like we were worthless ugly stepchildren," Pratt said. "Or if they had paid us more."

To keep Pratt and Montag loyal to MTV, the network told them that they would be getting a spin-off that would start with six episodes, according to Pratt. Furthermore, he claimed they were paid $1 million each for the spin-off contract for a show that would never materialize.

"That's how they make sure you won't leave," Pratt said. "They give you a contract for $1 million and promise you more shows to keep you around."

Throughout it all, Pratt and Montag were spending their own money to try to make Montag a music star. Pratt said Warner Bros. had offered them a 360-degree deal that would have given the label a cut of all Montag's projects in exchange for transforming her into a pop star. They decided not to take it and to produce on their own, paying top producers $100,000 to $200,000 to record singles with Montag. But without the millions in marketing that a label can pump into an artist, Montag's music career was going nowhere fast. So was the Speidi brand equity. America was growing tired of them, and the demand for their pictures, appearances, and secret endorsements had begun to fade by the time *The Hills* wound down in late 2009. With the overall economy in decline, the big money for photo deals had dried up too.

"We didn't understand the shelf life of the reality star, because we were in it before it was saturated," Pratt said. "We didn't know what to do then to make it last. We were like the cow that milked everything."

Not everything. One of the decisions that overexposed Montag was a *People* magazine cover story in January 2010, in which the twenty-three-year-old claimed to be addicted to plastic surgery and professed to have undergone ten surgical procedures in a single day. The story, intended by Pratt to humanize Montag's good looks by foregrounding her struggles with self-esteem and insecurity, instead made her a target for a virulent backlash, while *People* itself was lambasted for celebrating a culture of attention-whoring. The *People* cover hurt Heidi's brand, and ironically it was one of the few stories she was not paid for. Speidi had chosen the magazine because of its cachet, turning down millions from competitors, including *Us Weekly*, whose photo editor Peter Grossman had convinced the couple to go public with the information in the first place.

That's when Pratt says he really learned the game of getting paid big bucks for a magazine cover story. "They secretly pay, but they do it to charities in people's names. Now I wish we had started a charity—Heidi's Charity for Surgery Issues for Girls—and we would have gotten a couple million dollars," Pratt said.

The Hills ended on July 13, 2010. On July 30, Montag filed for divorce, citing irreconcilable differences. The pair received flak from the media for what they saw as a fake divorce, but Pratt thought divorcing Heidi would be the best thing for her personal brand.

"We were divorcing each other's brands, and in our world that was so logical," Pratt said. They also managed to get paid in the process. During the divorce the agencies started paying for their pictures again, and Pratt and Montag each signed on with Ad.ly, a company that paid celebrities to tweet on behalf of brands. Montag and Pratt endorsed different online dating sites and received payments in excess of $100,000.

The divorce story line didn't take, and by September the filing had been dropped. Then the pair dropped out of the spotlight.

Life Post-Reality

If you've been on television, you'll always be a little bit famous, even if that just means you're a little bit more famous than your mailman or a little bit more famous than your fourth-grade-teacher friend, Sally. And even a touch of fame can translate into cash rewards for a long time after the spotlight dims.

In 2004, Jessica Sierra was working as a nanny in central Florida and making $24,000 a year plus room and board. An aspiring singer, Jessica was the third finalist eliminated from the fourth season of *American Idol*. Her spot in the top ten earned her a slot on the post-show national tour, where she took a percentage of ticket sales and merchandising. Sierra told me she made $200,000 for her time on the tour. She then sang in a series of concerts with sponsor Kellogg's that paid $15,000 a pop. She did independent gigs touring the Middle East, singing to troops in Iraq and performing at a wedding in Kazakhstan. Sierra estimates that this made her $500,000. Then things went downhill. Bad management decisions caused Sierra to lose her earnings. She took a job at Hooters. She started drinking.

But when you're a little bit famous, even bad decisions can pay off. In 2007, two years after her stint on *American Idol*, the Oxygen network wanted to sign Sierra for a new reality series, *Bad Girls Club*. VH1 offered her a spot in their new program *Celebrity Rehab* with Dr. Drew Pinsky. Sierra says that she opted for *Celebrity Rehab with Dr. Drew* not because she knew that she needed treatment for her substance abuse but because "VH1 was a bigger and better network than Oxygen." She was paid $100,000 to tape the show. In 2010, she independently released a single via her Myspace page and was preparing to release an album. She was still offered an occasional appearance fee in the $2,000 to $5,000 range.

Sierra did make it into the final ten on the most-watched talent competition in the world, so it made some sense that her fifteen minutes of fame would stretch beyond *Idol*. She was a singer after all, someone who actually had talent.

Yet even reality stars without a talent can go on to capitalize far beyond their time on television screens. NBC launched *The Biggest Loser* in 2004 as a reality competition in which contestants compete to lose extreme amounts of weight. The show's first female winner, Ali Vincent, parlayed her success into a bestselling book, *Believe It, Be It*, and endorsement deals from 24 Hour Fitness, The Biggest Loser Protein, and Infinity Insurance. Three years after the show, Vincent could still command speaking fees of up to $20,000.

"Ali Vincent is like the *American Idol* winner of *The Biggest Loser*," Nicole Michalik, the thirteenth contestant cut on Season Four of the show told me.

Michalik wasn't a moneymaker like Vincent, but she still benefited monetarily from being a little bit famous. A DJ from Philadelphia, Michalik didn't win on *The Biggest Loser*, but four years after competing on the show in 2007 she still commanded speaking and appearance fees of between $300 and $500 a couple of times a month. She became a local semi-celebrity in her hometown of Philadelphia and describes the recognition that comes from being on the show as a whirlwind as addicting as fast food. In fact, Michalik thinks that some *Biggest Loser* contestants replace their food addiction with an addiction to attention. "When you're on the show and right after the show, you're in magazines and on television, and everyone is giving you all of this attention and you have a little bit of money, and a year later it goes away. And two years later it goes away even more. It's interesting that people get so caught up in it, because we're not *American Idol*. We don't have a talent. We were fat and we went on a treadmill."

Taking Reality Seriously

It took a long time for Hollywood to embrace the reality star as a viable moneymaker, but in 2008 the tide began to turn. Notable publicists began picking up reality stars as clients. Speidi signed with Cindy Guagenti of BWR Public Relations, who at the time represented A-level talent like Brad Pitt. Over the next year Guagenti would also acquire Patti Stanger, the reality matchmaker on the Bravo network, as a client. All of the major talent management agencies started to groom agents specifically to deal in the "reality" sector.

In 2009, the *Hollywood Reporter* named a crop of hungry young reality agents as the next big thing in the business. Leading the list was William Morris agent Josh Pyatt. Six months after becoming an agent in 2005, Pyatt packaged and sold his first series, the George Foreman vehicle *Family Foreman*, to TV Land. Pyatt went on to sign lucrative deals with a range of non-scripted bigwigs, including production powerhouses the Magical Elves (*Top Chef, Project Runway*) and Thom Beers's

Original Productions (*Deadliest Catch*, *Ice Road Truckers*, and *America's Toughest Jobs*).[3]

The agencies finally saw reality stars and producers as moneymakers. Even though they made less per contract than major movie stars, the opportunities for ancillary revenue streams from endorsements, product placements, book deals, and picture sales all added up to serious cash. And these were people who would do anything for a paycheck. On the production end, representing the makers of reality TV translated into major dividends, as a reality trope could be repackaged for global franchises. *American Idol* has more than thirty international franchises, including *Idols* in Malaysia and Kazakhstan. There have been more than forty international versions of *Survivor* and nineteen versions of *Project Runway*.

The rush of brands to contract reality talent to endorse their products was also due to how cheap they were in comparison to movie stars or established television stars. A brand can't sign an endorsement package with a movie star for under $1 million, but a reality star would accept a tenth of that. Brands also found that consumers related better to reality stars than they did to movie and traditional television actors. As of this writing, it remained to be seen whether "relateability" sells products as well as aspiration always has.

Flooding the market with cut-rate talent, however, has had the same kind of effect Wal-Mart had on mom-and-pop shops. The pricier, classier outfits have to fight for their survival and many of them lose so much revenue that they can't survive in the new marketplace. That's the reason we see the Jennifer Anistons of the world rushing to do a viral video on Funny or Die (funnyordie.com) with the likes of reality star Tila Tequila, or why country music sensation Shania Twain was willing to stage her comeback with a reality program on the Oprah Winfrey Network (OWN). They're leveling the playing field with the reality foot soldiers.

Enter "Snooki"

The problem with *The Hills* was that it was boring. No matter how many fights Pratt picked with Conrad, the drama wasn't titillating enough to keep the show going past its sixth season. Pratt thinks that the show may have been too tightly controlled and scripted. "The producers were writing it, and that's why I am glad it's not still on," Pratt said. "These producers were too obsessed with making *90210* and *Gossip Girl*, but it was never as good. They always worried about jumping the shark. They surfed the shark."

To stick with their carefully crafted plotlines, the producers didn't follow the cast around after midnight and rarely taped them partying, which meant they missed out on the kinds of real sparks the audience craved.

"The girls on the show, except for Heidi, didn't believe they weren't actors," Pratt said. "I would tell them, 'Play yourself. You're hoes.'"

Still, the show served as a launch pad for the young women on the program to go on to bigger projects. Lauren Conrad developed her own clothing line and became a bestselling fiction author. Audrina Patridge was given her own spin-off show.

For MTV, the plan post–*The Hills* was obvious. The network had seen firsthand that the ugliness of Pratt and Montag's antics gained ratings. Yuck-o sold. What if they replaced *The Hills* with something more raw? What if they compiled an entire cast of jerks who would behave badly all the time?

Jersey Shore first aired in December 2009, just as *The Hills* was wrapping up. The show featured eight housemates sharing a residence in the seedy beach town of Seaside Heights, New Jersey. It immediately met with controversy for using the terms *guido* and *guidette*, matching derogatory terms for male and female Italian-Americans.

The show's main action centered on the cast getting drunk, fighting, publicly urinating and defecating, and having sex on camera. Ratings went through the roof. It premiered with back-to-back episodes watched by approximately 1.3 million viewers as it teased an episode where Nicole "Snooki" Polizzi was punched in the face on camera. The Season One finale drew 4.8 million viewers. The premiere episode of Season Three was viewed by 8.45 million viewers.

From the start, the entire *Jersey Shore* crew co-opted the Speidi model, behaving badly and then milking the cash cow for all it was worth. By the fourth season of the show, the cast members were each making $100,000 an episode, a number it had taken Montag and Pratt six seasons to reach. In 2010 alone, cast member Mike "The Situation" Sorrentino made a reported $5 million from show fees and bonus incentives; product lines based on his much-discussed fitness regime, including an abs video and a supplement line with GNC; a book deal with Gotham Books for an autobiography entitled *Here's the Situation*; his own vodka line; and endorsements with Vitaminwater and Reebok.

On April 7, 2011, MTV announced that it had picked up twelve episodes each of two spin-off shows that would feature cast members Jenni "JWoww" Farley, Nicole "Snooki" Polizzi, and Paul "DJ Pauly D" DelVecchio.

That was two years into the cycle of fame for these young reality stars.

Conclusion

Pratt and Montag had a celebrity shelf life of four years, during which they made an estimated $10 million together. By the time the kids hit the *Jersey Shore*, reality programming was a viable moneymaker for everyone involved. Montag was one of the first reality TV stars to appear on the cover of *Us Weekly*, but reality stars now dominate the tabloid market. That means that even if the staged-photo prices aren't as high as they once were, the income stream still remains.

Companies are no longer afraid of partnering with reality stars, and the endorsement and licensing field has been cracked wide open. Whereas Pratt and Montag were given secret endorsement checks, the cast of *Jersey Shore* was openly endorsing products.

Speidi helped to pioneer the model, in other words, but they never got to take full advantage of it.

The payout for reality just keeps climbing. The $5 million estimated annual salaries made by the *Jersey Shore* cast is forty times the median household income in the United States. The Kardashian franchise pulled in $65 million in 2010. Bethenny Frankel, who got her start on Martha Stewart's much-panned version of *The Apprentice* and then shot to fame on Bravo's *The Real Housewives of New York City*, used reality TV to bolster her brand of Skinnygirl lifestyle products. In 2011, her

Skinnygirl margarita was acquired for $120 million by the world's fourth-largest spirits company, Fortune Brands' Beam Global Spirits & Wine, distributor of Jim Beam bourbon and Sauza tequila. In 2011, Frankel appeared on the cover of *Forbes* magazine for the publication's annual "Celebrity 100" list.

"I went on the show [*Real Housewives*] single-handedly and exclusively for business," Frankel said. "I knew it was a risk and I had the most to lose, because I already had a platform. When I went on the show, no one was going on for business, no one had done anything."[4]

In 2011 Pratt and Montag, at ages twenty-seven and twenty-four respectively, were semi-retired and ready for Act 2, during which they hoped to make Frankel-size money. Sure enough, in March Montag was cast in a new VH1 reality show with two other former reality stars, Danielle Staub from *The Real Housewives of New Jersey* and Jake Pavelka of *The Bachelor*. The show focused on the D-level celebrities competing to turn a restaurant into a Hollywood hotspot. As a prize the winner would receive an ownership stake in the property. Also starring on the show would be Ashley Dupré, the high-priced call girl who brought down New York governor Eliot Spitzer in 2008. Then the ABC reality competition *Dancing with the Stars* came knocking on Montag's door. They were considering her for their next season.

Meanwhile the photo agencies wanted Speidi pictures again. Pratt received an email from one agency while I was meeting with him over breakfast in April 2011, weeks before the wedding of Prince William and Kate Middleton:

> *Hi Mate,*
>
> *How bout this? We have some William and Kate masks in the office. Think it would be a really good idea if you two would don the masks. It would make for a good photo and the UK newspapers would love it. Let me know if you're both up for it. Cheers.*

Even without doing much, Speidi continued to be paid to be a little bit famous.

1   Carter, Bill. "Reality Shows Alter the Way TV Does Business." *The New York Times*, 25 January 2003.

2   Hirschorn, Michael. "The Case For Reality TV: What the Snobs Don't Understand." *The Atlantic*, May 2007.

3   Andreeva, Nellie. "America's Next Top Agents: Rising Reality Reps Are Maturing with the Genre." *The Hollywood Reporter*, 18 May 2009.

4   Bruce, Leslie. "How Bethenny Frankel Used Her Reality Show to Make $120 Million." *The Hollywood Reporter*, 21 April 2011.

3

Valerie Bertinelli:
Turning Pounds into Dollars

When the personal trainers, private chefs, surgeries, and cleanses don't work and the pounds pack on, celebrities prove they are not "Just Like Us." Most people struggle and spend to drop unwanted pounds. Celebrities actually experience a windfall from getting fat, as marketers pay millions to exploit their weight gain and loss, packaging it to consumers with inspirational can-do story lines.

Americans are obsessed with obesity. The country's preoccupation with body fat fuels a $40 billion weight-loss industry that churns out dietary supplements, self-help books, weight-management programs, and fitness centers. At the heart of the diet industry's marketing are endorsement deals worth $500,000 to $2 million a year for celebrities willing to publicly lose weight. Over the last twenty years, Hollywood has perfected the process through which a celebrity's personal weakness can generate value. In the celebrity market, pounds become dollars quicker than donuts become unwanted inches.

For example, beginning in April 2010, Weight Watchers launched a new marketing campaign featuring Academy Award–winning actress and former *American Idol* contestant Jennifer Hudson. The company experienced a 2 percent boost in gross profits right after signing her. Hudson benefited from her association with Weight Watchers as well; her total weight loss was a reported sixty pounds, and based on Hudson's multimillion-dollar deal, it earned her approximately $33,000 per pound.

The fact that a performer can be paid by the pound like a side of meat is Oprah Winfrey's fault. The talk show queen pioneered the trend of bald-faced oversharing about fat when in 1988 she dressed in snug size-10 jeans and wheeled a wagon loaded with sixty-seven pounds of animal lard onto her stage to represent her recent sixty-seven-pound weight loss. At that moment of what was then rare and news-making candor, Oprah's fans became emotionally invested in the talk show host's struggle with her weight and in Oprah herself. While her openness about size fluctuation certainly isn't the secret to all her success, Oprah's ability to project that vulnerability has certainly helped cultivate her $2.7 billion in net worth and massive media empire.

As her *O, the Oprah Magazine* began to lose steam in the fourth quarter of 2008, Oprah revisited the weight issue. The cover of the January 2009 issue of *O* featured two Winfreys: a svelte Oprah in 2005 as well as a considerably chubbier Oprah in 2008, when she again surpassed the two-hundred-pound mark. That issue sold 1.1 million copies on the newsstand, making it the bestselling issue of *O* in three years.

After Oprah's first weight confessional, Sarah Ferguson, Duchess of York and former wife of Prince Andrew (fourth in line to the British throne), became one of the first big names to enter the celebrity weight-loss endorsement game. She turned to Weight Watchers in 1996, after the nasty British press nicknamed her "the Duchess of Pork," and proceeded to make more than $2 million a year promoting the diet system for the next eleven years.

Next up was sitcom star Kirstie Alley, who signed an endorsement package with Jenny Craig in 2004.[1] From 1987 to 1993, Alley was beloved by Americans for her portrayal of Rebecca Howe on the sitcom *Cheers*. She won an Emmy and a Golden Globe and parlayed her television success into big-screen triumphs with the *Look Who's Talking* movie franchise. From 1997 to 2000, Alley played the title character in the NBC sitcom *Veronica's Closet*. Then, as happens for comedic actresses approaching middle age, her career hit a lull. Even if Alley had stayed thin, the roles would no longer have come in so quickly. But Alley's weight gain was the secret to her career's second life. She was able to parlay it into a Showtime series entitled *Fat Actress*, a sitcom loosely based on Alley's own trials and tribulations. The Jenny Craig endorsement kept the buzz for the show strong, and Alley even managed to work the program into her Jenny Craig press materials. "I had a great time getting fat and now I'm going to have an even greater time losing weight," Alley said. "Since I started working with the Jenny Craig team, they've supported my unconventional, hopefully humorous, approach to coming to grips with the fact that I'm certifiably fat. I goof around with that on my show, *Fat Actress*."[2]

At the time, Alley was by far the highest-profile Hollywood celebrity to sign with Jenny Craig. The gamble proved win-win for Alley and the diet industry. Then all of a sudden Alley became a cautionary tale for celebrity endorsements when in 2008 she regained the weight and Jenny Craig terminated their partnership. "Fired for Being Too Fat," screamed the *National Enquirer* headline. At one point Alley had lost seventy-five pounds on the program, but by the time she and Jenny Craig parted ways, she had gained back more than half of the weight. The business model had some kinks that still needed to be worked out.

Picking the Right Porker

The celebrities who work best for a diet company aren't necessarily the most famous. They're the most relatable. That's because it is hard to imagine Jennifer Aniston eating pre-packaged frozen meals when you know she has a personal chef on retainer. 1970s singer and TV personality Marie Osmond wasn't a household name when she signed with Nutrisystem in 2007. She was famous with the demographic of over-forty women that the weight-loss company was looking to target, but her face wasn't splashed on the covers of tabloids and she wasn't acting in blockbuster movies. The diet company pursued her anyway. Osmond had recently been cast on *Dancing with the Stars*, and Nutrisystem learned she was trying to lose weight before the competition. They approached her and asked if she would like to be a spokeswoman while she lost the weight.

"There is a science behind selecting our spokespeople," Nutrisystem's senior director of public relations, Susan McGowan, told me. "We run the ad and then track how many people respond to it. Marie's ads continue to poll better than any of our other celebrities'. She has been someone our customers really respond to." Around 800,000 people will sign up for the Nutrisystem program a year, paying more than $300 for a month's worth of food. The average time on the program is ten weeks.[3] In weeks when celebrity ads are in heavy rotation, sign-ups can increase by as much as 25 percent.

It isn't just women who are influenced to lose weight by celebrities. In 2006, Miami Dolphins Hall of Fame quarterback Dan Marino approached Nutrisystem and became its first male spokesperson.

"Prior to that time [our men's business] was nonexistent," McGowan recalled. "From the minute we signed him, we became the leading men's diet program in the diet industry, and we have had him as our main celebrity spokesperson since then. The key with men is finding somebody that is aspirational to men. With men especially, we find that the sports figures really work well."

But since only 15–20 percent of diet product consumers are male, according to John LaRosa, the research director for independent market research firm Marketdata Enterprises, female celebrities overwhelmingly command the big money weight-loss deals.

Diet companies can and will actively recruit celebrities and work with them to lose the weight. Larger brands have a celebrity wrangler in-house, but smaller companies often hire an outside gypsy consultant who is familiar with striking celebrity deals to help them find their ideal weight-loss talking head.

In 2007, the weight-management company Medifast recruited PR and media consultant Michael Sands to help them hire a celebrity endorser to push their brand outside doctors' offices. Though they had been in the weight-loss business for twenty-five years, they didn't enjoy the sizable consumer market share that Nutrisystem or Jenny Craig did. "I figured the best way to put them on the map was to use the B-list celebrity endorsement," Richard Zeeb, former executive vice president of marketing for Medifast told me.

Zeeb was thumbing through *Soap Opera Digest* magazine when he came across a picture of soap actress Genie Francis.

"I said, 'That's who I want!'" Zeeb later recalled. "She was overweight and didn't look good. And she was in the age group we were trying to reach."

Genie Francis had played Laura Spencer on the daytime soap opera *General Hospital* for eighteen seasons. Francis may not be recognizable to women under thirty, but she is considered one of the most beloved soap opera stars of all time and a reminder of a not-so-distant past when soap operas enjoyed significantly greater cultural currency than they do today. Francis's 1981 on-screen wedding as Laura to the character Luke was one of the most-watched television events in history. Approximately thirty million Americans tuned in for that episode of *General Hospital*, more than typically tune in for an *American Idol* finale.

Medifast gave Sands a list of ten names—all women over forty who weren't huge stars but who resonated emotionally with women in that demographic. Among the names were Francis, *All in the Family* star Sally Struthers, and *Sex and the City* star Kim Cattrall.

Francis was the only one who said yes to Medifast. Semiretired from acting, she was living quietly in Maine and selling antiques. She told the company that she had put on thirty-five pounds and was looking to lose it anyway, so she figured she might as well get paid to do it. Sands structured a contract for Francis that paid her approximately $50,000 a month for twelve months. In exchange, she was to appear in TV commercials and print advertisements as well as participate in press opportunities such as interviews with *People* magazine and the television show *Access Hollywood*. She would receive a six-figure bonus if she met her weight-loss goals. Francis lost those thirty-five pounds and was paid more than $700,000 for her Medifast deal, or a little more than $17,000 per pound.

Most celebrity endorsement packages are structured similarly. The endorsement is built with an up-front fee, a yearly contract, and incentive riders. Endorsement fees can range from the $700,000 paid to Francis to the $2 million a year paid to Sarah Ferguson.[4] A celebrity earns their full paycheck when they meet the weight-loss goals announced at the commencement of the campaign. The average amount of weight a celebrity will lose as a spokesperson is thirty pounds. With an average endorsement fee of $1 million, this makes each pound gained and lost worth approximately $33,000.

The payout often continues when a celebrity manages to maintain their target weight. Keeping a celebrity endorser on retainer is a smart strategy for customer retention, provided that celebrity isn't compromising the brand message. That's where things went sideways with Alley's contract.

After parting ways with Alley, Jenny Craig snatched up former child star Valerie Bertinelli and soon expanded their celebrity stable to include spokespeople from different demographics. They signed deals with *The Cosby Show* star and Tony Award–winning actress Phylicia Rashad, *Less Than Perfect* actress Sara Rue, and *Seinfeld* actor Jason Alexander.

Exhibit A: Diet Company Ad Spend in Millions 2007-2008

*Figures courtesy of Mintel/*Brandweek

	2007	2008	Change
Nutrisystem			
Nutrisystem Advanced Weight-Loss Program	$5.7	$109.4	1,799.7%
Nutrisystem Nourish Weight-Loss Program	$117.6	$41.1	-65.0%
Nutrisystem Website Weight-Loss Program	$35.2	$12.2	-65.3%
Nutrisystem Weight-Loss Program	$12.0	$11.5	-3.6%
Weight Watchers			
Weight Watchers Weight-Loss Center	$85.1	$61.7	-27.5%
Weight Watchers Smart Ones Entrées (Frozen)	$8.8	$26.6	199.9%
Other			
Jenny Craig Weight-Loss Center	$66.3	$59.1	-10.9%
LA Weight-Loss Center	$52.2	$11.6	-77.8%
Medifast Weight-Loss Program	$28.7	$10.5	-63.2%

In a 2010 brand analysis, consumer product and research firm Mintel categorized the segmentation of Jenny Craig's spokespeople as follows:

- Valerie Bertinelli is the friendly, approachable neighbor with a perky, can-do attitude. She's the brand cheerleader.
- Jason Alexander is the everyman nebbish.
- Phylicia Rashad is the elegant black woman who appeals to affluent women of this demographic.
- Sara Rue is the spunky character who brings levity to the challenge of weight loss.

By 2010 the marketplace for publicly losing weight had grown to include all ages, genders, ethnicities, even personalities. But the product endorsement isn't the only way the Hollywood Industrial Complex has capitalized on weight loss.

Making More Money from Fat

The four major revenue streams that overweight celebrities can take advantage of, besides the product endorsements discussed above, are magazine stories, book deals, and reality TV contracts.

Magazines

People magazine knows what headlines sell weight-loss stories. (There's a reason they all sound the same.) On September 15, 2010, reality star and mother of eight Kate Gosselin declared "The Truth About My New Body" on the cover, with the inside tagline "I'm in the Best Shape of My Life." Earlier that year, on May 31, a headline had Jennifer Hudson announcing she was enjoying the "Best Shape of My Life." Two months prior, in March, former *Baywatch* babe Nicole Eggert declared, "I'm in the Best Shape of My Life." The fall before, Kim Kardashian revealed how she "Gets in the Best Shape of Her Life."

The words "best shape" have the psychological impact of invoking health and vitality. They also make weight loss aspirational. By appearing in these magazines, celebrities aren't simply raising the profits for whatever diet they are promoting, they are burnishing their own personal brands.

"The economic impact of coming clean and talking about your weight struggles is so beyond the endorsement deal you get," *People* senior editor Galina Espinoza told me.

But money is nice too. Even celebrities who don't have endorsement deals and just want to tell their diet story can negotiate deals worth between $10,000 and $50,000 just for pictures and an interview with a weekly magazine. They are asked to discuss how they gained the weight, lost it, and then kept it off. Each celebrity weekly has an editor who deals with "health" issues. While those health issues may occasionally enter the realm of celebrity disease or injury, these editors are mainly responsible for negotiating weight-loss stories.

Books

Of the top seven bestselling diet books of 2009, four were celebrity diet books: Dr. Ian K. Smith, the resident diet guru on VH1's *Celebrity Fit Club*, was number 6 with *The 4 Day Diet*; *The View* cohost Elisabeth Hasselbeck's *The G-Free Diet* was number five; *Clueless* actress Alicia Silverstone's *The Kind Diet* was number four; and hard-body fitness queen Jillian Michaels, from NBC's *The Biggest Loser*, had the number-one-selling diet book of the year with *Master Your Metabolism.*[5]

"The diet and weight-loss category definitely used to be more expert driven, and now it is definitely more personality driven," Julie Will, executive editor of Rodale publishing house, which specializes in health and wellness books, told me. "It is becoming a category dominated by celebrity. These used to be really private issues, but now it has become another way for the celebrity to become relatable to people and to put a dollar figure on it."

The economics of the publishing industry have contributed to the rise of the celebrity in the diet book category. As publishing houses have less money to spend on marketing campaigns, celebrities seem like a surefire way to get the kind of publicity needed for a book to make money.

By 2010, publisher demand for celebrity weight-loss books was so high that an author who would have gotten a $150,000 advance in 2007 could benefit from a bidding war that now raised their advance against royalties to $1 million.

Reality TV

In January 2005, VH1 aired its first episode of *Celebrity Fit Club*, a series that followed eight overweight celebrities trying to shed pounds.

The original cast was even lower on the rungs of the fame ladder than the types of people chosen for endorsement deals. They were somewhere around the E-level. The first season featured comedian Ralphie May, actor Joseph Gannascoli (Vito from *The Sopranos*), actress Kim Coles (of *In Living Color*), Wendy Kaufman (the overweight woman who once appeared in Snapple commercials), lesser Baldwin brother Daniel, rapper Biz Markie, and *Divorce Court* judge Mablean Ephraim.

In eight weeks the original group lost an average of twenty-five pounds. Contestants were paid up to $100,000 to participate.[6] Britney Spears's ex-husband Kevin Federline, who signed on for Season Seven, reportedly gained thirty pounds on purpose to be considered for the show. His $100,000 fee allowed him to cash in at more than $3,000 per pound.

But the real benefit of gaining and losing weight in the public eye isn't the money, it is the increased exposure, and no celebrity dieter exemplifies this dynamic better than Valerie Bertinelli.

Valerie Bertinelli's Gains from Weight Loss

Bertinelli was a child star originally known for her role on the 1975–1984 sitcom *One Day at a Time*, on which she played the daughter of a single mom struggling to raise two girls. She stayed in the spotlight by marrying rock star Eddie Van Halen, worked on two sitcoms in the 1990s, and had a small role on the drama *Touched by an Angel*, but she was far from a household name by the mid-2000s. That changed in 2007, when she signed on as a spokeswoman for Jenny Craig and lost fifty pounds.

Bertinelli's first Jenny Craig commercial debuted on April 7, 2007. Bertinelli and Jenny Craig's then-spokesperson Kirstie Alley were part of an integrated marketing campaign designed to last several months, in which Alley's initial seventy-five-pound weight loss and successful maintenance of that loss would be shown to be the inspiration for Bertinelli to adopt the Jenny Craig program.

"We are confident and excited that Valerie's interaction with Kirstie in our new campaign not only demonstrates Kirstie's new role as a mentor, but also gives people another opportunity to see a busy mom lose weight on national television," said Jenny Craig CEO Patti Larchet at the time.

The plan was for Bertinelli to lose weight "in real time" and tape frequent updates on her progress. In addition to appearing in a series of monthly TV and print advertisements, Bertinelli posted regular video and blog updates on the Jenny Craig website to relate her ongoing story and provide tips for success. She also recorded video email messages made exclusively for new and returning Jenny Craig clients. On April 16, 2007, Bertinelli appeared in *People* under the headline "I Know What You're Thinking—I'm Fat!" The issue sold 1.5 million copies, slightly above the single copy average.

That year, *Forbes* listed Bertinelli among its relatively small list of celebrities who were able to make an impact at the newsstand. Bertinelli was suddenly keeping brand-value company with Angelina Jolie, Reese Witherspoon, and Jennifer Aniston.

At an estimated salary of $1 million a year from Jenny Craig, including bonuses, as of 2010 Bertinelli had made—from her endorsement deal alone—$60,000 per pound for the fifty pounds she lost and managed to keep off on the program.

But while each pound gained and lost translates into several thousand dollars in endorsement and book deals, the goodwill and intimacy cultivated with fans become a transactional spillover—something impossible to put a price tag on but valuable nonetheless. Think of it this way. A beekeeper owns bees that pollinate surrounding crops. The beekeeper makes money from the honey produced, but the external benefit is that thousands of flowers also flourish, and the capacity for future honey is increased.

Losing weight with Jenny Craig helped Bertinelli score a lot of honey.

Since going public as weight-challenged in 2007, Bertinelli has written two books on the subject of weight management: *Losing It: And Gaining My Life Back One Pound at a Time* and *Finding It: And Satisfying My Hunger for Life Without Opening the Fridge*. In March of 2008, *Losing It* became a *New York Times* bestseller.

In 2009, Bertinelli was recruited for a starring role in a new TV Land series entitled *Hot In Cleveland*, a much-hyped show that also featured seasoned sitcom actresses Betty White and Wendie Malick. *Hot in Cleveland* debuted in June 2010, became the number-one sitcom on cable, with an average of 4 million viewers, and was picked up for a second season.

Bertinelli was again in high demand. She consistently graced the covers of magazines, including the January 7, 2011, cover of *People*, which featured Bertinelli and longtime boyfriend Tom Vitale's wedding album. Bertinelli was now a frequent talk show guest and often cohosted *The View*. She planned to launch an exercise and fitness DVD series and began billing herself as a weight-loss advocate in addition to her already lucrative roles as actress, former rock-star wife, and happy newlywed.

Conclusion

Bertinelli set the standard for what losing weight in the public eye could do for a celebrity. Today it is not unheard of for a talent agent to sit a washed-up client down and advise them to gain some weight. It is equally common for agents to sit fat clients down and say, "How do we monetize this?"

Losing forty pounds in the public eye had made Bertinelli a hero to American women and made the former child actress a mint. Celebrities have taken the hitherto embarrassing issue of weight loss and turned it into a portion of their business portfolio. Not only does capitalizing on weight loss shrink their bottom and bolster their bottom line, it also increases their brand value in other endeavors.

---

[1]   Founded in 1983, Jenny Craig, Inc., is one of the largest weight-management service companies in the world. The company offers a comprehensive weight management program, including pre-packaged food and weight-loss counseling and consulting. In 2006, Switzerland-based conglomerate Nestlé announced it was buying Jenny Craig for $600 million.

[2]   "'Fat Actress' Kirstie Alley Chooses Jenny Craig To Lose Weight." Jenny Craig press release, 20 December 2004.

[3]   Whelan, David. "Before . . . and After." *Forbes*, 30 October 2006.

[4]   Watson, Bruce. "The Princess Bribe: Will Fergie Recover from Latest Scandal?" *Daily Finance*. AOL Money & Finance, 25 May 2010.

[5]   Schrick, Jamey. "Best-Selling Diet Books of 2009." AOL Shopping, 5 January 2010.

[6]   Hazlett, Courtney. "K-Fed Eating Overtime to Prep for Reality Show." *The Scoop*. Today.com, 30 September 2009.

4

Oscar:
What's an Academy Award Worth?

You cannot win an Oscar without spending money. It doesn't matter who spends the most, but it does matter who spends it best. Oscar wins are the product of finely tuned and aggressive marketing machines that trump talent on Hollywood's biggest night. Why all the fuss? Because future dividends increase for studios, directors, actors, and actresses who win those little gold men. An Oscar tomorrow is actually worth more than an Oscar today.

A breathless Kathryn Bigelow took the stage to accept the 82nd Academy Award for Best Director in 2009.

"There's no other way to describe it. It's the moment of a lifetime," Bigelow said. "It's so extraordinary to be in the company of my fellow nominees, such powerful filmmakers, who have inspired me and I have admired, some of them for decades."

Bigelow was the first woman in the history of Hollywood's biggest awards to earn the top prize for filmmakers. Her film *The Hurt Locker* won Best Picture and four other Oscars. It was the lowest-grossing Best Picture winner of all time, shown on just 535 screens across the United States. It contained no big-name actors in major roles, and its competition was the highest-grossing movie in recent history, the 3-D science-fiction juggernaut *Avatar*. Going into the eighty-second awards season, *The Hurt Locker* had nothing going for it.

But as the year went on, it became clear that what *The Hurt Locker* did have was one hell of a high-end Oscar campaign. Its emerging young studio, Summit Entertainment, was flush with vampire money. Summit had been wildly successful with a franchise of teenage vampire romances called the *Twilight* series—the first *Twilight* film alone grossed more than $392 million. Studio execs knew that a movie about love-struck bloodsuckers in Washington State couldn't win an Oscar. A critically lauded war film, however, could, if only they got the right people talking about it.

The studio asked Cynthia Swartz of 42West (a New York–based film publicity and marketing firm that specializes in landing their clients Oscar wins) to make awards magic happen at an estimated cost of between $3 and $5 million for the entire campaign—a fraction of what the *Twilight* franchise pulled in for them.

Longtime film journalist Steve Pond, author of the Academy Awards history, *The Big Show*, said Summit's strategy riled a lot of folks in Hollywood. "They spent a hell of a lot more money than anyone was expecting, and it pissed people off," Pond said. "Not because Summit was doing anything wrong, but just because they were doing it in the first place."

While Oscar campaigns are nothing new, in recent years the transformation of independent underdogs into award bait has become a $100 million-a-year cottage industry within the movie industry. Part of today's American dream is believing that movies win Academy Awards based on merit alone. But thanks to the mastermind of the modern Oscar campaign, Harvey Weinstein, and the many subordinates he has trained through the years in his techniques, it has become standard practice to buy the benefits an Oscar can bestow.

A Very Brief History of the Oscars

Over an intimate dinner party in 1927, Metro-Goldwyn-Mayer studio chief Louis B. Mayer, the actor Conrad Nagel, director Fred Niblo, and producer Fred Beetson hatched the idea of forming an organized group to celebrate and benefit the film industry. A little like throwing a birthday party for oneself, it would be a big celebration of their general fabulousness. By March of 1927, the Academy of Motion Picture Arts and Sciences was created and the actor and director Douglas Fairbanks appointed its inaugural president.

The Academy's first charter expressed such lofty goals as promoting harmony among movie professionals, protecting the honor and reputation of the industry, and meeting outside attacks from church and state. The first awards ceremony was a banquet at Hollywood's Roosevelt Hotel for just 270 guests who had paid five dollars each for a ticket.

Today there are six thousand Academy members—actors, writers, producers, directors, composers, and all the way down the film production line—who determine both who is nominated for Academy Awards and who wins them.

The process is simple. In the first round of voting, each branch of the Academy offers nominations within its category. Any film that opens during that calendar year for at least a seven-day theatrical run can be considered. In round two, the full Academy votes in every category. In a perfect world, members would vote based on how much they loved a film. But Hollywood is far from perfect, and if there is a way to spend money to gain an edge, checks have already been signed.

Some Oscar historians contend that Mary Pickford, the wife of Academy president Douglas Fairbanks, launched the first Oscar campaign in the run-up to the second awards ceremony. Pickford's 1929 performance in the film *Coquette* had been skewered by critics, but since it was her first talkie, the actress wanted an award to prove that she could pull her weight in the new format. She invited all the new Academy members to her home for tea and wooed them, and ultimately the second Academy Award for Best Actress did wind up on her mantle.

While that campaign cost Pickford little except tea, crumpets, and some choice compliments, it set a model for flirting with Academy members that would only become more elaborate over the years.

Throughout the 1940s and 1950s, studios, actors, and actresses purchased advertisements in trade magazines to lobby for awards.

The most excessive and controversial of these ads came from the actor John Wayne, who lobbied for the Western epic *The Alamo* to win Best Picture for the year 1960. Wayne's ads suggested that it would be unpatriotic to vote against *The Alamo* and featured the *Alamo* cast praying for victory "harder than real Texans prayed for their lives at the Alamo." Much to Wayne's chagrin, the only Oscar the Western won was for Best Sound.

No movie has won Best Picture without launching some kind of dedicated campaign since the 1970s, but it was at the end of that decade that the modern Oscar campaign really emerged. The two critical factors shaping it were the advent of the VHS videocassette and the rise of Harvey Weinstein. The VHS, which hit the United States in 1977, made it easy to send a portable version of a movie to the thousands of Academy voters, leveling the field between the major studios, who could afford to hold special screenings for Academy members, and smaller independent studios, who could not afford to host such events. With VHS, an independent studio could place a copy of their film in the hands of each Academy member for a mere $250,000.

The result was a shift away from nominations just for the mainstream epics like the *Godfather* franchise (winner of Best Picture for parts I and II) and musicals like *Oliver!*, *My Fair Lady*, and *West Side Story* (all Best Picture winners in the 1960s) to lower-budget sleepers like *Annie Hall* and *Ordinary People*.

Weinstein's impact was less direct but more long-lasting. Having cofounded the independent Miramax studio in 1979, he is both credited with and accused of giving birth to Oscar campaigns characterized by expensive gift-giving, lavish parties, and a fleet of publicists tasked with manipulating the press and industry tastemakers from coast to coast. In other words, Weinstein made the race for an Academy Award much like a race for political office.

A Brief History of the Weinsteins

After a childhood spent in Queens, New York, brothers Harvey and Bob Weinstein cut their teeth in the gritty world of rock-and-roll promotion in downtown Buffalo, New York, where they had acquired the Century Theater as a venue for concerts in the late 1970s. To make a buck between concerts, they began showing movies in the space and eventually parlayed their love of film (and quest for more money) into a small film company they named Miramax after their parents, Miriam and Max. Longtime chronicler of film Peter Biskind describes the Weinsteins as bottom-feeders trolling for any intellectual properties the big studios wouldn't touch, many of them X-rated or foreign, or both. A less judgmental analysis would note that Miramax entered the scene as independent films were starting to build an audience. By loose definition, indie films were the antithesis of "Hollywood" movies. They stressed narrative and characterization and dealt with gritty, uncomfortable subjects. They were also cheap.

One of Miramax's earliest hits was a $100,000 feature on the lives of New York City hookers entitled *Working Girls*. The brothers paid $200,000 for the film, which they marketed to gross around $1.8 million during its 1987 release. The next year, Harvey Weinstein proved his knack for low-rent marketing genius when he spun *Pelle the Conqueror*, a film about a Swedish boy's struggle to free himself from indentured servitude in nineteenth-century Denmark, into commercial gold. Weinstein used a photo of a practically bare-breasted peasant girl in the ads and promoted it as an action movie. It grossed $2 million at the domestic box office and earned Miramax its first Oscar win, for Best Foreign Film.[1]

Miramax subsequently picked up *My Left Foot* (1989), a tearjerker about a disabled Irish drunk who learns to paint and write with his left foot. The film won Oscars for Best Actor and Best Actress and was nominated for three more, including Best Picture.

Harvey and Bob and Miramax didn't just send out screener videos, they sent elaborate screening packages with books and glossy photos so detailed that a voter did not have to actually watch the film to know what it was about and to like it immensely. Some years, the cost of those mailings ran more than $500 apiece. With more than six thousand Academy members, sending screeners could easily cost more than $3 million. To push *My Left Foot* for the 1989 awards, the Weinsteins shipped thousands of chocolate feet to voters.

Now that the studio was seen as a contender for awards, its efforts didn't end with elaborate mailings. Each year, Miramax hired a fleet of veteran Hollywood publicists to schmooze important Academy members with parties and dinners. No other studio hired as many outside publicists per campaign. "We are not in any way in the vote-buying business," said Mark Gill, president of Miramax/L.A. in 1999, "but we are very assertive about publicity and promotion for our movies year-round, including during the Academy season."[2]

The often-strained tone in pronouncements like Gill's stems from the fact that the Academy has strict rules about what's allowable. It is Ric Robertson's job as executive administrator of the Academy to keep campaigners in check. In 1994, Robertson gathered a group of marketing executives from the various studios to discuss how to rein in the out-of-control mailings.

"There was a point where it went from being a promotional item to something of value," Robertson told me, adding that the screenings came with things that looked, smelled, and (in the case of the gourmet appendages) tasted like a bribe. This was troubling. "The bottom line of this organization is to promote the notion that the Academy members make their decisions based on the quality of the films," Robertson asserted.

Most of the studios were exhausted by the constant one-upmanship too, but so embroiled in the game that no one would back down unless everyone backed down.

"It was like an arms control negotiation," Robertson said.

To ensure everyone would play by the same rules, the Academy wrote them down. Screeners were fine, but presents were not. The video packaging had to be very plain and not contain anything but the VHS tape, and later, the DVD. The DVD couldn't have extras on it like behind-the-scenes footage or interviews with the cast and directors.

Academy members could be invited to screenings but not screenings that included anything special like a director or cast Q&A, hand-pumping, or dual cheek-kissing sessions following the film.

"It shouldn't be about the charisma of the people involved," Robertson said.

But even the watchdog admitted that because of the way the movie industry is structured, rules would be broken. The major way around the rules was to cater to members of the Academy through their various trade guilds—the Directors Guild of America, the Writers Guild of America, and the Screen Actors Guild—by sending them special screeners and inviting them to special parties as guild members. The penalties for rule-breaking are also little more than a slap on the wrist. (The film loses a portion of its allotted tickets to the awards show.)

One example of rule subversion happened in 1998, when Miramax was in a fierce battle with DreamWorks for the Best Picture Oscar. Miramax's romantic period piece *Shakespeare in Love* (13 nominations) was pitched against DreamWorks'—and Steven Spielberg's—war film *Saving Private Ryan* (11 nominations).

After the nominations were announced, Miramax hired longtime movie publicist Bobby Zarem to throw a "Welcome to America" party for British *Shakespeare in Love* director John Madden at the legendary East Coast industry watering hole, Elaine's. Zarem was a valuable asset to Miramax, because his guest list for dinner parties typically included a slew of Oscar voters.

"I put together a dinner for John Madden comprised entirely of Oscar voters and apparently that was a no-no," Zarem told me years later, after he'd retired from planning New York dinner parties and was living in his family's home in Savannah. The night before the dinner at Elaine's, Miramax's head of marketing and public relations called Zarem in a panic, saying that they were being accused of holding a dinner just for Oscar voters. He told Zarem to scramble to get nonvoters in there, so the publicist called mustachioed former baseball star Keith Hernandez, septuagenarian humorist Art Buchwald, and real estate mogul Donald Trump to dinner. Zarem estimated that it probably cost the studio $10,000 for the dinner, open bar, and his fee, but creating an intimate connection between Academy members and Madden was priceless.

Weinstein blew off the presence of Academy voters at Zarem's dinner as mere coincidence.

"I'm sorry there were three Academy members present," he petulantly told *New York* magazine's Nikki Finke. "But it was a press event, and you have to have celebrities at a press event to get the press there."

In the same column, Finke accused Weinstein of personally launching a word-of-mouth campaign to discredit *Saving Private Ryan*, alleging that Harvey was peddling his personal opinion to critics that the war film peaked in the first twenty minutes. Weinstein denied those allegations as well.

Industry experts estimated that Weinstein spent around $5 million to win *Shakespeare in Love* its Best Picture Oscar. Miramax disputed that number, saying that their film was in wide release during the Oscar campaign and its typical marketing efforts simply mixed with the campaign organically.[3]

Yet within the industry, opinion was nearly unanimous that the campaign bought *Shakespeare in Love* its Oscar. "*Saving Private Ryan* seemed the safe front-runner throughout that summer, but Miramax kept spending more and more money, forcing DreamWorks to spend more and more money," Hollywood journalist Steve Pond told me. "That campaign took Oscar campaigning to a level that hadn't been seen in the past and it certainly bothered people in the Academy. There were some people in Hollywood who said, 'Look, this has gone too far.' But at that point, you just can't turn back."

Courting the media was another game that Harvey Weinstein elevated to an art form. He made a point of staying on the friendlier side of the gossip press, who he knew planted the seeds for the national news. He once asked Richard Johnson, then-editor of the *New York Post*'s Page Six gossip column, to write a script for a movie that Weinstein had optioned. For a longtime newspaper scribe, the chance to transition to screenwriter would be difficult to pass up. But Johnson never took him up on the offer. When Weinstein learned *Premiere* writer Peter Biskind was penning an exposé of Miramax's role in the independent film industry, he invited Biskind to his Tribeca offices and offered to publish a pet project Biskind had been nursing for years in exchange for dropping the story. Biskind turned him down. Yet aspirational bribery, when successful, was a handy way to court favor for himself personally and also to ensure that he could plant positive press for his films.

Weinstein's campaigns may have skewed dirty but they weren't frivolous. Miramax also set the precedent of opening Oscar-worthy films late in the calendar year, a practice that is now industry standard—and the reason why movies released January through June are relative stinkers compared to the ones released later in the year. A holiday-season release means that the publicity efforts aimed at the general ticket-buying public complement the screenings, Q&As, screener mailings, and press plants that build buzz among industry insiders. A studio could easily spend $15 million on a marketing campaign at any time of the year, but Miramax would roll out the general campaign and the Oscar campaign as one neat package. Executed correctly, chatter would peak at the exact time Oscar ballots went into the mail.

The Campaign for *The Hurt Locker*

Cynthia Swartz joined Weinstein's Miramax studio in 1989 and went on to lead campaigns for *Pulp Fiction*, *The English Patient*, *Shakespeare in Love*, *Chicago*, *Gangs of New York*, *Cold Mountain*, *The Aviator*, and *Finding Neverland*. In all, Miramax films received more than 150 nominations during her tenure.

Two decades after she first worked with Miramax, Swartz and her team at 42West positioned *The Hurt Locker* as "the other" in relation to box office behemoth *Avatar*. The "other" strategy was a longtime Miramax trope. It works like this: If you don't like the violence of *Saving Private Ryan*, then vote for the plucky Elizabethan love story *Shakespeare in Love*. Or if you don't like the weird family drama of *American Beauty*, vote for the quaint John Irving adaptation *The Cider House Rules* (and just ignore the whole illegal abortion part while you're at it). This strategy was successfully replicated in the *Hurt Locker* campaign: If you don't want to vote for the outsize most-expensive-movie-of-all-time, then vote for this gritty little film about the Iraq war.

The Hurt Locker was, in fact, the perfect other. Not only was it an independent, low-budget film with a somewhat controversial message about a war America was still fighting, it just so happened that director Kathryn Bigelow used to be married to *Avatar* director James Cameron, a story that 42West trickled into the press during the fall lead-up to awards season. As a woman, Bigelow was herself an other in comparison to Cameron, and the press couldn't resist two exes going head-to-head for an Oscar. No other film seemed to matter once that card was played in the media.

The Economics of a Good Oscar Campaign

Why launch an Oscar campaign in the first place?

From the distribution side the answer is twofold. Jason Cassidy, long-time head of marketing for Miramax, views the goal of an Oscar campaign as value extraction during each step of the movie distribution process.

"The goal is to maximize the value of each movie in the current theatrical market as well as the after-market. You want to get the theatrical gross as high as you can while balancing how much you spend," Cassidy told me. "Based on how successful you are in the Oscar race, the ancillary revenues of your product will go up in the after-markets."

Seasoned Oscar campaigners agree that there is no single strategy for a successful Oscar campaign. Each one develops organically, and successful campaigners claim to rely on gut instinct. Swartz told me she relied on her gut with every campaign to win a film an award, including the one she and her team crafted for *The Hurt Locker.*

"Once that path is obvious, the most important factor is momentum," Swartz said.

A film needs momentum at the right time. Peak too early and excitement peters out; peak too late and the company has spent millions of dollars without enough time to get Academy voters invested. Building momentum often involves racking up accolades and awards from individual guilds and film festivals prior to the nomination voting in January.

Exhibit A: 2010-2011 Awards Season Schedule

November 2010

Thursday, November 11 - Golden Globe Cecil B. DeMille Award announcement

December 2010

Friday, December 10 - Golden Globe nomination polls close

Monday, December 13 - Screen Actors Guild Awards nomination polls close

Tuesday, December 14 - Golden Globe nominees announced

Thursday, December 16 - Screen Actors Guild Awards nominees announced

Sunday, December 19 - Satellite Awards (International Press Academy)

January 2011

Tuesday, January 11 - National Board of Review Awards Gala

Wednesday, January 12 - Golden Globe voting polls close

Friday, January 14 - Oscar nomination polls close

Saturday, January 15 - Critics' Choice Movie Awards (Broadcast Film Critics Association)

Sunday, January 16 - 2010 Golden Globe Awards

Saturday, January 22 - Producers Guild Awards

Tuesday, January 25 - Oscar nominees announced

Friday, January 28 - Visual Effects Society VES Awards

Friday, January 28 - Screen Actors Guild Awards voting polls close

Saturday, January 29th - Directors Guild of America Awards

Sunday, January 30 - Screen Actors Guild Awards

February 2011

Saturday, February 5 - Writers Guild of America Awards

Sunday, February 13 - BAFTA Awards (British Academy of Film and Television Arts)

Saturday, February 19 - ACE Eddie Awards (American Cinema Editors)

Sunday, February 20 - Golden Reel Awards (Motion Picture Sound Editors)

Tuesday, February 22 - Oscar voting polls close

Sunday, February 27 - Academy Awards

The Golden Globes, which are voted on by an obscure body of international journalists called the Hollywood Foreign Press Association, are another opportunity to build momentum. Winning a Golden Globe provides name recognition, which is always helpful when courting votes, but it doesn't guarantee an Academy Award win: From 2001 to 2010, Best Picture Globe winners went on to win an Oscar only 50 percent of the time.

A multipronged outreach approach to winning an Oscar typically starts nine months before the Academy Awards ceremony in February or March. The campaign is looking to reach three groups: Academy voters, press who cover film, and consumers of film.

The hope is that reaching the first two groups will affect the bottom line through the third. It is also assumed that reaching the second will influence the first.

The great thing about press is that, aside from publicists' salaries and costs, it is free. But there are plenty of other places to spend campaign dollars. There are six major costs inherent in any Oscar campaign, and the ultimate price of the campaign depends on how much effort is expended in any one of these six categories.

1. Consultants

Gypsy publicists, rogue party planners, and entire full-service consultancies will work exclusively on retainer to push a movie into Oscar contention territory. Firms can charge as much as $300,000 per film, individual operatives between $50,000 and $100,000. An intricate web of all these operators can run more than $2 million.

2. Mailings

A DVD can be mailed for less than two dollars. With elaborate packaging, express mailing, and hand delivery, the cost can increase to $200 per piece. With six thousand Academy members, that translates to a total of more than $1 million.

3. Parties and Dinners

One of the stealth tactics of good campaigners is the third-party Oscar party, where someone who is not in the Academy hosts an event celebrating a film starring one of their good friends. An example is when Larry King just happened to throw a bash for his pal George Clooney, who just happened to be in Oscar contention in 2005 for two films: *Syriana* and *Good Night, and Good Luck*. The third-party host can also invite their friends who just happen to be members of the Academy. The expenses of these campaign parties and dinners can easily run to $2 million, which is often somehow subsidized by the studio.

Studio marketing executives liken this part of the campaign to hand-to-hand combat. For a good campaign, you need to be on the ground driving home your message. The cast needs to be tirelessly glad-handing voters and going to every event to talk about their film. If a movie's main players aren't willing to commit to living and breathing and fighting for their film for the two months leading up to the Oscars, they can forget about taking home a statue.

4. Screenings

Starting in September, campaigners begin organizing screenings for press and for members of the Academy. The average screening costs between $3,000 and $10,000 to organize. The price increases for a screening that involves the actors and directors appearing for a Q&A session afterward. The costs include renting the theater, sending invitations, and paying the expenses for the major players to come and speak. There can be as few as two screenings (one in New York and one in Los Angeles) or as many as fifty. Some campaigners organize screenings in places where Academy members vacation between Christmas and New Year's, like Aspen and Hawaii.

5. Appearances

Expenses for making sure movie stars appear on talk and radio shows can be negligible or run to several million dollars for a high-profile star who takes a private jet and requires accommodations for their family and a large entourage.

6. "For Your Consideration" Advertisements

Full-page ads in trade magazines like *Variety* and the *Hollywood Reporter* can cost $25,000 apiece, but insiders know how to negotiate these prices lower. If the studio logo isn't used in the ad, the cost drops by about half. "You can also negotiate and tell them you have no money and call late in the production schedule. They need to fill the space, so those ads that are supposed to go for $25,000 a page don't go for anywhere near that," Steve Pond said.

Ad budgets can range from $15,000 to $1 million. But with the rise of Oscar blogs and the subsequent decline in importance of the trade magazines, the importance of ad campaigns in said magazines has diminished over the years.

Exhibit B: Oscar Campaign Costs Expressed as Percentages

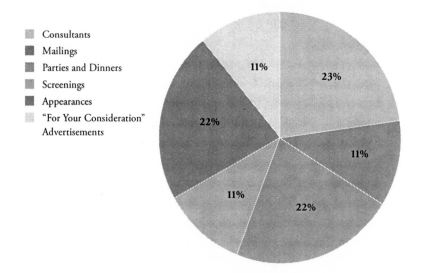

Consultants
Mailings
Parties and Dinners
Screenings
Appearances
"For Your Consideration" Advertisements

The professionals in the Oscar campaign business are paid quite handsomely to maximize value from each of these activities.

Is It Worth It?

An Oscar bump is the increase in profits following a nod from the Academy.

Oscar nominations and wins help convince the consumer that a film has value. They are a seal of approval, like a Food and Drug Administration (FDA) stamp, or a mark of quality, like an Intel processor. Brandon Gray, the president and publisher of the box office calculation firm and website Box Office Mojo, told me that the effect an Oscar win has on the box office gross is both ephemeral and erratic.

"There is also a bit of a chicken and an egg kind of thing," Gray said. "When a movie gets the nomination there is a big marketing push behind it. So you don't know if the movie is being bumped because of the nomination or because all of a sudden there is a big marketing campaign."

Some films definitely benefit from the combination of the nomination and the marketing that comes with the Oscar campaign. Up until nominations were announced for the 2008 Academy Awards on January 22, 2009, the independent feature *Slumdog Millionaire* had made only $44 million at the box office over nearly four months. In the little more than a month prior to the Oscars, the film grossed $53 million. After winning Best Picture it brought in another $42 million. Post-nomination, it was also released in more than triple the number of theaters it had occupied pre-nomination, going from 614 theaters to 2,244. *The Hurt Locker*, on the other hand, enjoyed a far more modest Oscar bump. It grossed just $12.6 million prior to its nomination. Post-nomination and post-award gross was only $3.7 million in additional revenue.

The general rule of thumb is that box office hits will continue to be hits after the nomination and that indies will see a bump. A movie like *The Departed*, the Martin Scorsese gangster movie that won Best Picture for 2006, was already a commercial success leading up to its nomination and only gained an additional $10.5 million after the nomination, or about 8 percent of its total box office gross. Harvey Weinstein famously likes to brag that *Chicago* received a $100 million Oscar bump, going from $64 million pre-nomination to $170 million total gross following its win in 2003. The famous campaign that drove *Shakespeare in Love* to win over *Saving Private Ryan* garnered the film $63 million in additional revenue post-nomination, or about 60 percent of the gross.

Exhibit C: Best Picture Winners' Box Office Grosses and Number of Theaters Pre-Nomination, Post-Nomination, and Post-Award

Figures courtesy of BoxOfficeMojo.com

	Year	Pre-Nomination Gross	Post-Nomination Gross	Post-Award Gross
The Hurt Locker	2009	$12,671,105	$2,028,895	$1,700,000
Slumdog Millionaire	2008	$44,711,799	$53,642,596	$42,965,533
No Country for Old Men	2007	$48,899,543	$15,391,636	$9,992,446
The Departed	2006	$121,756,022	$10,049,275	$579,018
Crash	2005	$53,404,817	N/A	$1,175,483
Million Dollar Baby	2004	$8,499,006	$56,352,732	$35,640,465
The Lord of the Rings	2003	$338,345,008	$25,770,604	$12,911,713
Chicago	2002	$64,568,153	$69,446,381	$36,673,984
A Beautiful Mind	2001	$113,704,771	$40,999,880	$16,037,690
Gladiator	2000	$186,610,052	$260,325	$835,050
American Beauty	1999	$74,681,000	$33,787,063	$21,628,538
Shakespeare in Love	1998	$36,549,292	$36,643,453	$27,125,049
Titanic	1997	$338,710,764	$156,862,280	$105,215,144
The English Patient	1996	$42,319,574	$21,218,055	$15,138,796
Braveheart	1995	$67,047,523	$6,277,314	$2,285,108
Forrest Gump	1994	$300,565,286	$16,899,392	$12,229,821

	Year	Pre-Nomination Theaters	Post-Nomination Theaters	Post-Award Theaters
The Hurt Locker	2009	535	274	349
Slumdog Millionaire	2008	614	2,244	2,943
No Country for Old Men	2007	1,348	1,273	2,037
The Departed	2006	3,017	1,453	274
Crash	2005	1,905	0	206
Million Dollar Baby	2004	147	2,125	2,375
The Lord of the Rings	2003	3,703	2,558	1,903
Chicago	2002	1,841	2,600	2,701
A Beautiful Mind	2001	2,250	2,220	1,560
Gladiator	2000	3,188	41	577
American Beauty	1999	1,553	1,662	1,990
Shakespeare in Love	1998	833	2,030	1,931
Titanic	1997	2,956	3,169	3,265
The English Patient	1996	1,042	1,186	1,409
Braveheart	1995	2,037	792	491
Forrest Gump	1994	2,365	1,119	1,135

In 2010, the ten movies nominated to win awards for 2009 averaged an increase of 6.89 percent in gross box office receipts between the time the nomination was announced and the awards were broadcast.

Exhibit D: 2010 Best Picture Nominees' Opening Stats and Box Office Grosses Pre-Nominations, Through Awards Night, and Post-Awards Night

Figures courtesy of Hollywood.com

	Distributor	3-Day Opening Gross	Opening Number of Theaters	Opening Rank
Avatar	Fox	$77,025,481	3452	1
Up	Disney	$68,108,790	3766	1
Inglourious Basterds	Weinstein Company	$38,054,676	3165	1
District 9	Sony/TriStar	$37,354,308	3049	1
The Blind Side	Warner Bros.	$34,119,372	3110	2
Precious	Lionsgate	$1,872,458	18	12
Up in the Air	Paramount	$1,181,450	15	13
A Serious Man	Focus	$251,337	6	29
An Education	Sony Pictures Classics	$159,017	4	39
The Hurt Locker	Summit Ent.	$145,342	4	26

	Gross Pre-Nominations	Gross Through Awards Night	Gross Post–Awards Night
Avatar	$595,752,416	$720,607,444	$124,855,028
Up	$292,979,556	$292,979,556	N/A
Inglourious Basterds	$120,523,073	$120,523,073	N/A
District 9	$115,646,235	$115,646,235	N/A
The Blind Side	$237,914,805	$250,467,047	$12,552,242
Precious	$45,447,889	$47,395,661	$1,947,772
Up in the Air	$73,273,658	$83,011,223	$9,737,565
A Serious Man	$9,190,525	$9,190,525	N/A
An Education	$8,795,228	$12,042,219	$3,246,991
The Hurt Locker	$12,647,089	$14,700,000	$2,052,911

"It depends where the picture is in its life cycle, but in general the Best Picture win is clearly the most valuable, followed by the Best Picture nomination (when there were five) if it's in theaters," former Miramax marketing man Jason Cassidy told me. "Then the major acting awards have the next most value. But getting people to the box office is about the top awards."

The Academy Award stamp of approval means even more in the international market. If a studio is willing to take a risk, they wait to release a film in the international market until after nominations are announced. Timed right, this can result in a major boon at the international box office.

The value-added of a Best Actress or Best Actor win is more subjective. Hollywood agents and managers say their clients experience a 20 percent bump in their asking price for the next film they negotiate immediately following a Best Actor or Best Actress win, which translates into at least $1 million for most actors. It also makes a difference in the types of material for which they're considered. Directors and producers start to look at a younger actor like *The Hurt Locker*'s Jeremy Renner in a new light. For established players like Colin Firth, an Oscar solidifies their brand as the gold standard of acting and, hopefully, box office returns. Banks provide studios with better lines of credit for films that contain Oscar winners. They're proven, time-tested, and reliable, which translates into good interest rates.

A strong Oscar-centric marketing push for a young director, actor, or actress brings future value to a studio that has contracted that fledgling talent for multiple projects. By crafting the marketing campaign around Matt Damon and Ben Affleck as screenwriting wunderkinder during the *Good Will Hunting* era, or around a young Gwyneth Paltrow during *Shakespeare in Love*, then signing them for multi-picture deals, Weinstein made an investment toward future profits generated by that talent.

Another trend Oscar watchers have noted is that the Best Actress winner sometimes enjoys a big payday on a bad movie following her Oscar win. After Halle Berry won the award in 2001 for her performance in *Monster's Ball*, she took on the title role of *Catwoman*, for which she received a reported $14 million paycheck and a Razzie.[4] After Charlize Theron won for *Monster* in 2003, she accepted a role in the sci-fi stinker *Æon Flux*, with a reported payday of $10 million. Industry rule of thumb is that a stinker is forgivable if you recently walked away with a little gold man, so it makes sense to cash in.

"After you win, you will get probably some of those offers to do something big and stupid, because the studio wants your Oscar-winning name in there and they're willing to pay for it," said Steve Pond. "But any change in what you get paid really has to do with what stage you are at in your career and what role you won the award for."

Conclusion

Examine the Oscar statuette closely, and the irony is apparent. The little gold man is thrusting a spear into a reel of film. He is skewering the film industry.

Still, the Oscar bump for a film is real. And in an industry that adores labels and titles, the future benefits of an Oscar are worth more than the immediate returns. "Academy Award winner" becomes an actor, writer, director, or producer's cobrand into perpetuity.

"Once you're nominated, forever thereafter Oscar will be included in all of your publicity material. It's a label that will be stamped to your name and career, giving each subsequent film the ability to use that brand," veteran campaigner Murray Weissman told me. "Once something receives Oscar nominations and/or wins, we have no idea of the value of it in the future. We've seen them go from films in theaters, sold to television, and put into home entertainment. Who knows what their future holds? They will be packaged and repackaged." ACADEMY AWARD WINNER will appear on every DVD cover and in every trailer for every film an actor or director works on for the rest of their careers.

However, the value of using a previous winner or nominee in a project may be inflated. In fact, when it comes to box office gross, having a winner or nominee is a crapshoot. In 2010, 85 percent of the top-grossing twenty movies for the year (according to BoxOfficeMojo.com) contained at least one Academy Award nominee. And eight of those top twenty contained at least one Academy Award winner. Of the twenty lowest grossing films of the year, 50 percent featured at least one Academy Award winner.

Nabbing Oscar-approved talent for a film by no means guarantees monetary success. *The American* starred George Clooney and yet it grossed only $35 million in 2010, making it the eighty-third ranked film of the year by gross. Similarly, the romantic comedy *How Do You Know*, starring two previous Academy Award winners—Reese Witherspoon and Jack Nicholson—as well as previous nominee Owen Wilson, ranked ninety-fourth for the year, grossing a little more than $30 million.

In some instances, an Oscar tomorrow can be worth more than an Oscar today. In the nine months following *The Hurt Locker*'s Oscar win, the film sold more than $31 million in DVDs in the United States, according to the data compilation site The Numbers (the-numbers.com). That represented 214 percent of its United States box office gross of $14.7 million. In comparison, *The Hurt Locker*'s main competitor, *Avatar*, grossed only 19 percent of its total box office gross, or $147.5 million, in DVD sales in the United States.

After their win, director Kathryn Bigelow, actor Jeremy Renner, and screenwriter Mark Boal benefited from the Oscar cobrand. Bigelow and Boal were paired again by Paramount for a much bigger-budget project—a film called *Triple Frontier* that was courting the likes of Tom Hanks (Oscar winner) and Johnny Depp (Oscar nominee) to star.

The *Hurt Locker* campaign involved a modest monetary expenditure, probably about $3 million. The additional $3.7 million at the box office and the $31 million in DVD sales following its win represented a return of more than 1,000 percent on the investment. Oscar may be the ultimate vanity prize, but at the end of the day, it is worth the funds it takes to procure it.

[1]   Biskind, Peter. *Down and Dirty Pictures.* New York: Simon & Schuster, 2004.

[2]   Finke, Nikki. "Much Ado About Oscar." *New York*, 15 March 1999.

[3]   Finke.

[4]   Razzies (Golden Raspberry Awards) are given out during Oscar season for the worst performances of the year.

5

Kim Kardashian Versus Paris Hilton: Innovation in the Celebutante Market

Celebrity years are like dog years. One year of fame equals seven years of regular life. In those terms, the decade that Paris Hilton spent dominating our collective consciousness through her assault on the media and demure good taste was a lifetime. Hilton pioneered the market for the celebutante—the celebrity famous for being rich, pretty, and overexposed—in the early 2000s. Kim Kardashian entered the market as a second mover and changed the way the game was played. Everything Paris did, Kim did better. She was a recession-friendly substitute for a digitized audience hungry for the next best thing.

Paris Hilton was practically shoved to the ground when her former friend Kim Kardashian swept into Las Vegas nightclub Lavo amid a melee of fans, photographers, ever-present camera crew, and assorted Kardashian family members on an August night in 2010.

Hilton's ego continued to be bruised as the evening wore on and the Kardashian crew commanded all the attention. Once the reigning princess of Las Vegas nightlife and the woman who pioneered the Vegas appearance fee, Hilton was now relegated to the rear of the VIP section, where she drowned her sorrows in cocktails.

The icing on the bitterness cupcake came when Hilton learned that Kardashian had been flown in on a private jet to the party at the nightclub's expense. Hilton had flown commercial, and that detail alone seemed telling enough. Was Hilton's turn as Hollywood's reigning celebutante coming to an end?

Celebutante (n) \'suh-leh-bew-tänt\ – A person (typically female, exception to the rule: Brody Jenner) who is famous for being famous. Originating from a wealthy and/or famous family, gestated in reality television, the celebutante becomes a brand by virtue of a continued assault on the consumer market through the entertainment news media.

The world was introduced to an eighteen-year-old Paris Hilton in 1999. For better or worse, the celebrity business hasn't been the same since. Her early hard partying earned her the nickname "feisty New York debutramp." The young hotel heiress became known for being willing to do anything for attention, including parading topless around the Hard Rock Hotel pool in Las Vegas and flaunting two high-profile relationships, first with fashion model Jason Shaw and next with Backstreet Boy Nick Carter. That willingness to constantly put herself in the glare of the spotlight made her a lot of money. In 2005, Paris Hilton earned $6.5 million.[1]

Like most successful businesses, Hilton spawned a host of imitators who, because of their family money and good looks, believed that they also had a shot at fame. But none constituted a real threat. Brittny Gastineau wasn't rich enough, Nicole Richie wasn't pretty enough, and Tinsley Mortimer wasn't scandalous enough. None had that X-factor that commanded attention, money, and magazine covers. Enter Kim Kardashian, who at the time was working as a wardrobe organizer for her more famous friends.

Kardashian was determined to reach Hilton levels of success. She used the Paris Hilton business model of personal exploitation coupled with the distribution platform of reality TV to sell herself and related products. Kardashian's advantage was that as the second mover in the market, she was able to learn from Hilton's abundant mistakes. She had the X-factor plus something more—an entire family willing to push the boundaries of personal exposure for the sake of bolstering brand Kardashian. Most importantly, Kardashian had her mother, Kris Jenner, unquestionably the wizard behind it all.

By 2010, it was impossible to pass a newsstand without seeing Kim Kardashian's face on at least one magazine cover. High-minded publications referred to her as a "businesswoman" and "entrepreneur." She hobnobbed at the White House Correspondents' Dinner. Hilton, meanwhile, made headlines that year only for getting busted with cocaine in Las Vegas. In the years BK (Before Kim), Hilton's negative headlines benefited her brand. All press had been good press in Hilton's world. But with Kardashian as a substitute in the market, consumers no longer had to tolerate Hilton's bad behavior. Kardashian was a guilty pleasure who inspired less guilt.

A big difference between the two, beyond a bottle of peroxide, was that Hilton had been deemed a magazine-cover liability. Former *OK!* editor in chief Sarah Ivens told me Hilton was a sales buzzkill. "I learned very quickly not to have her as a main cover. Women don't love or hate her enough to shell out four dollars for something with her on it," Ivens said. In 2007, *Us Weekly* editor in chief Janice Min actually proudly announced a "Paris-Free Issue." Kardashian, on the other hand, was a huge boon for the magazine market. *Shape* magazine had its bestselling issue of 2010 when it featured Kim Kardashian on its cover. Her *Allure* cover was the third-bestselling issue of the year, and a naked "art" photo for *W* tied for second.

Kardashian was a perfect product substitution for Hilton because she was the same, but better. Goods are classified by how demand for them fluctuates in relationship to one another. A substitute good can replace one that doesn't evolve as quickly as the marketplace changes. Classic examples are the Discman replacing the Walkman and DVDs replacing VHS tapes. When demand for one increases, demand for the other decreases. As Hilton's behavior became increasingly erratic and she refused to evolve, demand for Kardashian skyrocketed. Kardashian also comes with a slew of complementary goods. Khloé and Kourtney Kardashian were like the beer to Kim's pizza. Increased demand for one increased the demand for all. That was proven in 2011, when the Kardashian family made $65 million.

There may be a handful of celebutantes famous for being famous, but there is only room at the top for one. Hilton and Kardashian competed for top spot and for mindshare of the celebrity consumer. By 2011, it was clear that Kardashian was the superior product.

The Origins of Brand Hilton and Brand Kardashian

There are two main economic drivers behind Hilton's rise to celebutante status. She emerged as a public figure at a time when demand for stars began to outstrip supply. The year 2003 saw the beginning of excess in the celebrity weekly magazine market, and Internet gossip was becoming big business. Online celebrity news outlets multiplied by a factor of a hundred within a year, and their consumers wanted news and updates every time they logged on. Traditional celebrities could no longer fill the gigantic news hole that was growing wider by the week. Movie stars and rock stars just didn't do enough public stuff on a daily basis to meet the demand. (Some of them, in fact, were too busy working.) But Paris Hilton caused enough drama to fill several news columns and glossy pages every week.

Hilton's rise also coincided with the rise of reality TV, a programming format that networks began churning out at a fraction of the cost of traditional scripted shows.[2] Reality shows didn't have high production overheads, and because they often used "real" people instead of established actors, salary costs were low. When Hilton was cast on the Fox show *The Simple Life* in 2003, she joined a revolution of reality show "characters" supplanting professionals in the celebrity market.

Hilton's wealthy upbringing as the great-granddaughter of hotel baron Conrad Hilton had prepared her for the spotlight. Growing up, she shuttled between a suite at the Waldorf Astoria in Manhattan and a mansion in Beverly Hills, and rubbed elbows with other children of privilege. At nineteen, Hilton began working as a model with Donald Trump's modeling agency. Enter Hilton's wizard, manager Jason Moore, who joined her team in 1999 and stayed by her side until he quit in 2009. A hippie surfer dude, Moore studied film at the University of California–San Diego and decided to be a Hollywood manager when a big-time manager visited his college film class. The other students booed her off the stage as yuppie scum. But Moore was intrigued. An artist at heart, Moore believed he could paint a celebrity into fame as long as he had a blank canvas. Hilton proved ready and willing.

By 2001 Hilton was a gossip column staple. The *New York Post*'s Page Six gossip column regularly ran stories about her as an out-of-control party girl whom anyone who was anyone was talking about. Then came *The Simple Life*, the premise of which was that Hilton and then–best friend Nicole Richie would work and inevitably flail and fail at a series of menial jobs across the country, providing a stark contrast between the coddled heiresses and blue collar America. The show ran for five seasons, first on Fox and then on the E! Entertainment network. The show's debut coincided with the release of a sex tape featuring Hilton and her former boyfriend Rick Salomon. Hilton claimed to be outraged and tried to suppress the tape, but many believe that it was a savvy business move on her part. It certainly furthered her name recognition. The tape sold more than 600,000 copies, and according to Lola Ogunnaike of the *New York Times*, it established Hilton "as a kind of postmodern celebrity."[3]

Now witness a few parallels.

Born in 1980, Kim Kardashian is the daughter of the lawyer Robert Kardashian, famous for defending O. J. Simpson during his 1995 murder trial, and the stepdaughter of Olympic gold medalist and motivational speaker Bruce Jenner. She grew up in California, dabbled in modeling, and became a household name after a sex tape with her former boyfriend, the singer Ray J, was mysteriously leaked then sold through Vivid Entertainment in 2007.

Prior to the tape's release, Kardashian's mother, Kris Jenner, had decided her family would be famous. She had been shopping the concept for a reality show centered on her blended family, using Bruce's name to get producers interested. Kim Kardashian and her siblings were to be secondary characters when Kris first peddled the idea to Ryan Seacrest of the E! network. Post–sex tape, the reality show was sold on Kim's name.

Kris, who claims never to have seen the tape, said she initially thought it had ruined their chances. "But you can either be a problem maker or a problem solver. And I'm a problem solver. My job as her mom and manager is to take care of the problem, whatever it is. I had to cry and get upset in the privacy of my own room and then come out and help her, because she's my daughter. What's that Kenny Rogers line? 'You got to know when to hold 'em and know when to fold 'em.' All I knew was that I had to make some lemonade out of these lemons fast. Real fast."[4]

The lemonade took the form of a $5 million settlement from Vivid in exchange for the rights to distribute the tape. The first episode of *Keeping Up with the Kardashians* debuted on October 14, 2007, and documented the lives of Kim, sisters Kourtney, Khloé, Kendall, and Kylie, brother Robert, and of course, Kris and Bruce. *Kourtney and Khloé Take Miami*—a spin-off of the show, starring Kourtney and Khloé Kardashian—began airing in 2009.

Kris is the family matriarch and business manager and a guiding force for the entire Kardashian empire. As manager, she takes 10 percent of the family's earnings. "We face fifteen challenges a day," Kris told me. "I have to have a good head on my shoulders and put out fires all day long." Her attention to detail and willingness to work her entire family to the bone have proven instrumental to her success. Both Hilton and Kardashian entered the market through a well-timed sex tape and a reality show, but after their fame was solidified, their business strategies proved entirely different.

Paris Hilton's Brand Strategy

Hilton used the publicity from her sex tape and the foray into reality TV to launch brand Paris Hilton. In 2004, Hilton commanded between $150,000 and $200,000 to appear at a club for twenty minutes. She received more money if that club was in Japan. (For decades the Japanese market has been obsessed with American pop culture. When a celebrity says they're big in Japan, it's probably true.)

Hilton's compensated club appearances coincided with the 2004 publication of *Confessions of an Heiress: A Tongue-in-Chic Peek Behind the Pose*, which she co-wrote with Merle Ginsberg and for which she reportedly received a $100,000 advance. The book was panned by critics but became a *New York Times* bestseller. Hilton followed it up with a designer diary, also co-written by Merle Ginsberg, called *Your Heiress Diary: Confess It All to Me*.

That same year, Paris launched her line of Paris Hilton perfumes, marketed through Parlux Fragrances. The business community was initially skeptical of the partnership. Writing for *Fast Company*, business writer Kathryn Tuggle questioned Hilton's ability to successfully sell a lifestyle brand, given her scandalous history and well-publicized hard partying lifestyle: "If Parlux plans to make a successful brand out of panty-less Paris, they should probably buy her some undergarments before she starts making public appearances. I'm wondering what market Parlux will target for the Paris line. Moms with tweens may be hesitant to purchase it, and the 18–24 market is already pretty comfortable with brands like Maybelline and Clinique."[5]

But Hilton's fragrances have been her biggest successes by far. According to its 2005 annual report, Parlux experienced half of its annual sales growth from the launch of its first Paris Hilton fragrance.

Exhibit A: Parlux Net Sales and Percentage Generated by Paris Hilton 2005-2009

Figures courtesy of Parlux Fragrances, Inc.'s 2009 annual report

	Net Sales	Hilton's Sales
2005	$25,064,000	55%
2006	$106,364,000	68%
2007	$134,365,000	56%
2008	$153,696,000	69%
2009	$151,155,000	11%

That first fragrance achieved gross sales of $11 million from the time of its launch in November 2004 through the end of 2005. The business community would never discount someone on the basis of a sex tape again—to Kardashian's future advantage.

By 2010, Hilton had a stable of ten fragrances with Parlux, two of them for men. In 2009, she generated $85.4 million in sales for the company, most of which were overseas.[6]

Early on in her career, Hilton had set her heart on acting. In 2005, at age twenty-four, she signed with Endeavor, a Hollywood talent agency, in the hope of launching a movie career. She went with Endeavor because, in her words, "they know how to do branding and they're really smart." She had a small role in the 2005 horror film *The House of Wax*, which grossed $68 million worldwide.[9] She then executive-produced two movies in which she also appeared: 2006's *Pledge This!* and 2008's *The Hottie & the Nottie*, both of which made a little more than $1.5 million worldwide.

Hilton told the *New York Times* that she was modeling her career after moguls like Sean Combs and Donald Trump. "Puffy is a genius. He does everything. Music. Clothing. I totally look up to him and Donald Trump because he's built this whole empire—hotels, casinos, resorts, a television show."[7]

But unlike those businessmen, Hilton had difficulty cultivating a long-term strategy. She was consistently getting in the way of manager Jason Moore's plans to build her brand. In 2005, Hilton opened a chain of nightclubs with Florida businessman Fred Khalilian. The first property was Club Paris in Orlando, and Hilton was paid seven figures to sign on the dotted line with Khalilian, the plan being to split future profits down the middle. Khalilian claimed that Paris was trouble from the start. She arrived six hours late for the club's grand opening and, according to Khalilian, ceased communications with him shortly afterwards. The businessman announced through the media that he planned to "fire" Hilton and end her involvement with his nightclub ventures.[8]

Despite her claims that she wanted to be a business mogul and her successes with fragrance branding, what Hilton really wanted was fame. Perhaps because she grew up so wealthy, fortune was an ancillary concern.

In 2006, Hilton released her first album, *Paris,* on Heiress Records, a Warner Bros. sub-label she created in 2004 to support her music ventures. The album sold 75,000 copies in the first week but was classified as a flop by the industry and in December 2008, Hilton and Warner parted ways. Hilton said she had plans for a second album, but that it would be independently produced. As of 2011, no album had been released.

But for a while her dreams of fame were granted. A modern art exhibit that spent a year in galleries in Southern California required visitors to swipe their credit card or driver's license to see where they ranked in a globe-spanning Internet index of fame. Rank was determined by how often a person was mentioned on the Internet and how often their name was searched by Internet users around the world. The top two slots were consistently taken by Jesus and Moses. Paris Hilton was third.

Hilton was so famous—or rather faux-mous—that simply banning her from a gossip column brought the columnist a certain cachet, as my former *New York Daily News* colleague Lloyd Grove can attest. Because Hilton's presence in the media was so ubiquitous, Grove was hard-pressed to ban her from his column, "Lowdown," but he did it and was praised for his initiative.

In 2008, Hilton launched a new reality show on MTV, *Paris Hilton's My New BFF*, a spin on reality dating shows. In it, Hilton searched for a new best friend, a not-so-veiled reference to the friendships she had lost on her path to stardom. The show aired for two seasons on MTV before moving into the international market. International markets like Asia, Australia, the UK, and even the Middle East have been fascinated by Hilton from the beginning of her rise. But brand Hilton was perhaps a little too diffuse—and a little too American—for Americans to truly love her.

Kim Kardashian's Brand Strategy

Kim Kardashian's greatest asset isn't her much talked-about backside. Her greatest asset is a business model that uses *Keeping Up with the Kardashians* as a hub for all her family's other business ventures. It is a centralized distribution system through which the family sells products, stories, and themselves. Kardashian and her sisters jokingly refer to it as "the mother ship."

"These shows are a thirty-minute commercial," said Khloé Kardashian, costar of the first spinoff, *Kourtney & Khloé Take Miami*, and her own spin-off with her husband, Los Angeles Lakers basketball player Lamar Odom.[9] They have become expert at parlaying the familiarity that the show breeds into lucrative magazine covers. When *Redbook* decided to publish their first-ever "family" issue, a group shot of a beaming Kourtney, Khloé, Kim, and mom Kris was their first choice. Kourtney's 2009 pregnancy sold in a package deal for $300,000 to *Life & Style* magazine. Khloé's wedding to Lamar Odom also sold for $300,000.

But early in the Kardashian family's rise to fame, Kris was frazzled. At one point she asked her stepson Brody Jenner's buddy Spencer Pratt, who would later shoot to reality TV fame on *The Hills*, to act as Kim's manager. Some sources claim that Kris orchestrated the release of her daughter's sex tape, an allegation the family has vigorously denied. Yet following release of the tape, she brokered a deal for Kim to appear in *Playboy*, which kept Kardashian buzz strong despite being a questionable strategy for Kim's long-term image. It was one of the few times that Jenner focused only on the short-term, and given the legions of shady characters who had approached her offering sketchy deals, *Playboy* may have seemed the most reasonable option.

Then in 2008 Kim Kardashian got her first real modeling endorsement, when she became the face of Bongo jeans. By then, Kardashian was a staple in weekly magazines and on nightly entertainment shows (both the lifeblood of the celebutante who, unlike an actor or a musician, doesn't promote herself around a movie or an album). She then branched out into the consumer products market.

In 2009, Kardashian took advantage of the copious amounts of press about her curvy figure by creating a partnership with GNC to launch a diet cleanse called QuickTrim, a product plugged on *Keeping Up with the Kardashians* and used by the entire family. The promotional opportunities were endless, especially when the girls were constantly being photographed in barely-there bikinis and talking about how they kept "a bikini bod" or "got in the best shape of their lives." In 2009, Kardashian launched the ecommerce site ShoeDazzle, a Los Angeles–based high-end online shoe rental site, and struck a deal to promote the fast food chain Carl's Jr.'s new healthy option—grilled chicken salad. (Back in 2005, Carl's Jr. had hired Hilton for a similarly steamy ad.) The Kardashian ad generated 258 million media impressions (the number of times the ad was viewed or mentioned in the media), more than three times the quantity achieved by any of the chain's previous celebrity commercial stars and more than all of them combined.

Taking another page from Hilton's playbook, in February 2010 Kardashian released her first fragrance, Kim Kardashian, in partnership with Lighthouse Beauty, a company partially owned by Hilton's fragrance house, Parlux. Kim Kardashian's fragrance went on to become the cosmetics chain Sephora's bestseller that year. Just in time for the holidays, Kim released her first book, *Kardashian Konfidential*, co-written with sisters Khloé and Kourtney. They received a reported $150,000 advance. It sold 275,000 copies.

Kardashian improved on Hilton's business model by working harder than the heiress ever had. In the fall of 2010, Kardashian executive-produced her first TV series, *The Spin Crowd*, starring the publicist Jonathan Cheban, her longtime friend. She received a $180,000 producing fee. The show was the highest-rated program in the history of its 10:30 p.m. time slot on E!—for its eight-week run it received an average of 1.5 to 2 million viewers. Cheban had not expected Kardashian to be hands-on, but she surprised him with the amount of love she gave to *Spin Crowd*.

"She is the busiest woman I have ever met, and yet once the show started, she was out promoting it on the *Today* show and on Twitter. She never flakes on you. That's what sets her apart. Her business model is about morals and standards, never screwing anybody and never flaking," Cheban told me.

That the Kardashians are exceptionally industrious young women is a theme hit by several celebrity industry insiders. "They work until they fall down at night," *Redbook* editor in chief Jill Herzig reported after the Kardashian cover shoot. She saw Kim tweeting from a Golden Globes party at 3:00 a.m. and then fresh-faced and ready to go at 6:00 a.m. the next morning.

By 2010, Kim Kardashian's revenue streams were similar to Hilton's— book sales, fees, and television revenues—but with a heavier emphasis on endorsement deals and product sales. However, while a good year for Hilton meant $10 million, a good year for the Kardashians was six times that. Kardashian had learned from Hilton how to use her club appearances to her advantage, and in 2011 Kim commanded a personal appearance fee of $100,000 to $250,000 domestically and $1 million abroad. "The appearances are good moneymakers," she told *Cosmopolitan*. "And they're also a great way for me to connect with people in places like Oklahoma, where I never would go otherwise. Those girls going to the clubs will be buying my perfume."

The smallest of the five streams was actually payment from *Keeping Up with the Kardashians*, for which the three sisters each made around $20,000 per episode. But the show was merely a vehicle to promote the Kardashian brand and sell its many products. The economics of abundance grew absurd in the market for faux fame.

None of the Kardashians' revenue streams would have been realized if it were not for the reality shows. The shows, all airing on E!, do well because they are fun to watch and the family is relatable. The public enjoys the aspirational intimacy. Whereas Hilton's reality show was alienating (it showed how different she was from the rest of America), Kardashian's was inclusive. "The glamour of the family is fascinating, but when you peel back the layers you see they are really devoted to each other in complex ways," Herzig said. "I think there is an honesty about them that contrasts in an interesting way with how stunningly gorgeous they all are, and I think that is what clicks with the American public. They're real. They show their flaws."

Prior to launching *Keeping Up with the Kardashians*, E! was the thirteenth-rated cable network with women aged eighteen to forty-nine on Sundays. By 2011, it had moved into the number one slot. The Season Four finale of the show drew 4.8 million viewers, making it the most-watched broadcast in E!'s history.

"It has changed the face of E!," said Lisa Berger, the network's executive vice president of original programming. "We were a place to report on celebrity; we weren't a place to break and make celebrity, which is now the whole idea of the E! brand."[10]

The Kardashian business strategy has always been brand first, fame second. That's a major diversion from Paris, who wanted to be famous more than anything else. The celebrity brands that have thrived over the past several decades are run by women who have put their brands first, some to the point of losing their fame altogether. Cases in point are Jaclyn

Smith, Kathy Ireland, and Daisy Fuentes with their clothing lines. Even Jessica Simpson, whose clothing line was worth a reported $1 billion in 2010, put her fame on the back burner to become an entrepreneur.

Hilton-Kardashian Product Differentiation

In many ways, fame-whoring and overexposure killed the Hilton brand in the United States. But more than anything, what made Hilton riskier and "more expensive" to deal with in the celebrity market was her refusal to play nice and behave. To that extent, Kardashian's long-term lifestyle strategy further differentiates her from Hilton. Whereas Hilton was a sexy bad girl, Kardashian is a sexy good girl. Kardashian does not drink to excess, does not do drugs, and doesn't party. In order to strictly control her image, she will not be photographed at a club unless she is being paid to appear at that club and even then she will be out of there before midnight and exercising early the next morning.

Kardashian rose to fame amid the worst recession America had experienced in seventy years, and her tremendous success as a substitute good is in many ways a product of that recession mentality. Hilton represented all the excess of Bush-era wealth and conspicuous consumption, whereas Kardashian, despite her upper-class income, displayed a work ethic worthy of the middle class. Ask any one of the Kardashians about their success and they will pepper their answer with work, work, work.

"There was just a desire to work hard and do good work; the goal was to produce things," Kris told me. "When we realized there was an audience and people were excited about watching the show, it made me so happy to know that what we were working hard at was paying off." Independently of her mother, Kim said to me later, "You know it's just a lot of work that goes into this whole thing that might not be so visible to the public eye. I think hard work pays off, and I think having a strong work ethic. No matter what, we have to stay focused."

The parties that were fun for Hilton are work for Kardashian. Kim typically arrives at a red carpet an hour after the expected call time, to ensure that everyone is ready and waiting for her, spends an hour on the red carpet, doing interviews with absolutely every outlet that came to cover the event, then she mingles for between five minutes and an hour before leaving. None of it is fun.

Because Kardashian came into the game later than Hilton (and several years older), she learned from Hilton's mistakes. She doesn't have many friends besides her four sisters. She trusts next to no one except her family members. She's also nice. Speak to Hilton for any length of time and she will rarely look you in the eye. Hilton rolls her eyes, plays on her phone, and speaks in classic distracted Valley Girl cadences. Kim may speak in a childlike register but she smiles at you and makes eye contact the entire time you speak to her.

Kardashian even charmed business reporter Stephanie Dahl of *Forbes* with her overwhelming niceness.

"I was initially skeptical and then I started researching what she did and how many different business ventures she had and I was stunned," Dahl told me. Kardashian did make Dahl wait about an hour for her interview, because she wanted to make sure the paparazzi got pictures of her aligning her brand with *Forbes*. But she won Dahl over when she stayed after their meeting to make conversation with and sign autographs for the building's doormen and maintenance staff, proving that every fan counts in Kardashian-land.

Positive media impressions drive the Kardashian brand, whereas Paris clawed and scratched her way into news stories. Hilton's brand was built on feuds, both verbal and physical, with friends and enemies alike, almost as much as it was on her illicit sex tape. Though sources claim she was in on the joke and not the airhead she was often reported to be, Hilton was never mistaken for nice. In 2007, in a candid moment, a seemingly self-satisfied Hilton was caught on video dancing around with her sister Nicky to the Notorious B.I.G. song "Hypnotize" and referring to a male friend as a "faggot." She made further Internet waves by approaching the camera and proclaiming, "We're like two niggers." She added more fuel to the fire by describing another woman at the party as a "fuckin' hoodlum, broke, poor bitch from like, Compton, public-school bitch."

By 2010, Hilton was still driving publicity through negative media impressions. That September, Wynn Resorts Ltd. spokeswoman Jennifer

Dunne told the Associated Press that Hilton was banned from Wynn Las Vegas and Encore, following her arrest outside the hotel for drug possession. Hilton eventually struck a plea deal that knocked off the more serious felony charge in return for pleading guilty to two misdemeanor counts of drug possession and obstructing an officer.

Another avenue where Kardashian has superseded Hilton is in the realm of social media. She and her sisters were early adopters of the Ad.ly model, whereby brands pay celebrities up to $25,000 to tweet on their behalf. Kardashian's $25,000 tweet for Armani drove forty thousand users to the Armani website in less than twenty-four hours.[11] For the fourth quarter of 2010, Kim and Khloé Kardashian were the second and third most influential celebrities in Ad.ly's network.

Cementing her place on top of the celebrity pyramid, the Microsoft search engine Bing announced in December 2010 that Kardashian was the most searched person of the year. Hilton was forty-third on the list, a far cry from her days trumping biblical figures.

Conclusion

It's often said that Kim Kardashian stole Paris Hilton's business model. Or worse, that she is a counterfeit of Hilton—a product seemingly identical to the original that has actually damaged the original brand because it is a poorly made substitute. True, Hilton was the first mover in the celebutante market. Yes, Kardashian's entrance did detract from Hilton's consumer mindshare. But Kardashian is not evolving as a counterfeit. She is a pure second mover and substitute in the market who creates new opportunities in that market as her business grows.

When Kim first sat down with her mother to talk business in 2007, they agreed there was no business model they could follow. Hilton's was a good start, but it didn't go far enough.

"My mom and I talk about it all the time. We have just done what works for us and stuck by that. . . . We make our own model," Kardashian told me.

Kardashian blows off comparisons to her predecessor: "I definitely respect everything [Paris] has done. She's very cool and has done so much in her life, and she's taught me so much, just being a friend for so long. But I don't look at it like that." Kardashian added that she could see reasons for the comparison, but that she has never aspired to be Hilton.[12]

In 2011, 90 percent of the U.S. population had some idea who Kardashian is, while 97 percent knew of Hilton. But Kardashian's Davie Brown Index (DBI) scores from The Marketing Arm, a firm that helps companies determine what value a celebrity will add to their brand and their campaign, topped Hilton's in every other category. Kardashian had a stronger appeal score (59 vs. 45 out of a possible 100), was more likely to be a trendsetter (66 vs. 55), had more endorsement potential (63 vs. 48), and was more aspirational (56 vs. 42).

More brands wanted to sign Kardashian for endorsement deals, more consumers wanted to buy products that would allow them to be like her, and the public simply liked her more than they liked Paris Hilton.

As Kardashian's star rose, Hilton began moving aggressively into international markets—ceding the domestic market to her former friend. Her remaining fan base was abroad. Countries like Japan and India saw Hilton as the embodiment of American chic and glamour, and just didn't care about the negative baggage being reported in the U.S. press. After all, what was more American than a little hubris and bad behavior?

In 2008, Parlux sublicensed the international rights for a Paris Hilton line of handbags. In 2009, they sublicensed the worldwide exclusive rights for Paris Hilton sunglasses through 2012. Hilton began traveling abroad more often, and when her second venture in reality TV, *Paris Hilton's My New BFF*, didn't achieve tremendous success in the domestic market, she launched an international version, *Paris Hilton's British Best Friend*, which premiered in early 2009 on ITV2 in the UK. Later that year she began work on *Paris Hilton's Dubai BFF* and announced plans to continue her reality search for a soul mate across new continents.

Hilton is wise to turn BFF into an international franchise and to capitalize on opportunities abroad while her star power is still strong around the globe. With her mindshare cannibalized by Kardashian in the United States, becoming an international brand is the most lucrative option for Hilton.

Her former manager Jason Moore parted ways with Hilton in 2009 amid reports that his wife was jealous of all the time he spent with his client. Moore concedes that he was just tired from a decade traveling around looking for the next opportunity to make a buck. There was talk that he would write a tell-all memoir about his time with the heiress. He has no interest in doing so.

"Why would I destroy the painting?" Moore asked me over mimosas at a bar near his Venice Beach apartment, where he was basking in his semi-retirement.

Should she choose to fight to retain her domestic brand, Hilton has no choice but to innovate. As 2011 progressed, it appeared she was making inroads. Hilton took a few months out of the spotlight and prepared for the launch of *The World According to Paris* on the Oxygen network. Now it was Hilton taking a page out of the Kardashian playbook about how to relate to fans. The new show was a candid look at Hilton's life, which more than one critic described as a Kardashian rip-off before the show even aired. But it was a smart business move on Hilton's part; when a substitute takes over a product's market share, the original reinvents and repositions.

Still, Hilton has yet to find Kardashian-level success with her latest venture. In July 2011, she stormed off the set during an interview with ABC News when reporter Dan Harris asked her if she thought her stardom had been eclipsed by Kardashian, leading her own celebrity moment to pass.

Kardashian will be smart to study Hilton's decline. Fame is a cycle, and though it may seem like forever, Team Kardashian has only been around for three years. There's always someone younger and prettier and smarter in Hollywood who wants it more. The day will come when someone will not just keep up with but surpass the Kardashians. Kris jokes that the future stars will be her teenage daughters with Bruce: Kylie and Kendall Jenner.

"My fantasy is to have *Keeping Up With Kardashians*, Season 26," Kris said. "Who knew it would be this profitable? I should have had more kids."[13]

1   "Paris Hilton, Forbes Top Celebrities." Forbes.com, June 2005.

2   The average episode of reality television typically costs around $500,000 to produce, whereas a scripted program can run as high as $2 million.

3   Ogunnaike, Lola. "Sex, Lawsuits and Celebrities Caught on Tape." *The New York Times*, 19 March 2006.

4   Newman, Judith, and Leslie Bruce. "How the Kardashians Made $65 Million Last Year." *The Hollywood Reporter*, 16 February 2011.

5   Tuggle, Kathryn. "Paris Hilton Launches New Business Venture." *Fast Company*, 29 November 2006.

6   Parlux Fragrances, Inc.'s 2005 annual report.

7   Ogunnaike, Lola. "Paris Inc." *The New York Times*, 2 May 2005.

8   *Showbiz Tonight*. HLN, 5 January 2007.

9   Newman and Bruce.

10   Newman and Bruce.

11   Shepatin, Matthew. "Kim Kardashian's a Ca'rear' Woman." *New York Post*, 18 July 2010.

12   Elfman, Doug. "Pool Pays Kardashian to Create Buzz." *Las Vegas Review-Journal*, 30 March 2009.

13   Newman and Bruce.

6

Tim McGraw:
Using Fragrance to Maximize
Customer Lifetime Value (CLV)

Celebrity fragrances can be an ATM for famous people—paying high dividends for very little investment of time or money. Done well, they also cement brand loyalty and provide a national marketing platform from which to sell a celebrity brand to consumers outside its niche market. Tim McGraw has harnessed the power of fragrance to transform himself from mere country singer to mainstream, multiplatform star.

By any account, Tim McGraw was one of the most successful country music stars in America in 2006. In April of that year, McGraw and his wife, fellow country music sensation Faith Hill, began a fifty-five-city, seventy-three-concert tour that grossed nearly $89 million on sales of more than 1.1 million tickets, making it the top-grossing tour in Nashville history. The previous year, his song "I Like It, I Love It" played every halftime on *Monday Night Football* broadcasts. McGraw had even branched out into acting, playing the dad in the family film *Flicka*, a modest success in theaters and a hit on DVD.

McGraw liked it, he loved it, and he wanted a lot more of it. He wanted to transition from a singer who dabbled in acting to a full-fledged celebrity brand. He knew this process would require cultivating new fans outside the country demographic, without alienating the loyalties of old fans. It required a delicate repositioning. He would have to find a way to get city slickers interested in country and let country folk know he was still their cowboy.

This was when McGraw's management team approached longtime talent and branding consultant Michael Flutie. At first glance, Flutie seemed an odd choice. A former modeling agent, Flutie got his start branding celebrities when he dated the interior designer Thom Filicia, whom he helped turn into a bankable name on the cable TV makeover show *Queer Eye for the Straight Guy*. Always impeccably dressed, Flutie talks like a primetime game show host, often finishing people's sentences. When they approached him, the McGraw team knew only that they wanted to get the singer's name and face in front of as many people as possible. Ford truck endorsements had given McGraw's country compatriot Toby Keith a significant exposure boost, but McGraw's team knew that Keith's strategy wouldn't gain them much traction north of the Mason-Dixon Line. During their first meeting with Flutie they asked him what he would do. His answer may have surprised them.

"I told them we just had to do a fragrance for Tim," Flutie related to me. (Over the course of my research, Flutie was open about his McGraw branding strategy. The McGraw team and fragrance house Coty declined invitations to comment.) "I said, 'I think that Tim McGraw is an icon in America and there is no person that represents the heartland of America better—the flyover states—in a way that is so aspirational.'"

Flutie's reasoning was that a fragrance could be used to extract more value from existing fan loyalty and also serve as a foundation for marketing a McGraw lifestyle, one defined by success in a white T-shirt and jeans, marriage to a beautiful and equally successful woman, and a confident masculinity unafraid of a hint of lavender behind the ears.

Along the way, a fragrance would boost the performer's bottom line by giving him entrée to the $25-billion-a-year fragrance business. A fragrance would pollinate a relationship with McGraw fans, planting seeds for future dividends.

Customer lifetime value (CLV) is the net present value of the cash flows attributed to the customer. In the celebrity industry, the customer is someone who buys the things that a celebrity produces, be it music, DVDs, or concert tickets. Put simply, the customers are fans. The push to maximize CLV is often a question of deciding what else the loyal fan will buy. If a concert T-shirt, how about a refrigerator magnet or a ringtone? If the image of a good ol' boy country crooner, how about the image of a country crooner gone a little bit metrosexual? Could Flutie "Queer Eye" one of the straightest red-blooded American men in show business and make him even richer and more popular?

The Celebrity Endorsement Meets the Fragrance Market

Since the birth of radio in the 1920s, celebrities have attached themselves to products through what is known as the celebrity endorsement. Ads paid for radio programs to be produced, and recognizable famous voices on air brought in listeners. In short, the celebrity endorsement made radio lucrative.

Strictly speaking, the celebrity endorsement today involves a celebrity appearing in an ad—be it in print, on the radio, or on television—announcing that they enjoy a particular product and encouraging the world to like it too. For decades, however, there was no consensus as to the celebrity endorsement's effectiveness. David Ogilvy, of mid-century Madison Avenue behemoth Ogilvy & Mather, was famously skeptical. "Testimonials from celebrities get high recall scores," he maintained in his 1985 book *Ogilvy on Advertising*, "but I have stopped using them because readers remember the celebrity and forget the product. What's more, they assume the celebrity has been bought, which is usually the case."[1]

But prevailing opinion shifted, and today more than 15 percent of advertisements in the United States contain a celebrity. The nature of the endorsement itself has also evolved. Instead of simply expressing a preference for, or attaching their face to, a particular product, many celebrities now choose licensing and cobranding deals that give them partial ownership and/or a percentage of sales, making brand and celebrity more personally and professionally intertwined.

This also creates a bigger payday. Whereas an endorsement grants a celebrity a flat upfront fee for lending his or her image to an ad campaign, the licensing deal is a longer brand alliance that pays on performance. The additional revenue stream is a boon to celebrities at a time when CD sales are plummeting, movie studios pay out less upfront, and TV shows have lost ad revenue to websites. The licensing deal also benefits companies, because the celebrity now has greater incentive to work very hard promoting their product. For example, the hip-hop mogul Sean Combs has rarely been seen drinking anything but Cîroc vodka since he took a 50/50 stake in Diageo's ailing grape liquor in 2007.

Within the world of endorsements and licensing deals, celebrity fragrances are big business. Sales of fragrances associated with a celebrity approached $1 billion dollars in 2005 and are the fastest-growing segment of the global fragrance industry.[2]

Perfume bottle designer Kenneth Hirst believes that the use of celebrities derives from the fact that they provide a ready-made marketing platform in a glutted industry. Before the 1990s, fewer than a hundred fragrances would launch in the United States each year. In 2009, by no means a banner year for the global economy at large, 245 new fragrances entered the market.

With a celebrity, the image and consumer fan base already exist. "That reputation is built through the media with the bombardment of coverage," Hirst said. "That's free advertising for the fragrance companies."[3] And free advertising for the celebrity too.

Rochelle Bloom is the president of the Fragrance Foundation, a nonprofit whose goal is to educate consumers about the fragrance industry. Its yearly event, the FiFi Awards, is considered the Academy Awards of fragrance. Stars like Usher, Kim Kardashian, Fergie of the Black Eyed Peas, Mary J. Blige, Antonio Banderas, and Tim McGraw regularly walk its red carpet. Bloom was with Estée Lauder for twenty-seven years before joining the nonprofit, and her irritation shows when she talks about how many new fragrances are released each year.

"It has become very bottom-line driven and not emotional, and I think the consumer got confused and was attacked when every day there was a new fragrance. [Companies] went from building brands to just throwing them out there to see what stuck," Bloom said.

The marriage between fame and fragrance goes back decades, to the

1930s, when the fashion designer Elsa Schiaparelli designed a curvy perfume bottle modeled after the actress Mae West's figure. In the 1950s, Givenchy created a scent for film star Audrey Hepburn that was musky and powdery, and in the early 1980s, *Dynasty* stars Joan Collins and Linda Evans promoted fragrances linked to their primetime soap opera. Elizabeth Taylor's scent, White Diamonds, has been an Elizabeth Arden top seller since it launched in 1991, grossing more than $1 billion in sales and providing a nice revenue stream for an actress who was no longer spending much time in front of the cameras.

Through much of the 1990s, the fragrance aisles were dominated by fashion brands like Giorgio Armani and Calvin Klein. In 2000, that tide turned. The market for designer fragrances was saturated, and fragrance houses turned their attention back to Hollywood. Elizabeth Arden hired Welsh actress Catherine Zeta-Jones and Chanel hired Nicole Kidman. But it wasn't until Coty, a company founded in 1904 and the world's leading maker of mass-market perfumes and colognes, struck a deal with Jennifer Lopez that the celebrity fragrance renaissance truly began.

In 2002, Lopez was a gigantic star marred by scandal. Her relationship with Sean Combs, who had recently been charged and later acquitted in a nightclub shooting, had tarnished her brand.

Coty executive Catherine Walsh met with Lopez during her honeymoon with her first husband, the dancer Cris Judd, in Venice. The singer, fresh out of the shower, remained in her bathrobe while she sketched a curvy bottle, reminiscent of her own voluptuous frame, for Walsh. She wanted the fragrance to smell like soap. The result of that meeting was Glow, which Coty sold exclusively in department stores. They wanted older store regulars and also to attract Lopez's young followers to fragrance counters.[4]

Coty's success with Lopez inspired a rush to sign younger celebrities to fragrance deals. Elizabeth Arden signed Britney Spears. Her scent, Curious, launched in 2004 and achieved $100 million in sales in its first year alone. Estée Lauder signed Beyoncé Knowles and Enrique Iglesias to reposition its Tommy Hilfiger fragrances. In 2009, a grand total of sixty-two new celebrity fragrances were unleashed on the market, an increase from a mere ten fragrances just ten years earlier.

Exhibit A: Number of Celebrity Fragrance Launches by Year

Figures courtesy of Michael Edwards and the Fragrances of the World database

	Male	Female
1999	4	6
2000	4	4
2001	3	6
2002	4	8
2003	2	9
2004	5	15
2005	12	19
2006	12	36
2007	16	34
2008	17	40
2009	18	44

"The celebrities saw it as a revenue stream without a lot of responsibility, and the manufacturers saw it as a revenue stream to help their bottom line. They started signing people like crazy," Rochelle Bloom said. A celebrity can expect to make between 5 percent and 10 percent of the sales for licensing their name to a scent, in addition to an upfront payment between $3 million and $5 million. Bloom likens a celebrity signing a fragrance licensing deal to going to an ATM: "low personal investment, high ROI [Return on Investment]."

Not all celebs just sit back and collect their checks, however. McGraw involved himself intimately in the process of fragrance development and marketing each step of the way.

Development of the McGraw Fragrance

Whatever turns it may have taken, the fragrance category remains consistently aspirational. It represents a persona in an emotional and tangible way. A consumer feels more connected to a star through their fragrance, which in turn allows the star to bank some major brand equity with that consumer. When a consumer looks at the celebrity as a friend, they want to support them. Fans can't exactly ring them up to say "good luck with your movie." They vote with their wallets.

Everything today is about the brand. In the fragrance market, how a brand is perceived is heavily tied to distribution.

There are three tiers for fragrance distribution in the United States:

Tier 1: High-end department stores. At the top of this category are Bergdorf Goodman and Barneys. It continues down through Bloomingdale's and further on down to Nordstrom and Macy's.

Tier 2: J.C. Penney, Sears.

Tier 3: Pharmacies, Walmart, Target, Kmart.

What tier a celebrity sells in says something about whom they want to reach. When Jennifer Aniston released her fragrance Lolavie in the European market before launching in high-end Tier 1 stores in the United States, it showed she was currying favor for her brand first with the very lucrative international market and then with the high-end consumer in America. Why did that make sense for Aniston? The lower end of the consumer spectrum already loved Jennifer. The high-end consumer wasn't a frequent reader of the tabloid magazines that relayed Aniston's every coming and going as if she were a close friend. The distribution platform expanded Aniston's reach.

Once Flutie was signed to pursue the fragrance deal, he and the McGraw team needed to determine their distribution plan in order to start marketing both McGraw the cologne and McGraw the multiplatform superstar.

Flutie first approached the major fragrance houses of Estée Lauder, Coty, and Liz Claiborne. Because of its distribution arm and strong marketing plan, Flutie and McGraw chose to go with Coty.

Coty's brands included not only Jennifer Lopez, but JOOP!, Jovan Musk, Rimmel, and Vivienne Westwood, as well as the hugely popular mass-market cologne Stetson. In 2005, Coty had gone upmarket with its purchase of the prestige Calvin Klein fragrance brand. But even as it grew its prestige business, Coty knew its bottom line was bolstered by the masses. For Coty the McGraw partnership made good sense.

"Tim represented an opportunity for Coty," Theo Spilka, the vice president of new business development for Firmenich, the international perfume house, told me. "Tim helped to balance out Coty's portfolio in men's fragrances and gave them another mass-market brand besides Stetson."

McGraw's fragrance would be Stetson updated for a new generation of cowboy.

Both McGraw and Faith Hill were involved in each step of the development process. They completed an intense olfactory investigation that consisted of weeks of questions about what each liked in a scent, including: What did your first girlfriend/boyfriend wear? What did your mom wear? What foods do you eat?

They visited factories and chose the packaging and designs. They motivated the local sales forces by offering them freebies like CDs and concert tickets.

"My wife and I had a great time just sitting and going through things and working on what we liked the best," McGraw told *Women's Wear Daily*. "She had a lot of input into it. I took stuff home, we tried things out and we gave samples to her friends."[5]

Once the fragrance was developed, the team needed to decide where to sell it and for how much.

A conjoint analysis showed the potential McGraw consumer wanted a low price point, but they also wanted to feel like they were getting a prestige brand. To do that, the group opted for a Tier 2 and Tier 3 distribution strategy at stores like J.C. Penney and Sears as well as drugstores, entirely bypassing the option of launching in Tier 1, a move that saved them the marketing overhead of in-store advertising, table purchase, and catalog fees associated with the first tier.

"I really believe that understanding the audience and distributing products where your audience shops is one of the most important aspects of launching a brand. It is all about location, location, location," Flutie told me. "If the Tim McGraw fragrance were put in Tier 1 at Barneys it would not sell, because of the price point and the competing fashion brands."

Based on the importance of low price points and a wide distribution plan, Flutie and the team created what they called a "mass-tige" product. It would sell at mass market prices (between $15 and $30 for 1.7 fl. oz.) but would have the look and feel of a prestige brand, achieved by lowering the product costs by having the fragrance available in 28,000 locations as opposed to the 250 locations pertinent to a Tier 1 distribution plan. Those economies of scale allowed them to manufacture the packaging and the product in the United States, another factor important to the McGraw consumer, and to shoot the advertising campaigns with glitzy fashion photographer Michel Comte, who had shot for Armani and Dolce & Gabbana.

The scent launched in the fall of 2008. The rectangular glass bottle featured a silver cap and a black leather-like collar to suggest the brim of McGraw's cowboy hat. The carton had a matte black texture with a silver embossed guitar pick on top, and a rope running along each panel. Cupped in the hand, it felt heavy and manly.

A second McGraw scent, Southern Blend, was launched in fall 2009, and that year McGraw won the FiFi in the "Men's Popular Appeal" category. His fragrance was ranked number one in the men's mass-market category, and Hill made a plan to enter the market herself with a signature scent that the team viewed as an extension of the McGraw brand, as well as a vehicle to build her own brand awareness and cultivate consumer intimacy. "Faith Hill" was a more feminine version of McGraw's fragrance. In 2010, Coty launched McGraw Silver, and McGraw and Hill began making plans to launch a joint fragrance.

The bottom-tier distribution platform was regarded as critical to their success.

"It's what makes me so special," Flutie bragged. "I understand that most people want to be in Bergdorf and Barneys, but let me tell ya, most people are not buying celebrity fragrance in Bergdorf. The difference between Bergdorf and Walmart is not quality, it's price."

Why Fragrance Means Money

The growth of the fragrance market can largely be attributed to a shift in the consumer's attitude toward fragrance. Gen-X and Gen-Y consumers have a more truncated loyalty than their parents did, meaning that rather than stick with a single signature fragrance for their entire lives, they are far more apt to adopt a "wardrobe" of several different scents. The market today is segmented in order to give this younger generation more options.

It is also segmented to capitalize on an intense feeling of intimacy. McGraw the fragrance helped to make the consumer the country music star's compatriot, willing to support him in whatever he does. The intimacy comes from the nature of fragrance as a product. It is something you wear on your body. That tangible connection creates a feeling of camaraderie and friendship that translates into fan loyalty and future value.

Flutie knew that customers were motivated primarily by three things: price, function, and psychology. Customer analysis can be made by posing the following questions:

1. Who are they? Many of McGraw's original customers were his music fan base, middle-class Americans who enjoyed country music and worked hard. They are women like Madeline D'Alessandro, age fifty-four, from Levittown, Pennsylvania, who works as a sales associate in a Walmart where McGraw is sold.

2. How do they choose? The ultimate owner of the McGraw fragrance is a man largely influenced by the woman in his life, a woman who is highly influenced by the power of celebrity in the consumer products marketplace. "Women love Tim, and part of the purchasing power for men comes from women," Flutie said. "The mass-market audience is truly influenced by their female counterparts. In prestige, a man will go buy his own Dolce & Gabbana scent, but in the mass market, women shop for the husbands and their sons."

There are two types of buyer for the McGraw fragrances: the user and the giver. In short, the man and his partner. So the advertising has to appeal both to men who want to smell like Tim McGraw and to the partners who wants their men to smell like Tim McGraw. D'Alessandro is a giver. She buys McGraw fragrances for all three of her sons, aged twenty-six, twenty-four, and eighteen. "I love Tim McGraw and so do my boys," D'Alessandro said from her job in the Walmart fragrance aisle. I bought it for them for Christmas and now it is all that they wear. I think it smells pretty good. But they like it and I like it because it comes from Tim."

3. Where do they buy? The McGraw consumer is buying fragrance at Walmart, drugstores, and occasionally at Tier 2 outlet J.C. Penney.

4. When do they buy? Because the McGraw customer often buys a fragrance as a gift, it is important to increase promotional activities and launches around the holiday season. D'Alessandro first bought her sons McGraw cologne around Christmas 2008, when she saw sales for the fragrance ramping up in her store and noticed that it came with a free CD.

5. What are they worth? Fragrance buyers can become fiercely loyal and will return to the product over the course of their lifetime even if it is no longer the only fragrance in their stable. Not only will they return to the product, they will return to all aspects of the brand. Loyal customers will buy the McGraw fragrance, buy tickets to his concerts, see his movies, and buy his albums. Since D'Alessandro bought her sons their original McGraw colognes, her boys have each become loyal customers of the fragrance and even more loyal customers of the McGraw brand. "They buy it on their own now," D'Alessandro said. "And we're loving him in the movies."

The fragrance contributed to McGraw's Customer Lifetime Value by making loyal fans out of D'Alessandro's entire family. The intimacy it generated meant that instead of just buying CDs and concert tickets, the D'Alessandros would buy tickets to McGraw's movies, which would in turn net McGraw more film projects. Ultimately it probably made D'Alessandro five times more valuable to McGraw.

Conclusion

Since the launch of his fragrance, Tim McGraw successfully positioned himself as an actor, mainly due to the success of the 2009 film *The Blind Side*, in which he played a supporting role. Was the fragrance a causation or correlation? All we know is that the fragrance sold like gangbusters and *The Blind Side* made more than $309 million at the box office.[6] Today McGraw remains a dominant force in country music, but Flutie's fashion friends in New York City don't scratch their well-coiffed heads in confusion when he mentions the singer.

Because it's his job, Flutie naturally believes the fragrance started it all.

"If you really reach that Walmart consumer at the counter, then they will support you as an actor, and that support will help you to sell movie tickets. It increases your audience. The fragrance and his transition to movies happening at the same time helped to change the public's perception of Tim," Flutie said. "He is no longer just a country music singer. Through the aesthetic promoted by his fragrance he represents somebody who has a wide range of tastes, who appeals to a wide audience."

In 2010 McGraw filmed two movies, one with Gwyneth Paltrow, entitled *Country Strong*, the other called *Dirty Girl*, starring veteran actors William H. Macy and Mary Steenburgen and model-turned-actress Milla Jovovich. Film directors were taking the country singer seriously.

Since launching his fragrance, McGraw's brand awareness has grown by 13 percent and his appeal to marketers by 6 percent, according to private marketing firm The Marketing Arm and its Davie Brown Index, which measures how useful a celebrity will be to a brand. In terms of brand strength, McGraw now ranks much higher than most conventional country singers in his age range.

Exhibit B: McGraw DBI Scores in Comparison to Other Country Artists
Figures courtesy of The Marketing Arm

	DBI Score	Attribute Average	Awareness
Carrie Underwood	80.57	73.24	85.46
Alan Jackson	53.98	70.88	42.71
Reba McEntire	83.62	68.25	93.87
Tim McGraw	80.81	67.17	89.91
Dolly Parton	84.57	67.11	96.07
Shania Twain	79.68	66.57	88.41
Brad Paisley	67.00	65.16	68.22
George Strait	66.55	65.07	67.54
Martina McBride	64.25	64.77	63.91
Willie Nelson	69.90	63.89	73.90
Kenny Chesney	64.79	58.75	68.82
Keith Urban	63.11	57.41	66.91
Dwight Yoakam	51.07	53.56	49.4
Tim McGraw (March 2006)	74.36	71.56	76.22
Tim McGraw (March 2010)	80.81	67.17	89.91

As the music industry continues to struggle amid declining album sales, a takeover by digital media, and the decreasing strength of the label system, a musician's other business ventures are what will not only generate revenue but also prop up the rest of their brand.

McGraw now has revenue from a variety of streams: movies, music, and consumer products. The brand has diversified its portfolio and solidified the future of McGraw's fame and income. Done right, fragrance is a win-win for the companies who produce the products and for the celebrities and their lavender-laced dreams of Americana.

[1]   Ogilvy, David. *Ogilvy on Advertising*. New York: Vintage Books, 1985.

[2]   Boorstin, Julie. "The Scent of Celebrity." *Fortune*, 14 November 2005.

[3]   Horyn, Cathy. "The Sweet Smell of Celebrity." *The New York Times*, 30 January 2005.

[4]   Boorstin.

[5]   Naughton, Julie. "Coty's Just Got to Have Faith—Faith Hill That Is." *Women's Wear Daily*, 5 December 2008.

[6]   *The Blind Side* (2009). Box Office Mojo. IMDb.com. Retrieved 2010-7-2.

7

50 Cent:
The Evolution of the Hip-Hop Beef

For the past thirty years, hip-hop stars have built their names based on feuds, also known as "beefs." The original beefs were violent and sometimes lethal. Back in the day, beef sold albums. Today, as a new generation of consumers view music as a public good, artists need to sell much more than albums to maintain their celebrity. Just as Tim McGraw tried to transition beyond the country market with his fragrance, in 2007 the artist known as 50 Cent was looking to move beyond the hip-hop beef to sell himself as a viable global brand.

In 2007, the author Robert Greene, who a decade prior had penned a best-selling tome on the dynamics of political and social power, *The 48 Laws of Power,* began hanging around the rapper Curtis Jackson, better known as 50 Cent, with the idea to write a book about what made the man tick. What drove him? Why was he so successful? How was he different from the rappers who came before him?

Greene followed Jackson for months, into business meetings, through a manufactured crisis that the rapper had engineered to drive publicity for one of his products, to his childhood home on the south side of Queens. Greene was impressed with Jackson from the start, calling him "a master player at power, a kind of hip-hop Napoleon Bonaparte." The pair ultimately collaborated on a hybrid how-to/motivational tome called *The 50th Law*, which was published in 2009.

In 2007, while Greene conducted his research, Curtis Jackson was preparing to release his third album when his rival, the rapper Kanye West, announced plans to release his own upcoming album, *Graduation*, on the same day as Jackson's.

One of the maxims of which Jackson would later write in *The 50th Law* was the importance of turning lemons into lemonade, or in this case, beef into filet mignon. "Every negative is a positive. The bad things that happen to me, I somehow make them good. That means you can't do anything to hurt me," Jackson wrote. And so a modern day beef was born.

"Let's raise the stakes," Jackson shot back at West when he learned the albums would launch on the same day. "If Kanye West sells more records than 50 Cent on September 11, I'll no longer write music. I'll write music and work with my other artists, but I won't put out anymore solo albums."

Of course none of this was true. Neither Jackson nor West had any plans to retire, but by starting a fight, the pair grabbed headlines for their simultaneous releases. Competition-crazed fans eagerly chose sides, while the entertainment media hyped the feud to the hilt. The artists appeared on the cover of *Rolling Stone*, menacing eyeball to menacing eyeball, above the cover line "Showdown! 50 Cent vs. Kanye West—Who Will Be the King of Hip-Hop?" It was a question that had been asked a decade earlier, when a previous beef between the rappers Tupac Shakur and Christopher "Biggie Smalls" Wallace had gone horribly wrong.

The rap dictionary defines beef as "to have a problem with someone." Used in a sentence, it goes something like this: "Me and that boy got beef." Beef has been the preferred term for a rap feud since as far back as the 1980s. No one can remember who started using it or why, but the preference for the term over "feud" or "fight" comes from its flexibility. It's a noun and a verb that makes a distinct and evocative connection. There is also something scrappy and grassroots about the word, despite the fact that many beefs have been little more than a corporate invention.

"Rap music was built on being competitive — MCs from back in the days battlin' and trying to be the best," the rap artist and business mogul

Shawn Carter, better known as Jay-Z, said in 2001. "But now you've got money involved, so you take that competitive fire and you add it along with money, and you got a lethal combination. But it's good for rap music."

When asked in 2011 what the term "beef" meant, Curtis Jackson echoed Carter's statement, adding that what was known as "battling" ultimately became conflated with the more violent "beefing."

"They [the media] started calling it beefing after Tupac. The culture is so competitive in hip-hop, you had to be prepared for battling all the time to see who could rock a crowd better than other [sic]. But then they [the media] used the same terminologies. 'Beef' is when you're in an altercation with another person and it is actually violent versus artists just competing with one another," Jackson said.

Jay-Z defined what it meant to be both a rapper and a businessman. Today's hip-hop artists are entrepreneurs like him. Kanye and 50 Cent's beef was a postmodern brawl, not fought through lyrical jousting or with guns but rather on magazine covers, on websites, and on Facebook pages, and with consumer mindshare as the ultimate prize. The beef has always been about making money. But because digital downloads and pirating have cannibalized CD sales, and a new generation of consumers came of age genuinely believing that music should be free—that it is a public good like law enforcement, tap water, or fireworks—today's artists cannot maintain either their bank accounts or celebrity status on music sales alone.

The twenty-first century of social media and marketing has made the music ancillary to the brand as a whole. Whereas Jay-Z used his music to stay relevant, 50 Cent uses the Internet and social media to maintain his relevance. But before 50 and even before Jay, there was just beef in the streets.

What's the Beef?

Hip-hop beefs are an internecine web of disses, comebacks, and brawls that some speculate have resulted in several deaths over the last twenty years.

"Exchanging broadsides and comparing your greatness to others' became a way to get people interested in what you were doing. You wanted to prove who was the toughest and had the greatest skills. The ways to do that were to boast and to insult—twin sides of the same stylistic coin. That was the straight original hip-hop beef," rap scholar Adam Bradley, the editor of *Book of Rhymes: The Poetics of Hip Hop* and coeditor of *The Anthology of Rap* told me.

Jay-Z calls this the most familiar refrain in rap: "Why I'm dope."[1]

What we recognize as hip-hop today began on the streets of New York City in the 1970s. Because the genre was new, delivering music to the consumer wasn't easy. The record industry was still high on the fumes of disco and the burgeoning punk market. They had little time for or interest in music that was emerging from urban communities.

But being a little bit scrappy worked. In 1979, future Def Jam cofounder Russell Simmons passed out his 12-inch vinyl rough-cut album to DJs in clubs across the city. He wrote on the album that DJs who liked his music and wanted to know more should just contact PolyGram Records. PolyGram had no idea who Simmons was and certainly didn't have him on their roster. But the label eventually received so many phone calls that they bought the album. Decades later, in 1994, PolyGram would acquire 50 percent of Simmons's label, Def Jam, for $33 million. Simmons found his early success as a promoter launching artists like Kurtis Blow, his younger brother Joseph "Run" Simmons, and his friends Darryl "DMC" McDaniels and Jason "Jam-Master Jay" Mizell, who became the East Coast rap group Run-DMC.

In the late 1980s, in response to being ignored by the majors, a handful of independent labels sprung up on the East Coast, Simmons's Def Jam included, and began producing albums on their own. Out on the West Coast, Ruthless Records and Death Row Records were also run by the hip-hop artists and promoters themselves.

That decade also saw the emergence of the subgenre of "gangsta" rap, which reflected the violent lifestyles of America's inner cities. It was first popularized in 1987 by N.W.A, a group that used gangsta rap to differentiate itself from both the flashy, disco-influenced old-school rap of artists like Grandmaster Flash and the Furious Five, and from the likes of New York's college-educated Run-DMC.

N.W.A stood for Niggaz With Attitude. The original group was assembled by Compton-based drug dealer Eazy-E, cofounder of Ruthless, and consisted of himself and the artists Arabian Prince, DJ Yella, Dr. Dre, Ice Cube, and the D.O.C.

"They wanted shock value and they wanted a way to brand themselves," Alonzo "Lonzo" Williams, a West Coast promoter, DJ, and hip-hop artist who used to run with N.W.A, recalled. "They were looking for something that hadn't been exploited yet and that was it. Crack cocaine was just hitting the streets and there was no theme music for it." Their single "Fuck tha Police" off their first album, *Straight Outta Compton*, made Los Angeles law enforcement agencies so angry that they refused to provide security for N.W.A events. The FBI sent them a letter stating that they did not approve of the violence advocated in their music, and *Straight Outta Compton* was one of the first albums to carry a Parental Advisory warning label.

This new rap genre also bred a more confrontational style of rivalry. The FBI letter and the consistent negative press only generated more publicity for N.W.A, propelling *Straight Outta Compton* to double-platinum status. Being bad was good for album sales.

"What you started to have was a hip-hop version of the WWF [World Wrestling Federation]. It was the same mentality. You created two combatants and put them in the arena to sell tickets or in their case to sell albums," Williams said.

In 1991 Andre "Dr. Dre" Young split from N.W.A to form Death Row Records with the concert promoter Suge Knight. One of their first artists was Tupac Shakur, the son of two Black Panther activists, an introspective rapper and poet who penned lyrics about running afoul of the law. He would later become involved in the most famous rap beef of all time.

In 1993, fledgling A&R executive and record producer Sean Combs (who would later change his name to Puff Daddy and then P. Diddy), a high school football player raised in a comfortable Westchester County suburb—far from the rough and tumble streets featured in rap music—started the New York–based label Bad Boy Records, which released early tracks from the Brooklyn-based rapper Christopher "the Notorious B.I.G." Wallace.

It remains unclear how real the feud between Shakur and Wallace was in the beginning and how much record executives like Knight and Combs had to do with playing up a rivalry to keep their artists in the press. Yes, people were really shot, injured, and, finally, killed, but how these stories were spun may have had more to do with cold, calculated marketing than with real beef.

Shakur and Wallace were once good friends, but by 1994 their rivalry would form the backbone of the East Coast–West Coast "rap wars." That year Shakur was shot five times and robbed in the lobby of a New York City recording studio. He accused Wallace and Combs of being involved.

Shortly after the shooting, Wallace released his "Big Poppa" single with a B-side track called "Who Shot Ya?" Regardless of whether it was planned, it was a brilliant marketing ploy by Bad Boy and Combs and brought their artist a whole lot more attention. Shakur subsequently included antagonistic lyrics aimed at Wallace and Bad Boy Records on tracks he released in 1995 and 1996, including taunts about sleeping with Wallace's wife, the singer Faith Evans. During this time, the media dubbed the rivalry a coastal rap war and fans took sides. Media attention only fueled the fires, driving both the real and imagined feuds to dangerous new levels.

"The two of them were friends before that. With the media fanning the flames, Tupac even bought into it. He was convinced that Biggie had something to do with him being shot," explained Cathy Scott, the author of *The Killing of Tupac Shakur* and *The Murder of Biggie Smalls*. "I think the record companies may have been behind part of it to sell records, and that was unfortunate. You couldn't tell what was real and what wasn't real, because it had become real regardless of whether it was the record companies trying to hype it up."

In March 1996, during the Soul Train Music Awards ceremony in Los Angeles, guns were drawn in the parking lot in a confrontation between the respective entourages of Bad Boy and Death Row.

On September 7, 1996, Tupac Shakur was shot four times by one of four men driving by in a white Cadillac. He died from his wounds six days later, and rumors persisted that Wallace was somehow responsible. Wallace gave interviews saying that he feared for his life, and on March 9, 1997, his concerns proved justified when he was shot in Los Angeles following a *Vibe* magazine party. He was pronounced dead on arrival at the hospital.

Regardless of whether media attention and the labels' desire to move albums created or escalated the feud, the sales that came out of the rivalry as well as the postmortem album sales for both Shakur and Wallace proved that death and tragedy compelled consumers to purchase albums.

The first week of commercialization is typically when an album peaks, and those early sales tell us a lot about the effect a publicity campaign, beef, or tragedy has had on consumers' purchasing behavior.

Exhibit A: Rap Artists' First Week Album Sales

Figures courtesy of Nielsen SoundScan

	Album (Year)	First Week Sales
Tupac Shakur	Me Against the World (1995)	240,000
	All Eyez on Me (1996)	398,000
	The Don Killuminati (1996)	664,000
	R U Still Down? (1997)	549,000
	Still I Rise (1999)	408,000
	Until the End of Time (2001)	426,000
	Better Dayz (2002)	364,000
	Tupac Resurrection (2003)	437,000
	Loyal to the Game (2004)	332,000
	Pac's Life (2006)	159,000
Biggie Smalls	Ready to Die (1994)	56,000
	Life After Death (1997)	689,000
	Born Again (1999)	485,000
	Duets: The Final Chapter (2005)	438,000
Jay-Z	Reasonable Doubt (1996)	43,000
	VOL 1 - In My Lifetime (1997)	138,000
	VOL 2 - Hard Knock Life (1998)	352,000
	VOL 3 - Life and Times of S. Carter (1999)	463,000

Jay-Z (continued)	The Dynasty (2000)	558,000
	The Blueprint (2001)	426,000
	The Blueprint 2 (2002)	545,000
	The Black Album (2003)	463,000
	Kingdom Come (2006)	850,000
	American Gangster (2007)	425,000
	The Blueprint 3 (2009)	476,000
Nas	Illmatic (1994)	60,000
	It Was Written (1996)	269,000
	I Am (1999)	471,000
	Nastradamus (1999)	232,000
	Stillmatic (2001)	343,000
	God's Son (2002)	156,000
	Street's Disciple (2004)	232,000
	Hip Hop Is Dead (2006)	355,000
	Untitled (2008)	187,000
50 Cent	Get Rich or Die Tryin' (2003)	872,000
	The Massacre (2005)	1,141,000
	Curtis (2007)	691,000
	Before I Self Destruct (2009)	66,000
Kanye West	The College Dropout (2004)	441,000
	Late Registration (2005)	860,000
	Graduation (2007)	957,000
	808s and Heartbreak (2008)	450,000
	My Beautiful Dark Twisted Fantasy (2010)	496,000

Sales of Shakur's catalog titles spiked by 332 percent overall in the week following his death, with two albums spiking by more than 1,000 percent. Posthumous releases were even more successful. *Don Killuminati* sold 664,000 copies in its first week in November 1996. It entered sales charts at number one and generated the second-highest debut-week sales total for the year. In comparison, Shakur's previous album, *All Eyez on Me*, sold 398,000 in its first week. By 2010, *Don Killuminati* had sold nearly 3.5 million copies.

As for Wallace, catalog title sales spiked by 379 percent the week following his death and, like Shakur's, his posthumous titles sold extremely well. The album he was promoting before he died, *Life After Death*, sold 689,000 copies in its first week, up from the 54,000 sold of his previous album, *Ready to Die*, released in 1994.

"There were elements of the Tupac and Biggie feud that were real tensions, but there was also an aspect of commerce," Adam Bradley told me. "Consumers wanted to follow the artist and be a part of the controversy themselves. Diddy has always been a master of taking the controversy and turning it into commerce." The more consumers played into the controversies, the more the labels built them up. Combs crafted a marketing campaign surrounding the death of Biggie Smalls that essentially turned him into rap's great martyr.

"Anytime there is any publicity around a feud there is a boost in sales," said Dave Bakula, the senior vice president of analytics for Nielsen Entertainment, which calculates album sales. "The more you get the word out there, the more you rally the fans to say 'I am a fan' of this side or that side. Fans want to choose sides."

Following the deaths of Wallace and Shakur, however, some industry insiders feared the potential collapse of hip-hop as a viable mainstream business. They were worried that at some point, violence and negative attention would overpower talent and product. Industry executives began talking about how to use feuds to keep sales strong while keeping violence to a minimum.

"That's when we saw a fundamental difference in the beef. It began to develop through lyrics, and it produced some amazing songs," Bradley said.

The Beef Remixed

The next major hip-hop rivalry evolved in the realm of mixtapes, freestyling on the radio, and verbal assaults. When the industry searched for someone to fill Wallace's big shoes as the reigning monarch of NYC hip-hop, attention was showered on Shawn Carter, a.k.a. Jay-Z, and Nasir bin Olu Dara Jones, a performer better known as Nas, and the two fought for East Coast supremacy through ever-more-elaborate disses. At the 2001

Hot 97 hip-hop festival, Jay-Z recited the lyrics to the first single off his new album, *The Blueprint*. They ended with the line, "Ask Nas, he don't want it with Hov, No!," a bait contending Nas couldn't compete with Jay-Z lyrically. *The Blueprint* was released in September of 2001, sold 426,000 copies in its first week, and went on to sell 2.66 million copies as of 2010.

Nas responded with an attack on Jay-Z during a radio freestyle session and with the single "Ether," which mocked Jay-Z as a misogynist and accused him of exploiting Christopher Wallace's legacy. On his album *Stillmatic*, released in December of 2001, Nas implied that Jay-Z was gay. *Stillmatic* sold 343,000 copies in its first week, up from the 232,000 copies sold in the first week of Nas's previous effort, *Nastradamus*, in 1999.

Days after that album's release, Jay-Z released a freestyle track called "Super Ugly," in which he claimed that he and the basketball player Allen Iverson had both slept with Carmen Bryan, the mother of Nas's daughter Destiny. Jay-Z's mother, Gloria, was so appalled that she forced her son to publicly apologize.

In 2001, the singer Jadakiss tried to pull back the sirloin curtain and expose these beefs for what they were: a way to make money by getting radio play.

"Most of the beefs you hear about . . . are phony because the people you hear talking about each other, you can catch them downtown having a [hand]shake over some seafood, and it's not that serious. Usually everything is to make money," he explained. "People are going five platinum."[2]

The following year, Hot 97 Summer Jam refused to allow Nas to burn an effigy of Jay-Z on the stage. The rapper instead appeared on the rival radio station, Power 105, and attacked the music industry's control over hip-hop. On and on it went. Jay-Z attacked Nas on the next album, *The Blueprint 2: The Gift and the Curse*, dissing his street credibility, his stinginess, and his spirituality. *Blueprint 2* sales were the highest Jay-Z had experienced since 2000—selling 545,000 albums in the first week, up from the prior album's first-week sales of 426,000. On his next album, *God's Son*, Nas bit back by comparing himself and Jay-Z to characters in the movie *Scarface*, alleging Jay-Z was weak. But *God's Son* sold only 156,000 copies in its first week.

By the end of 2002, the feud had fizzled. Jay-Z had won. The beef went unmentioned for years, but when Nas signed with Def Jam in 2006—during which time Carter was president of the label—it was most definitely over. That signing proved that the beef had never been as serious as it was played up to be in the media.

Radio airtime at the end of the 1990s and into the 2000s was the platform on which albums were sold and artists were turned into stars. So it was no accident that Carter and Nas used rival radio stations as the platform for their beef. It's also not surprising that the beef waned as the battlefield for consumer mindshare began to move online. The whole music industry was in trouble. The real money was now in touring and product endorsements. The hip-hop stars of the 2000s became business-people and brands, making petty squabbling, armed or not, look more and more like child's play.

Virtual Beef

By 2007, an artist could use the Internet to reach a wide audience through the portals of MySpace, Facebook, or even their personal websites before being signed to a major label. Gone were the days of pay-to-play radio airtime and the need to get a mixtape into the right DJ's hands at the right time. Label reps who toured the country in search of the next big thing were rendered obsolete.

It was time for the beef to be reborn in a modernized, virtual way. That's when Kanye West and Jackson, a.k.a. 50 Cent, stripped the beef of all remaining artifice and made no bones about the fact that beef was about album sales alone.

West and Jackson couldn't have had more disparate upbringings, and yet both have come to represent the new breed of artist in the digital age. They embrace Internet-driven album sales, understand that atten-tion drives those sales, and know how to attract copious amounts of this attention.

Kanye West was raised in middle-class suburban Chicago, where his mother was a college professor. He began his career as a producer for Roc-a-Fella Records, working with Jay-Z, Alicia Keys, Ludacris, and Janet

Jackson, before releasing his debut album, *The College Dropout*, in 2004 and a follow-up, *Late Registration*, in 2005. Jay-Z was then head of Roc-a-Fella and skeptical of West's move from producer to artist. Several marketers expressed concern at West's lack of street cred and his dandy style of dressing. Others likened his chartreuse polo shirts and argyle sweater vests to those of the uptight brother Carlton on the early 1990s sitcom and Will Smith vehicle *The Fresh Prince of Bel-Air*.

Jackson had a much rougher narrative. Born in Queens, New York, Jackson began dealing drugs when he was twelve years old. He never knew his father, and his mother was murdered when he was a child. As an aspiring rapper in 2000, Jackson had a record with Columbia in the works when he was shot nine times in an attack many speculated was payback for his 1999 song "Ghetto Qu'ran," which named several prominent Queens drug dealers. Columbia promptly dropped Jackson from its label, proving that violent beef was no longer in vogue. Not to be deterred, Jackson began a concerted mixtape campaign, producing his own songs with money he made hustling drugs and distributing his music all over New York. He encouraged bootleggers to pirate his songs, in the hope it would get them into the right hands. It did. In 2003, Jackson was discovered by the rapper Eminem (whose driver was playing a 50 Cent mixtape) and signed to his and Dr. Dre's labels, Shady Records and Aftermath Entertainment—a division of Interscope Records—for a five-album, million-dollar deal.

50 Cent's debut, *Get Rich or Die Tryin'*, was certified platinum eight times after its 2003 release. His next project, *The Massacre*, was the best-selling album of 2005 and sold more than 1.14 million copies within a week of its release. He spent his first $300,000 registering the "50 Cent" and "G-Unit" trademarks.

By 2007, he wanted to try something new. He was looking to reconnect with his old fans and build inroads with new ones. Frustrated with his label's refusal to face digital cannibalism head-on and in an effort to connect with his base, Jackson put together his own website as a hub for showing videos and soliciting fan feedback. It quickly evolved into a social network that brought his fans from around the world in touch with him and one another. It made him seem both intimate and aspirational at the same time.

To reach new consumers, Jackson agreed to pen a book with Robert Greene, hoping it would paint him as a serious businessman. Back when Jackson was selling drugs on the streets of Queens, he experimented with a handful of hustles—four or five at a time—hoping that one would work big and pay for the others should they prove unprofitable. This gave him options and room to move. By 2007, Jackson had about five hustles going in the business world. His beef with Kanye West over album sales was only one of them.

When West and Jackson released their albums on the same day, the game was actually rigged so that everyone would win. The beef not only boosted first-week sales for both artists, it also benefited Universal Music Group, the parent company of West's label Def Jam and Jackson's Interscope.

More so than beefs past, this beef made the consumer a direct participant.

Facebook users created more than 430 groups related to the Kanye–50 Cent "feud." The largest group, "!!Buy Kanye Wests [sic] Album so 50 CENT will stop rapping!!" had a membership of nearly eight thousand. A majority of the groups favored West over Jackson.

John Bartleson, vice president of digital media for Island Def Jam, wasn't surprised. He knew from the start that West's fans would provide powerful social media support.

"You close your eyes and envision the typical rap fan, and then you see Kanye, and they don't seem to match up," Bartleson said. "Who are the consumers? Where do they live? My answer is that they live on the Internet."

Jackson had his own online support. He played up the feud on his website, while Facebook hosted at least sixty groups betting that 50 Cent's album would outsell *Graduation*.[3] Those bettors lost. In the first week, Jackson's *Curtis* sold 691,000 albums, down from *The Massacre*'s 1.14 million week-one albums sold. Still, the album outstripped projected sales of 500,000 by a wide margin. Kanye's album *Graduation* did significantly better than *Curtis*, selling 957,000 albums in its first week, up from West's previous effort, *Late Registration*, which sold 860,000 albums during its first week in 2005. It was West's bestselling first week since his 2004 debut. "The industry as a whole does a good job at projecting sales, but both of these albums blew those projections out of the water. It was manufactured obviously, but whether it was a feud or not, that exposure drove these albums to a whole other level," Nielsen's Dave Bakula told me.

The extent to which the beef drove sales can be seen in the amount of decay in sales from week one to week two. A typical hip-hop release will see a 65 percent decline in sales from the first week to the second. For Jackson's *Curtis* that decline was 79 percent.

"It was a dramatic drop. That shows more of the sales were pushed into that first week because people were hyper-aware of the record coming out," Bakula explained. "I don't think there was a single fan of Kanye or 50 that didn't know the record was coming that week."

When it was all over, West didn't seek to maintain the illusion that the beef between himself and Jackson was in any way real.

"It was a complete publicity stunt. It was my idea," West later told *GQ* magazine. "I knew it was going to take off as soon as we were going to come out on the same date. Think about it. You got the two biggest shit-talkers in rap history. There's no one in rap history for talking more shit than me and 50. That's something I will stand on."

When asked about Jackson's vow to retire if he lost the battle, West said: "Oh man, he sold so many more records by saying that. Man, 50 is really one of my favorite rappers too. I almost feel bad [about beating him]."[4]

Jackson, of course, did not retire. In 2009, he released his fourth album, *Before I Self Destruct*. He was gracious in his perceived defeat. "I am very excited to have participated in one of the biggest album release weeks in the last two years. Collectively, we have sold hundreds of thousands of units in our debut week. This marks a great moment for hip-hop music, one that will go down in history," he told the Associated Press.

The double punch provided by the beef over *Graduation* and *Curtis* marked just the second time since 1991 that two albums debuting the same week had totals surpassing 600,000 albums in week one. (The record was first set when the rock band Guns N' Roses released two of their own albums, *Use Your Illusion I* and *Use Your Illusion II*, on the same day in 1991.) But while the West-Jackson beef translated into bucks, Jackson knew beef alone wasn't going to build him an empire.

Hustlers to Moguls

Today's hip-hop stars don't want to die for the chance to be the king of hip-hop. They want to be businessmen, moguls, and global brands, because that is where the money is. The most successful hip-hop artists and producers have branched out beyond making music and channeled the energy they previously used to gain street cred into building their business portfolios.

Changing the nature of the hip-hop beef was smart for another reason: An artist selling albums made record labels rich, but an artist selling himself made the artist rich. Violence could help sell albums, but it rarely sold artists as a consumer brand.

As Jay-Z often says: "I'm not a businessman. I'm a business, man." And Carter is adamant that rapping was a stepping-stone to a lucrative future. "I was an eager hustler and a reluctant artist," he said.[5]

"Today's artists are straddling a fine line between maintaining their authenticity with their hip-hop fan base and trying not to alienate potential endorsement partners," *Anthology of Rap* editor Bradley told me. And because the new generation of consumer views music as something that should be free, artists need to sell products.

Chris Atlas, senior vice president for marketing at Def Jam, told me that artists like Jay-Z and the up-and-comers following in his footsteps today are very careful to appeal to a general audience for this very reason.

"Certain artists have made a business model out of working with brands and becoming partners in brands," Atlas said. "The troublesome part for the brands with hip-hop is that if you associate yourself with a certain rapper, and they do something out of line, that is bad for the brand. Nowadays we see less rappers stepping far out of line."

Following his inclusion in the Christopher Wallace–Tupac Shakur beef, Sean Combs released several albums of middling success before going on to become an international businessman and fashion mogul. In 1998, still going by "Puff Daddy"—a nickname given to him on the football field of his private high school—he launched a fashion label entitled Sean John, his first and middle name. Combs's goal was to create a line that would fill a void in the market for well-made, sophisticated, fashion-forward clothing reflecting an urban aesthetic. Combs hired former Ralph Lauren executive Jeffrey Tweedy to help him create what *Newsweek* in its February 12, 2001, issue referred to as a "hip-hop-meets-Liberace" apparel label.

The Sean John men's sportswear line debuted in the spring of 1999 and approached $400 million in sales by 2003, when the Sean John brand was sold in more than two thousand retail locations throughout the country. In 2002, Combs was featured on *Fortune* magazine's 40 Richest People Under 40 list. That same year *Time* magazine named him one of its hundred most influential people.

"I watched too many other entertainers create something through their own hard work, only to see someone else profit from it," Combs said. "I decided to figure out how to do what someone else was going to do with my name and my brand anyway. Not just to make money for myself, but to build a lasting enterprise."[6]

Following his beef with Nas, Carter went on to found the urban clothing brand Rocawear with Damon Dash. In March 2007, he sold the rights to the Rocawear brand to Iconix Brand Group for $204 million. He also co-owns the 40/40 Club, an upscale sports bar in New York City that has expanded to locations in Atlantic City and Chicago. He serves as cobrand director for Budweiser Select and collaborates with the company on strategic marketing programs and ad development. Additionally he is a part-owner of the New Jersey Nets basketball team and the Manhattan bistro The Spotted Pig, as well as co-owner of the Carol's Daughter beauty line. He had a reported net worth of more than $450 million in 2010, and the *Wall Street Journal* called him an artist who "inhabits the rare zone where cultural cachet and corporate power meet."[7]

That zone was Jackson's long-term goal. Around the same time *The Massacre* was going platinum, Jackson invested in Glacéau, the makers of the drink Vitaminwater. The relationship began when privately held Glacéau saw Jackson pose with a bottle in a print ad for Reebok and learned that he was a fan of the sugary substitute for sports drinks. They offered him a minority stake in the company to pitch Vitaminwater. Jackson did print ads and promotions and even mentioned the drink in his songs. Jackson then helped develop his own Vitaminwater—the grape-flavored "Formula 50." When Glacéau was sold to Coca-Cola for $4.1 billion in 2007, Jackson received a cut of around $100 million.[8]

It was only one of the many hustles Jackson had going. He was working on *The 50th Law* with Robert Greene as well as a line of novellas and graphic novels. He also had an endorsement deal with General Motors and Pontiac.

"Those with truly savage breasts and literal *cojones* would have to find their high-testosterone hiphop elsewhere," Greg Tate wrote in the *Village Voice*. "Mr. Cent could care less for your love anymore. Certainly not after cashing in those Glaceau stock options; if hiphop is now more defined by the corporate game than the street game, that lucrative little coup just might be the definitive hiphop act of 2007."

Jackson's empire continued to grow from there. Following his feud with West, he paid a visit to mining baron Patrice Motsepe in South Africa to obtain an equity stake in his mine, with the hope of eventually bringing 50 Cent–branded platinum to the market. Jackson has also launched a fragrance (Power by 50 Cent), a 50 Cent G-Unit line of shoes with Reebok, a deodorant (Pure 50 body spray), and a line of condoms (Magic Stick).

Jackson has spent so much time building this brand that he is willing to take legal action to protect it. In 2009, the fast-food chain Taco Bell sent out a press release asking 50 Cent to consider changing his name to 79 or 89 or 99 Cent, to promote the chain's "79-89-99-Cent Why Pay More!" campaign. The company sent copies of the request letter to news outlets as well as to the artist to gin up attention. What they neglected to do was make any arrangements with Jackson about the rights to his name. Jackson filed a $4 million lawsuit against the chain. The suit was settled privately.

West has been relatively late to the brand-expansion game. He partnered with Fatburger in 2008 to bring ten franchises of the West Coast burger chain to his hometown of Chicago and the next year partnered with fashion label Louis Vuitton to produce a Kanye West line of footwear.

Conclusion

We have to use our imaginations to envision what kinds of business Christopher Wallace and Tupac Shakur would have taken up had they lived to see the evolution of today's hip-hop stars into moguls. They no doubt would have found success in production, fashion, and consumer goods.

Reflecting on the new hip-hop business model, Alonzo "Lonzo" Williams doesn't think things are all that different today than they were thirty years ago.

"The business model of hip-hop has always been the same. Everyone wants to get out of the ghetto and get paid. That's how gangsta rap got its wings, because it seemed like talking about killing people and selling dope was the fastest track to getting there," Williams said. "Talking about killing people used to be cool. Now being a businessman is cool. They're just playing to the consumer."

Def Jam's Chris Atlas says beef as a marketing tool has become largely moot—thanks mostly to Jackson setting the bar so high.

"I think 50 was the best who ever did it, used beef as a part of his marketing, but since then no one has been as good," Atlas said. "These new guys, they'll get maybe fifteen minutes of attention. But they won't become stars through beefs alone."

The West beef was just the latest in a series of challenges with which Jackson had been presented. When asked about his history with beefs at the 2011 Aruba International Film Festival, where he was promoting a film project and billed exclusively as "actor Curtis Jackson," the artist seemed resigned to his past and ready to move beyond it: "I have had beef my entire career, the reason being everyone wants the top position. If anybody else wants to be number one they have to knock me out of that position. I am the number one they feel like they can get to."

Jackson honed his hustling skills on the street, perfected them in the music marketplace, and now uses them to hustle online. He continues to connect with his fans on his website and through his Twitter account, where he has 4.5 million followers. He isn't above manufacturing a good feud to sell a few albums, but his legacy, unlike Tupac's or Biggie's, will go far beyond beef in the streets.

1   Jay-Z. *Decoded*. New York: Spiegel & Grau, 2010.

2   Reid, Shaheem. "Jay-Z, Jadakiss Say Beef Good, Violence Bad: The Mixtape Circuit Is a Swarming with Disses, but Rappers Insist It's Just Talk." MTV.com, 9 August 2001.

3   Joyner, April. "Did the Web Help Kanye Outsell 50 Cent?" *Fast Company*, 20 September 2007.

4   Heath, Chris. "Men of the Year: Graduate." *GQ*, December 2007.

5   *Decoded*.

6   Stein, Nicholas. "Celebrity Inc.: How Have So Many Entertainers Muscled onto This Year's List? By Transforming Themselves into Brands." *Fortune*, 17 September 2001.

7   Jurgensen, John. "The State of Jay-Z's Empire." *The Wall Street Journal*, 29 October 2010.

8   Howard, Theresa. "50 Cent, Glaceau Forge Unique Bond." *USA Today*, 17 December 2007.

8

Ashton Kutcher:
The Evolution of the Digital Celebrity

Starting in 2008, celebrity agents advised their clients that they had to have a "digital strategy" and "online presence." No one told them more than that. Some created Facebook pages or hired people to do it for them, the ambitious (Gwyneth Paltrow) blogged, and the even savvier created webisodes (Lisa Kudrow, Neil Patrick Harris). But tech geekery wasn't a revenue stream for celebs, despite the $35 billion a year that brands spent on digital media. If there's anything celebs disdain, it's doing things for free. Then Ashton Kutcher pioneered a way for celebrities to monetize their social media networks. What did he get in return? Competition that could cannibalize his share of the market.

A tall stranger wandered the Silicon Valley offices of Internet video start-up Ustream. He towered six inches above the computer wonks and smiled with incisors that gleamed unnaturally white. He had impeccable skin and his outfit, though disheveled, was too artfully styled as geek chic to belong to an actual geek.

Ashton Kutcher was meeting with Ustream founders John Ham and Brad Hunstable to discuss how to promote and exploit their burgeoning video-streaming platform, but first he wanted to gain street cred with the office underlings. Dozens of Ustream staffers crowded into a conference room, eager to glimpse an actor in the wild and see how he would behave in their world. The stargazing stretched all the way to Budapest, where the coding team responsible for the company's iPhone app was patched in digitally.[1]

Kutcher pumped a fist at the screen. "Hi Budapest," he said. "Can I get a *woot-woot?*"

"Woot, woot," came the reply. Budapest was easy.

In a manner of minutes, well-timed self-deprecating jokes about his being a hayseed from Hollywood visiting the big city lubricated the room. Ham asked Kutcher to share his thoughts on the future of web entertainment with the group, which was Kutcher's cue to prove his worth to the web entrepreneurs.

"Whoever gets live video right will win. YouTube? Fuck YouTube. YouTube's too big. It's not discerning enough with its content. There's no velvet rope to speak," Kutcher told the crowd.

The actor was protecting his livelihood. YouTube's content was curated by the average person. The videos weren't flashy and they didn't contain celebrities. YouTube represented a problem for Hollywood because it took celebrities out of the entertainment equation and made stars of laughing babies and guys getting hit in the nuts.

Kutcher courted the community of techies to save his skin and preserve Hollywood's place in entertainment. He knew that social media—a blanket term for online platforms that distribute content—was about to become the focus of consumers' leisure time, and he wanted to insert Hollywood into the new paradigm.

The short but eventful history of Kutcher's attempts to monetize social media for celebrities is instructive and surprising. Kutcher was the first A-list celebrity to stick his toe in the digital waters and then bill someone for it. He tried to determine how to baptize Hollywood for a generation that lives their lives online and eschews vowels in their tweets and text messages. Kutcher may have begun his investigations without a concrete business model, but he knew this: If Hollywood didn't start developing content online, its stars would eventually be supplanted by web personalities like CharlieIsSoCoolLike, the twenty-year-old vlogger

Charlie McDonnell who has become the most subscribed-to YouTube user in the UK for his videos of himself singing duets (with himself), baking brownies, and making balloon animals.

Kutcher is older than the generation that reveres CharlieIsSoCoolLike, but not by much. He could be their older brother, not their dad, and that was key. The network execs, studio bigwigs, and advertising suits plotting how to reach the youngsters from their corner offices in Manhattan and Los Angeles were old enough to be the kids' grandparents. Kutcher had come to Ustream because he knew he could make "cool" content that under-twenty-somethings would like. His plan was simple: Use his celebrity to obtain a large number of followers and friends in social media, then sell himself as a distribution platform for brands to convey their messages (read: sell things) to the online consumer.

His plan worked. Kutcher and his production company, Katalyst, created complex custom content for social media that brought together celebrities and brands, and they were paid in the seven-figures to do it. Today, thanks to Ashton Kutcher, a celebrity's digital strategy can be directly linked to a revenue stream.

What has Kutcher gotten for all his hard work? Competition.

In 2009, the start-up Ad.ly took Kutcher's model of marrying celebrity and social media and made it easy for both celebrities and brands to use. Ad.ly didn't bother with making original content, like shows or short webisodes. They took the simplest social media platform, Twitter, which broadcasts messages in 140 characters or less, signed up celebrities, and then, like Kutcher, used them as a distribution system for brands to deliver promotional messages. Ad.ly took all the work out of the equation and made it very simple for celebrities to be paid just for being popular online.

Kutcher's Online Strategy

Ashton Kutcher was just another exceptionally good-looking biochemical engineering student at the University of Iowa when a modeling scout picked him out of the corn-fed crowd in 1997. A year later, Kutcher moved to Los Angeles and landed the role of the lunkhead heartthrob Michael Kelso on the television series *That '70s Show*. In 2003, he catapulted himself to the A-list by marrying the actress Demi Moore, a woman sixteen years his senior and the mother of three kids.

It's easy to imagine that Kutcher is a pretty boy who consistently lands in the right place at the right time. But in Hollywood no one's luck is this good. Scratch a little deeper and you begin to realize he is the mastermind of his entrepreneurial destiny.

Fast Company magazine once asked Kutcher what scared him. "When I have a conversation with someone and they say, 'I'm not worried about monetization yet,'" Kutcher said.[2] Of course it did. Celebrities are used to being well compensated for their work, and Kutcher is no exception. At the peak of *That '70s Show's* popularity, Kutcher was making between $5 and $7 million a season.

Traditional advertising, which foots the bill for many celebrity paychecks (by generating income for television shows and through endorsement deals), has declined over the past several years. The global recession caused the U.S. advertising market to decrease from $77 billion in 2008 to $67 billion in 2009. Much of that was due to a dramatic drop in television revenue, which fell from $52 billion to $41 billion in a single year. Yet, despite the recession, Internet advertising grew from $24 billion in 2008 to nearly $26 billion in 2009.[3]

There has long been a belief that advertisers traded analog (read: TV) dollars for online pennies—meaning it was cheap to advertise online because it was new and untested. But by 2009 that axiom no longer rang so true. Online pennies quickly turned to nickels, dimes, and quarters, because the web offered advertisers something that traditional media didn't—consumer interaction and the ability to obtain extensive consumer buying information. Web advertising doesn't just get consumers to buy products, it generates data to help marketers immediately see which advertising campaigns are effective.

By 2009, social media had overtaken porn as the number one activity on the Internet. Sites like Facebook, YouTube, Twitter, and Ustream provided primarily user-generated content in the form of videos, status updates, and shared photos. The content was also distributed by the users to the people in their networks. Whether you realize it or not, when you consume a status update you are consuming user-generated entertainment, which then takes attention away from other forms of entertainment like movies and television. But advertisers are less interested in pictures of you and your friend Mary getting drunk last night or your cousin Peter's kids at the Grand Canyon. That's what Kutcher meant when he said that he was scared for folks who didn't talk monetization upfront—he was worried about those who didn't think about producing content that could be sold opposite ads on these hugely popular social media sites.

Kutcher then went about creating content specifically for the social web, to capitalize on the millions of consumers using social media and the brands that wanted to reach them.

He had the means and the infrastructure to do it through his own production house, Katalyst. The actor and a buddy, Bel-Air-born film and television producer Jason Goldberg, started the Katalyst Films production company in 2000 to exploit Kutcher's success on *That '70s Show*. Their first success was the MTV series *Punk'd*, a reality show that consisted of Kutcher playing practical jokes on celebrity pals like Justin Timberlake, Jessica Alba, and Shaquille O'Neal. It ran for seven years on MTV.

Katalyst gave Kutcher and Goldberg the autonomy to create the kinds of projects they liked, and in their first seven years they developed a dozen feature films and more than twenty television shows, some of which, like *Beauty and the Geek*—a reality dating show where nerdy men were paired with vapid women—made it to air. *Guess Who* (a comedy co-starring Bernie Mac) and *Killers* (a romantic thriller with Katherine Heigl), made it to the big screen. As in any production house, dozens of other projects ended up on the cutting-room floor, but Katalyst allowed Kutcher to get a bigger slice of the pie.

In 2007, with pilots in negotiations with ABC, NBC, and CBS, Kutcher and Goldberg decided they wanted to branch out as a full-service branding and marketing house with a focus on original online content for social media platforms.

First the pair had to wrap their heads around how to make money online. In 2007, celebrities just didn't do digital. Sure, they emailed and maybe played around with MySpace, but they lived their professional lives outside the virtual world. Kutcher was entering uncharted territory.

The two men began with a modest contract to develop online content for AOL that fizzled in its infancy. Next they managed to raise $10 million in funding from Tucson-based mortgage brokerage house Prime Capital. They attended tech conferences, took exploratory meetings with any tech expert who would see them, and they played around with producing different kinds of short videos for the web. At the annual TechCrunch50 conference in 2008, they unveiled their original web series, *Blah Girls*, quickie animated cartoons of teens that spoofed pop culture. Kutcher was looking for a buyer for the series when he ran into MySpace CEO Chris DeWolfe in the hallways of TechCrunch and managed to convince the executive that *Blah Girls* would be a great fit for MySpaceTV, then a social networking platform with 51 million unique video views. Two months later, Katalyst had its first online-only distribution deal.[4]

In 2008 Kutcher and Goldberg hired a real Silicon Valley pro, Sarah Ross, who had ten years' experience in marketing at Yahoo! and five start-ups under her belt, as their head of digital media.

Ross was no fan of Hollywood and thought Tinseltown's power players screwed up when it came to tech. "You've got to invest the time to become part of the community, and you have to earn web cred," she told the Katalyst boys. Ross's beef with Hollywood was that no one ever took the time to earn the trust of the online community.

As an early experiment, Ross brought in the Ukrainian-born computer scientist and cofounder of PayPal, Max Levchin, to speak to Kutcher and Goldberg, to gauge whether they would sink or swim. The pair was admittedly lost during parts of their conversation with Levchin, but they expressed a willingness to learn what he was talking about. That impressed Ross.[5] They weren't swimming yet but they could certainly stay afloat.

"I think Ashton was initially observed very cautiously by Silicon Valley veterans. A lot of Hollywood people come here and try to dazzle the locals with the celebrity lifestyle. Ashton was pretty obviously not interested in doing that. He also happens to be smart. . . . A lot of other Hollywood people find the Valley's sort of Asperger's level of honesty really off-putting. Ashton was able to roll with it," Levchin said.[6] His kind words proved true when he later partnered with Katalyst and the frozen foods brand Hot Pockets on a large-scale product-integration campaign.

Kutcher and Goldberg slowly gained credibility on the web as they listened to and chose as partners and advisors smart people who had been doing business online since Kutcher was doing keg stands at the University of Iowa. The actor began flying north from Los Angeles on Southwest Airlines, the no-frills unofficial carrier of the nerds. He attended more TechCrunch events and web conferences, and ate pizza sitting on the floor with upstart web monkeys. What sped the process for him was something Kutcher intrinsically understood: the power of celebrity. Nerds are starfuckers too.

In April of 2009, Ashton Kutcher became the first person to have one million followers on Twitter, in part as a result of a publicity stunt he arranged with CNN and a willing NGO. The Katalyst team, under Ross's direction, picked the brain of Ray Chambers, a friend from her days at Yahoo! and the United Nations' special envoy for malaria. That connection brought Katalyst into contact with another techie do-gooder, Malaria No More CEO Scott Case, who founded the travel website Priceline.com.

This conflux of tech, philanthropy, and celebrity gave Kutcher the boost he needed to become a major player on the then-still-new social media platform. Philanthropy made him seem kind, celebrity made him seem cool, and all the tech geekery made him seem smart. At 750,000 followers, Kutcher—under the name @aplusk (Ashton plus Katalyst)— began tweeting "Every 30 seconds, a kid dies of malaria. Nets save lives." Next Kutcher challenged CNN, which at the time was the next most popular tweeter, in a race to win one million followers. Kutcher declared that if he won, he would donate ten thousand mosquito nets (at ten dollars apiece) and encourage his celebrity friends to do the same.

It was a brilliant public relations move, because it suddenly made the world's best-known broadcaster part of the story. The Kutcher-CNN Twitter competition received airtime on *Larry King Live*, Wolf Blitzer's *The Situation Room*, and *Anderson Cooper 360°*. Simultaneously, Katalyst and Malaria No More blanketed the web with videos, tweets, Facebook updates, and blog posts. Kutcher emerged victorious—ninety-thousand mosquito nets were donated to Malaria No More, and Katalyst proved its mettle in the online social scene.

Kutcher's popularity online was undisputed. The question now was how to make money off being so popular on the interwebs. By 2011, the number of Kutcher's Twitter followers had swollen to more than 6.5 million. And besides the sheer volume of followers, Kutcher's Klout score was an impressive 97 out of a possible 100. Klout is a measure of how much people pay attention to you online. The Klout algorithm weighs twenty-five variables, including the size of the social sphere (number of followers) and the number of engaged followers and friends versus the number of spambots and dead accounts, to determine how influential a person is. One factor the Klout algorithm takes into account is how influential the other people in your network are and how often they rebroadcast your message. It isn't just how cool you are, but how cool your network is perceived to be. It is lunchroom politics boiled down to an algorithm.

A Klout score of 97 is considerable compared to President Barack Obama's 90, talk show host Oprah Winfrey's 65, and pop star Lady Gaga's 81. "Ninety-seven means that Kutcher is in the top .0001 percent of people on Twitter. Every tweet he does gets thousands of retweets, replies, link clicks, etc.," Klout CEO and cofounder Joe Fernandez told me. "It is really like a tsunami of activity with everything he does."

Exhibit A: Celebrity Twitter Influence Measured by Klout Score as of August 2010

Figures courtesy of Klout.com

	Klout Score		Klout Score
Justin Bieber	99	Perez Hilton	88
Conan O'Brien	99	Shaquille O'Neal	88
LeBron James	99	Khloé Kardashian	88
Ashton Kutcher	97	Bill Gates	87
Sean Combs	94	Terrell Owens	86
Kim Kardashian	93	Paris Hilton	84
Kanye West	92	Snoop Dogg	84
Barack Obama	90	Dane Cook	84
Jimmy Fallon	90	Nick Jonas	83
Alyssa Milano	90		

Kutcher's tweets resemble the chaos of a tidal wave. Interspersed between seemingly mindless tweets ("Sometimes I feel like rollerblading got the short end of the stick" and "Is it weird that quantas [sic] mascot is basically a gained [sic] jumping rat with a pouch"), Kutcher tweets pleas for his followers to support organizations that help combat sex-trafficking in the United States as well as links to live feeds from his office and the red carpet at movie premieres, and—most importantly for Katalyst's business model—he posts tweets championing brands that signed with Katalyst to take advantage of Kutcher's online distribution network. "My entire office is addicted to pop chips" was tweeted on behalf of Kutcher's client, the all-natural potato chip brand Popchips, though only the savviest consumers would know Kutcher was being paid by Popchips.

In just two years, Katalyst had evolved from a company producing big budget, often cheesy, Hollywood projects into a hybrid business focused on brand marketing and the creation of online content that was often cheesy but was still enjoyable. Its efforts didn't go unrecognized. In 2010, *Fast Company* magazine named it one of the top ten most innovative companies in marketing for its promotion of such brands as Pepsi, Nestlé, and Kellogg's. Within two years Kutcher had successfully monetized his web celebrity.

The Celebrity Advantage Online

"At the intersection of peak intimacy and peak virality is a movement, and that's what these marketers want," MySpace chief revenue officer Nada Stirratt told me when I asked her what kinds of online content get brands excited. "Marketers go to a social network to make something viral. It's easy to put something out there and get people to find it, but you also need to give people a connection to that content and get the consumers involved, and that's the intimacy."

In the beginning, Katalyst's competitive advantage was Kutcher, because he was intimate and viral at the same time. Because most consumers knew something about him—married to Demi Moore, in that movie with Bernie Mac, and on that silly stoner show—he was intimate. Consumers also knew he was huge on Twitter, and Kutcher's online

"Klout" created the virality that, as Stirratt explained, is intensely seductive to marketing executives. Kutcher was his own movement.

The program *Katalyst HQ* was an early example of using Kutcher's intimacy and virality to distribute a brand's message to consumers. Launched in February 2009, *Katalyst HQ* was a scripted "reality" web series about the activities at Katalyst headquarters in Los Angeles. It really just showed a lot of staff members playing pranks on one another and on Ashton (a small-scale *Punk'd*, as it were). But more importantly, it offered a voyeuristic peek behind the scenes of a Hollywood production studio, and that made it compelling.

Some of the five-minute videos bordered on the ridiculous. In one episode Kutcher buys a live turkey for Thanksgiving dinner but, after having second thoughts, makes the bird the office mascot. For the remaining four minutes of the video, Katalyst employees make funny faces at the turkey while it defecates around their cubicles.

The original sixteen-episode series, hosted on Facebook, was sponsored by the microwavable snack Hot Pockets. The entire production was a collaboration between Katalyst, Slide (a web company founded by Levchin of PayPal), the advertising titan Publicis Groupe, and Nestlé, owner of Hot Pockets. Business magazines were quick to call this a true marriage of Madison Avenue (advertising), Silicon Valley (tech), and Hollywood (celebrity).

Kutcher tirelessly promoted the videos on his Twitter account, and despite the often juvenile subject matter, Nestlé's group marketing manager, Mike Niethammer, was blown away by *Katalyst HQ* and the attention it brought his microwavable snacks. "There is really nothing like this out there," he said, referring to short video content that exploited a celebrity's star power and social media network in order to sell a product.

He was right. While in 2007 the actor-comedian Will Ferrell and writer Adam McKay launched the comedy website Funny or Die to make funny celebrity videos that would go viral—receiving venture capital funding and entering into a partnership with HBO—Katalyst was different, in that they first integrated sponsorship and then distributed the content through Kutcher's online "friends" and followers. That's where Katalyst was unique.

The Internet is a democratic medium. Consumers feel like they're interacting with the ads by "liking" them on Facebook or retweeting them on Twitter. The short videos produced by Katalyst are either sandwiched between product ads or incorporate products and product mentions into their content. They fall under the rubric of branded entertainment, which also includes product placement in movies and TV shows. *Katalyst HQ's* aesthetic, however, mirrors the kind of videos regular people upload to YouTube, but they include Kutcher and his flashy Hollywood office. It was the same junk available elsewhere on the Internet, but because it was junk starring Ashton Kutcher, it became aspirational and viral and was therefore attractive to brands.

Through 2009 and 2010, Katalyst worked hard to recruit new clients. Its new business approach involved reaching out to brands that the founders liked and believed had potential to grow through social media. That meant brands that were already "cool" and appealing to a younger generation. That was how Katalyst came to work with Popchips. "I reached out to the CEO and told him I had an interest in working with the business and making an investment in the company," Kutcher told *Fast Company* in 2009.[7] Kutcher claimed to have had three conditions for working with the snack company: He wanted to be president of Pop Culture, to oversee the social media for the brand, and to have an endless supply of Popchips to feed family and friends.

Being named the company's president of Pop Culture just meant that Kutcher took over the company's social media campaigns. His more than five million Twitter followers and three million Facebook followers were what the brand really wanted access to. The Kutcher/Katalyst advantage online was his vast distribution platform.

The Katalyst team walked into a pitch meeting with a potential new client armed with models, facts, and figures designed to knock the socks off well-established consumer brands accustomed to the traditional advertising models of TV and print. First Katalyst representatives would describe the social web. They explained how it is built of different networks and how each of those networks could be used. A potential client usually asked, "But who is doing it well right now?" To which a Katalyst exec had a pat reply: "No one. But you can."

About nine out of ten prospective clients Katalyst met with had yet to launch a serious digital campaign. Right off the bat, Katalyst stressed the importance of content sharing among consumers and the rule of 1 percent. With a million followers on a site like Facebook, if just 1 percent of content is shared by 1 percent of followers, then the number of people who view the content in some form already reaches into the millions. A share rate of 2 percent translates into the tens of millions. Kutcher's millions of followers gave brands a comfortable start in distributing their message with a high likelihood it would be shared.

Making More Money Online

In addition to exploiting Kutcher's vast social network, Katalyst experimented with using social media platforms to make money on shows that traditional media no longer wanted. In effect they created a secondary market for flops.

For the fall season of 2009, the company produced a primetime soap opera for the CW network called *The Beautiful Life*, about aspiring models trying to make it big in New York City. The result was a show about beautiful people with some very ugly ratings. *The Beautiful Life* survived for only two episodes on television, where it had 1.5 million viewers on the CW network for its premiere episode and 1 million for the second episode.

Most production houses would throw up their hands and accept a bomb. But Katalyst did something entirely unprecedented. They approached YouTube about airing full episodes and moved the show online, where they could offer deals to advertisers at a discounted rate yet still recoup some of their sunk production costs.

Hewlett-Packard stepped in as a sponsor, partnering on a "Create Change" philanthropic program that was meant to spark viewer participation and sharing. As part of the arrangement, the show's stars—Elle Macpherson, Corbin Bleu, Mischa Barton, and Sara Paxton—recorded video commentary for YouTube about how they planned to create positive change in the next year. YouTube users could upload their own videos about their personal goals. The hope was that all this sharing would go viral and encourage more sharing—creating the intimacy brands crave.

Five episodes of the series, including three that never aired on television, were posted on YouTube in mid-December. Kutcher set the modest goal of half a million views for the series when he made the executive decision to put it online. "I want this to be the first show ever that gets more viewers on the web than it did on terrestrial television," Kutcher said. The online episodes were viewed more than 3 million times in total.

In addition to generating extra revenue and bringing new eyeballs to already created episodes of *The Beautiful Life*, posting the show on YouTube was an invaluable investment in data-gathering for Kutcher and Katalyst.

YouTube collected information about the people who tuned in to the online episodes, including gender, age, even when they stopped watching, whether they started up again, and how often they rewatched certain scenes. That data would later inform the choices that Katalyst made on future projects.

Delivering the kinds of content that make the brands want to spend money online is far from effortless. First you need to woo the brand, convincing them you are bringing to the table an entirely unique skill set. Once the contract is signed, content needs to be created, and that involves writers, directors, and editors. Then inroads must be made with the social media platforms. That's why Kutcher was wandering the halls of Ustream back in 2007. That's why he challenged CNN to a Twitter duel, and that's why he flirted with Popchips. It was a lot of work, and not every celebrity was willing to work that hard. Not every celebrity looking to monetize his or her online presence has the time to do so.

Fortunately for the slackers, an upstart called Ad.ly came along to make monetizing online social networks very simple. In the process it stripped away some of the magic of Kutcher's unique position in the market.

Ad.ly Enters the Market

In the spring of 2011, the highest paid actor on television, Charlie Sheen, was fired from the number one sitcom on CBS, which caused him to lose a $2 million paycheck per episode. He needed to cobble together some new revenue streams. Sheen, forty-five years old, wasn't a big web guy, so he had a buddy of his reach out to a company called Ad.ly, which had been in the news for its business model of paying celebrities to tweet on behalf of brands. There was a dead Twitter account with the name @CharlieSheen attached to it, and Ad.ly was able to work out a deal with Twitter for Sheen to take it over. The actor went from zero to one million followers in twenty-four hours, setting a Guinness world record and proving that by 2011 celebrities no longer needed to try as hard as Kutcher had with his malaria campaign to be popular online.

The phones at the Ad.ly offices—four rooms in an office park in Beverly Hills with the overworked feel of a telemarketing hive—rang off the hook with questions about what Sheen would endorse first. There was speculation that the actor could make as much as $25,000 per 140-character tweet. It ended up being more.

Arnie Gullov-Singh, Ad.ly CEO for less than a year, needed to take a deep breath. Usually they had three to six months between signing up to work with a celebrity and pairing them with a brand. Celebrities like and need a lot of handholding, and Ad.ly wanted to give celebs a chance to get comfortable with social media before making endorsement deals for them. Now, for the first time in his life, Gullov-Singh was caught up in the fast-paced cycle of celebrity news, and it was overwhelming.

The company's founder and president was Sean Rad, a web genius in his early twenties who had dropped out of the undergraduate business program at USC to work on Ad.ly full-time. He already had one start-up, Orgoo.com, under his belt.[8] In addition to being a tech prodigy, Rad was also an accomplished singer and songwriter who at the age of twelve composed an original work that was recorded by the Bangkok Symphony Orchestra. Ad.ly debuted in 2009 with $1 million raised from angel investors to pioneer celebrity endorsements in social media. But Rad was too baby-faced to be taken seriously in meetings with big-time celebrity managers and the heads of brand marketing teams. So in May 2010, Ad.ly hired a CEO, News Corp. digital veteran Gullov-Singh, and raised another $5 million from GRP Partners and Greycroft Partners.

Gullov-Singh, who looks and sounds a little like a celebrity himself, with a well-carved face and posh British accent, had previously worked as the executive vice president of product, technology, and operations at News Corp.'s Fox Audience Network, which he cofounded and helped grow into one of the five largest display advertising networks in the United States. Prior to that, he held a similar role at Yahoo! and had worked to monetize MySpace, where he had been frustrated because, although it gave celebrities a distribution platform on the Internet, the company had not implemented a way to bring in revenue for the service it provided and neither had the celebrities who created the pages.

Ad.ly's goal was to make monetization of the distribution platform very simple. The company's business plan revolved around recruiting brands to pay to have celebrities distribute their messages to their millions of followers on Twitter, while Ad.ly took a percentage for bringing the brands and celebrities together. Twitter was the perfect platform, because it was social media that offered the ultimate in ease of use for a celebrity. There was no long drawn-out profile like on Facebook, and the celebrity didn't have to know how to build an html-based website like on MySpace.

Once a celebrity partnered with Ad.ly, they could sit back and collect checks on a monthly basis. Ad.ly employed a team of copywriters, three well-educated twenty-somethings who spent their days learning how to mimic the voices of celebrity tweeters like Tori Spelling and Snooki. Celebrities are paid a flat rate for their tweets, which can be adjusted monthly depending on how well previous campaigns do.

Among the first celebrities to adopt Ad.ly were reality stars Spencer Pratt and Heidi Montag, who crafted a campaign around their carefully orchestrated divorce. But soon, getting paid just to be online trickled up from the D-list to the A-list. The company began attracting higher quality talent like the rapper 50 Cent, tennis star Serena Williams, and comedian George Lopez.

On Monday, March 7, 2011, just a week after they got him online, Ad.ly ran their first endorsement with Charlie Sheen. With so much media attention on him, they eschewed the typical several months' wait and jumped right in bed with Sheen while his celebrity was hot from a protracted war with his network and an increasingly erratic media blitz. Ad.ly paired advertiser Internships.com with the actor. From Sheen's account they tweeted out the job requirements for his own social media intern and included a link to Internships.com. The tweet read:

> I'm looking to hire a #winning INTERN with #TigerBlood. Apply here – http://bit.ly/hykQQF #TigerBloodIntern #internship #ad

It generated 95,333 clicks in the first hour and 450,000 clicks in forty-eight hours, created a worldwide trending topic out of #tigerblood-intern, attracted 82,148 internship applications from 181 countries, and added an additional one million incremental visits to Internships.com.

Sheen received a six-figure deal for his tweets, but that was an anomaly. Celebrities are typically paid between $200 and $10,000 per tweet, with pricing based on number of followers and how those followers respond to the branded messages. It is Ad.ly's version of calculating Klout.

Ad.ly was producing content just like Katalyst. The difference was that its content consisted of 140-character tweets instead of videos, and its celebrity network spread farther than Ashton Kutcher, his wife, and his buddies. By 2011, Ad.ly was working with a network of a thousand celebrities on Twitter, including TV personalities, athletes, and artists. A brand pays Ad.ly on average $25,000 to $100,000 per campaign, but for more tweets and more celebrities they can pay up to $1 million or more. It's cheap, considering the typical celebrity endorsement deal for one celebrity starts at $100,000 and rises into the millions. Cost per click—literally how much it costs the brand to achieve a single click on a link—is a standard measurement of the effectiveness of online advertising, and Ad.ly delivers. Endorsements from celebrities on Twitter have a click-through rate between 5 and 10 percent, which is a hundred times higher than what you'd get with a typical Internet banner ad. Ad.ly's cost per click is in the range of $1 to $2.

An Ad.ly campaign typically consists of between six and twelve celebrities. A campaign for children's toys, for example, will have a grouping of celebrity moms, whereas a campaign for a dating website will focus on single celebs.

Campaigns can range wildly in scope and reach. A modest campaign for the website FamilyFinds.com included Tori Spelling (387,000 followers), Olympian Amanda Beard (18,000 followers), model and actress Ali Landry (18,000 followers), and "Real Housewife of Beverly Hills" Adrienne Maloof (77,000 followers). A high-end campaign for the Warner Bros. movie *Red Riding Hood* consisted of tweets from teen actor Chaske Spencer of the *Twilight* franchise (60,000 followers), reality starlet Lauren Conrad of *The Hills* (1.7 million followers), Conrad's former *Hills* costar and *Dancing with the Stars* contestant Audrina Patridge (1.4 million followers), and reality star Khloé Kardashian (3 million followers).

Ad.ly didn't require a production team to craft its campaigns. A handful of engineers and three copywriters could turn any celebrity into a revenue stream. The celebrities that perform best for Ad.ly and the brands that sponsor their tweets are not A-list by old Hollywood standards. Lauren Conrad and Khloé Kardashian, in fact, are among Ad.ly's top performers. Conrad was the company's most influential celebrity and Kardashian its third (right behind her sister Kim, who occupied the second slot) for the fourth quarter of 2010. If Kutcher and Katalyst wrote the bible for digitizing celebrity, Ad.ly created *Capitalizing on the Internet for Celebrity Dummies*.

Conclusion

Celebrities today have the opportunity to make millions online, and the savvy ones are already doing just that.

Kutcher pioneered the business model, using celebrity as a distribution system for brands to convey their messages to consumers through social media, and he was the first celebrity to start making real money online.

Since 2007, Kutcher has had his hand in each new evolution of the social web. First it was AOL, then MySpace, then YouTube, and then "fuck YouTube" and it was on to Ustream and Twitter. He's moved between these platforms seamlesssly, all the while figuring out how to put his celebrity distribution system to work to make him money.

Kutcher and Katalyst didn't join the digital world for the cute dork cachet. They got into it to make bank and they were successful. While branding and marketing were still a small percentage of Katalyst's revenue in 2011 (insiders estimated approximately 20 percent), their contribution was expected to continue growing.

Then along came Ad.ly, which improved upon the Katalyst model by making it incredibly easy for celebrities to make money online. Ad.ly did all the heavy lifting and a celebrity simply had to lend their name and network. Kutcher crafted the business model for digital celebrity; Ad.ly made it scalable.

Since he first started trolling tech conferences and playing with the Internet, Kutcher has called himself "The Connector." "I want to connect the creative talent with technology with the advertisers," he said. "I want the right people to meet the right people to get it done. And once I do that, you can find me on an island in the South Pacific."[9]

He continues to connect the worlds of celebrity and tech by investing (often through a partnership with billionaire Ron Burkle and Madonna's manager Guy Oseary) in start-ups that he believes have a future—"companies that solve problems in intelligent and friction-free ways and break boundaries."[10] Those companies have included the hyper-local location network Foursquare, photo-sharing app Path, budget travel site Airbnb, and Internet calling platform Skype.

It is entirely possible that Kutcher will become an early investor in the next big tech thing to again change how Hollywood interfaces with the consumer.

But for a time, Ad.ly became "The Connector," and brands reached a point where they were generally much smarter about knowing what to ask for online. By 2011, most brands knew to write a Twitter clause into any celebrity endorsement contract. Endorsers are now mandated to support the brand through their social media activities. As social media continues to evolve at a rapid pace, it remains to be seen whether Kutcher's entrepreneurial spirit will continue to evolve the business model for online celebrity, or whether he will be happy to have simply created the business model and retire to the South Pacific early.

[1] Brown, Scott. "Don't Laugh: Ashton Kutcher *Is* the Future of Video." *Wired*, 11 January 2010.

[2] McGirt, Ellen. "Mr. Social: Ashton Kutcher Plans to Be the Next New-Media Mogul." *Fast Company*, 1 December 2009.

[3] Howe, Carl. "2009 Advertising Forecast Update: Less TV, More Internet." Yankee Group, 6 April 2010.

[4] Arrington, Michael. "MySpace to Distribute Ashton Kutcher's Blah Girls." TechCrunch, 5 November 2008.

[5] McGirt.

[6] Brown.

[7] Glassman, Neil. "Kutcher's Klout Creates Cred for Crunch." SocialTimes.com. WebMediaBrands, 1 July 2010.

[8] A free service that allowed the user to get all email accounts, IM accounts, video chat, video email, and SMS integrated in one place online.

[9] Brown.

[10] Wortham, Jenna. "An Actor Who Knows Start-Ups." *The New York Times*, 26 May 2011.

9

Taylor Hicks:
Building a Career After *American Idol*

Though the wildly popular singing competition has launched a handful of popular stars, American Idol *has not proved to be the superstar-generating machine it was originally billed as. The launchpad that the show gave artists failed to catapult contestants from obscurity to the A-list 70 percent of the time. When what we call "the* Idol *Machine" takes its leave of an artist, says good-bye and moves on to the next act, what's a former Idol to do? Idol-winner, sales-loser Taylor Hicks had a few ideas.*

Approximately 63.4 million people voted for the winner of the fifth season of *American Idol* in 2006. "That's more [votes] than any president in the history of our country has ever received," announced the show's plucky host Ryan Seacrest, as he stood on the stage with finalists Taylor Hicks and Katharine McPhee.[1]

McPhee glowed like a beauty queen, chocolate curls falling over the shoulders of her champagne ball gown. Hicks, in a black shirt and black jacket, hair prematurely gray, clutched her hand in his sweaty palm, looking the part of a very fortunate prom date.

"The winner of *American Idol* Season Five is . . . Taylor Hicks!"

Hicks flung his arms in the air and hugged McPhee. The crowd in his hometown of Birmingham, Alabama, went Super Bowl–win wild.

"Soooooouullll Patrol," Hicks wailed, paying homage to his legion of fans, the self-described Soul Patrol, which catapulted him to his first-place finish.

Judges Randy Jackson and Paula Abdul gave Hicks a standing ovation. Their counterpart Simon Cowell stayed seated at the judges' table with a look that clearly insinuated he would have preferred McPhee to win. Cowell, a record industry executive and a raw populist at heart, who has been behind acts selling twenty-five million hit albums, had always considered *Idol* winners in terms of future record sales. The democratic notion of *Idol* viewers calling or texting their votes aside, Cowell suspected Hicks would have difficulty selling actual records to actual consumers.

Taylor Hicks doesn't look like a pop star. His gray hair, his soft belly, and the nervous tick that makes him say "you know" every few sentences while talking to a stranger, make him look and sound like a high school chemistry teacher.

Entertainment Weekly magazine once expounded on *American Idol*'s track record in translating fan-favorite status to blockbuster careers in the music business: "It's given us Kelly, Carrie, Daughtry, and J. Hud. *Idol* rules the reality roost because the winners of Fox's ratings juggernaut actually do go on to greatness. And Taylor Hicks? He's the exception that proves the rule."

Entertainment Weekly and the conventional wisdom about *Idol* are wrong. First of all, Chris Daughtry and Jennifer Hudson weren't *Idol* winners, but simply finalists—that means America didn't choose them as their superstars. And when it comes to post-show success, Hicks's experience of middling (let's call it D-level) celebrity is more the rule than the exception. Superstardom, as we popularly define it—sold-out stadiums, several platinum albums, an eponymous fragrance, and endorsement deals from Chevy—hasn't come to former winners Ruben Studdard, Jordin Sparks, Fantasia Barrino, David Cook, Kris Allen, or Lee DeWyze either.

American Idol is a moneymaking endeavor first, entertainer second, and star-maker third (in order of importance). Each Idol who signs a record deal following the show is a business unit in the asset portfolio of the label (Sony until 2010, then Universal Music Group) and *Idol* management company, 19 Entertainment. These two players invest money to harvest the unit and then wait to see if its value goes up or down. When it becomes clear to the label that a particular unit will no longer be profitable, they drop it or stop investing in it.

This is why *Idol* winners and runners-up lucky enough to obtain the coveted record deal can be analyzed with the Boston Consulting Group (BCG) growth-share matrix, which can predict, at the moment of their win, which Idols have the chance to be superstars and which will end up like Hicks. The tool, designed by Bruce Henderson of BCG in the 1970s, has traditionally been used to classify successful and unsuccessful business units in corporations by using market share and market growth. The matrix has four categories: Star, Cash Cow, Problem Child, and Dog. Stars make money, Dogs don't, and the other two exist in purgatory somewhere in between.

The *Idol* Machine, which consists of the record executives and 19's managers, marketers, and publicists is notoriously canine-averse. Once it smells a Dog, the machine stops investing in it—that could mean they are ignored or dropped altogether. Hicks was labeled a Dog relatively early on, as the look on Cowell's face clearly spelled out. But can a fallen Idol still be successful once they've been left behind? Taylor Hicks certainly hopes so.

Exhibit A: *American Idol* BCG Growth-Share Matrix

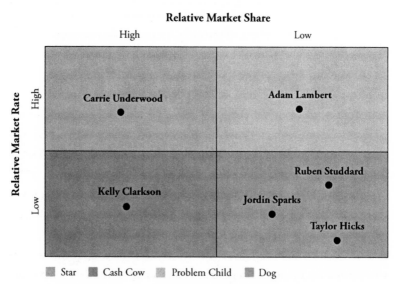

Relative Market Share

A History of *Idol*

At the turn of the millennium, advertising dollars on network television were in decline as TiVo allowed viewers to hop right over commercials and brands began turning their attention to cable and online. Meanwhile, the music industry was scrambling to combat online file-sharing and remain relevant. *American Idol* found a way to extract profits from both ailing industries.

Launched in 2002, the reality singing competition was the brainchild of British television producer and manager Simon Fuller, the mind behind the nineties girl-power juggernaut the Spice Girls. The goal of the show—a spin-off of the popular British program *Pop Idol*—was to find the best singer in the country, as determined by real-time audience voting. The original three judges were an admittedly odd mixture: record producer and bass player Randy Jackson, washed-up pop singer Paula Abdul, and *Pop Idol*'s sharp-tongued judge, the British music executive Simon Cowell.

They created a ratings monolith. Each season of *Idol* brought, on average, twenty-six million sets of eyeballs to television screens per episode. Because the show filled four hours of programming over two weeknights on Fox, other networks were forced to scramble to move their good programming or risk being eclipsed by this inexorable force.[2] In an unlikely shift, the show actually brought audiences that had migrated to cable back to network television.

Coca-Cola got in on the ground floor with the franchise in 2002, paying less than $10 million for an intense product placement that turned the show's greenroom into a "redroom" and had the judges sipping from Coke glasses each week. By 2010, the company was spending $60 million for that same placement. The show makes money hand over fist. In 2010, *Idol* raked in an estimated $7.11 million in advertising for the Fox network every half hour. The next biggest moneymaker in television was sitcom *Two and a Half Men*, with an estimated $2.89 million in advertising revenue for CBS per half-hour show.[3]

In addition to changing the television landscape, *Idol* had a considerable impact on the music business. A song sung on the *Idol* stage could enjoy a sales boost for up to eight weeks post-performance. When contestant Jason Castro performed Jeff Buckley's version of Leonard Cohen's "Hallelujah" in 2008, the Buckley download promptly moved to number one on the Hot Digital Songs chart, selling 178,000 copies according to Nielsen, fourteen years after its initial release and eleven years after Buckley's death.

And then there was the matter of star-making. Before appearing on television at all, *American Idol* contestants signed a contract that stipulated that Sony and 19 Entertainment would get a first-look record and management option. They can pass on whomever they want, and whether future contracts materialize depends on how well a first album sells. While there's considerable variation between contestants' album sales, the overall numbers for the group are good. According to Nielsen SoundScan, Sony has sold 126.5 million *Idol*-related albums, singles, and download tracks since 2002.[4]

More than 200,000 people audition for *Idol* each year. Of the two hundred individuals who meet with the executive producers, a handful will make it to the finals, where they compete in front of a live studio audience in Los Angeles.[5] It is at this point that a contestant's eventual place on the growth-share matrix—and their ultimate viability in the market—begins to become clear.

On *Idol*, the value of a singer's brand is determined by the viewers—more specifically, by the viewers who vote. Gaining America's support is a tightrope-balancing act. New York University cognitive psychology professor Scott Barry Kaufman has been studying *Idol* since Season Three. A former voice major at Carnegie Mellon University in Pittsburgh, Kaufman has also auditioned (unsuccessfully) for the show twice. Early on in his *Idol* fandom, and following his unsuccessful attempts to get on the show, Kaufman made a hobby of using his psychological profiling skills to analyze who won *Idol* and why. Kaufman told me the essential factors for getting votes—humility and uniqueness, in the right proportions. Musical talent, Kaufman claimed, has very little to do with an *Idol* win. This is one reason post-*Idol* album sales aren't always very high.

"Human beings react to others' successes so much better if they feel like the person who is succeeding is a person who deserves those successes," Kaufman explained. "You have to show that you are special and at the same time that you are relatable." And in this balancing act, it helps to suffer a little—or be seen to suffer—in the season's early episodes. "You can't peak too early. Peaking too early is the kiss of death. You have to be the underdog and grow slowly, and that is what makes America love you and vote for you."

Kelly Clarkson, one of the few superstars the show has created, exhibited the perfect slowly unraveling underdog narrative. Clarkson's audition wasn't even shown on the first episode of *Idol*. During her season—the show's first—all the attention was showered on the smooth-talking, wild-haired, boy-band clone Justin Guarini, who was hailed as the front-runner from the start. Guarini got loads more screen time than other contestants, and it wasn't until the semifinals that America finally met Kelly. It was then she wowed the crowd with her showstopping version of Aretha Franklin's "Respect," and even Cowell was impressed.

"You have a good voice but I honestly couldn't remember you from the previous rounds," the ornery judge said to Clarkson. Kelly had picked her spot and from there let her narrative of the down-on-her-luck Texas waitress who moved back home after a failed go at fame in Los Angeles unfold like a striptease.

Even when a contestant has won over America and finished high in the competition, they have only cleared two hurdles. The next challenge is to funnel value from the win into the marketplace. Following the show's finale, the *American Idol* Summer Tour sends the top ten contestants out on a grueling national tour that has them cranking through thirty-odd performances in six weeks. They can take a flat fee of approximately $200,000 or a percentage of ticket sales and merchandising revenues, which can yield as much as $500,000. The lucky one, two, or sometimes three singers who are given a record contract following the season put in the extra hours to produce an album by fall. They try to get it out between the start of school and the pre-holiday season. That's the *Idol* sweet spot.

Idol brings contestants into America's living rooms twice a week, giving artists a huge amount of primetime exposure and the consumer a high level of comfort with the performers and the brand. This is the *Idol* advantage—the thing that sets contestants apart from Joe Schmo playing guitar at his local pub. This is what gives them the chance to be famous. But sometimes it just isn't enough. *American Idol* was created to make two Brits—Simon Cowell, the record executive who would sign the artists to his label, and Simon Fuller, who would manage them for 19 Entertainment—a lot of money. In that respect it has been an overwhelming success. But it was also created on the claim that it could turn the winner into a superstar. These two goals can be at odds with one another, and the spotty success record for star-making has to do with maximizing profits for the franchise rather than for the winners.

Investing in Idols

In return for virtually creating a star out of nothing, *American Idol* contractually owns each of its contestants. That means contestants' fees for albums are fixed in a contract signed before anyone knows who will win that season. The winner is paid $175,000 when he or she starts recording their first album and another $175,000 when they deliver, for a total of $350,000 (almost seven times the median household income in the United States). If the winner records a second album with Sony, the contract fees rise to between $275,000 and $550,000, depending on the first album's success. The scale increases with each album until the sixth, which can yield a million-dollar payday.[6]

As of this writing, Clarkson was working on her fifth album and Underwood her fourth. As long as their albums continue to sell and their songs make it onto the *Billboard* charts, the *Idol* Machine will keep building the Idol's brand. How it determines who is lucrative enough to keep and who should be set free is a closely guarded secret and follows no strict formula. As one record exec put it, "We just let them go when we think they won't be profitable any longer." Once profits start to slip, an artist is either let go or kept on the roster with less money and less support available for them to grow.

In that way, each performer is considered like a business unit in the BCG matrix of Sony and 19's larger portfolio and is judged as such. Approached from this angle, it becomes easier to see how an Idol is tossed aside after experiencing lackluster album sales, so that the Machine's energy can focus on higher grossing performers—the Stars and the Cash Cows.

A Star is a performer in a high-growth market with a relatively high share of that market. Stars not only sell lots of albums, but they are also eminently likable and therefore salable across other platforms. They get lots of endorsement and licensing deals. They are, in short, a strong brand. Carrie Underwood is the epitome of a Star. It's all she has ever wanted to be. "If you were to ask me what I would be when I grow up when I was little, I would have been like, 'I want to be famous,'" Underwood has said. Not only has the diminutive blonde country powerhouse sold 11.57 million albums (which gives her a high market share), but her market—the hybrid of country-pop—was exploding in 2005.

Underwood released her first album at the end of that year. By the second half of 2006, country album sales were up nearly 18 percent over the year prior. And despite the fact that by 2010 the entire market for country music declined by 5 percent (rap was the only genre that saw any increase in sales that year), country-pop crossovers were still strong, with three of the year's top-selling albums (Taylor Swift, Lady Antebellum, and the Zac Brown Band) hailing from the genre. Underwood didn't release an album in 2010 but had plans for a 2012 release that would likely enter a market hungry for country-pop.

Underwood's brand strength also continues to grow through endorsement and licensing deals, because she is enormously likable. On the Davie Brown Index (DBI) of likability she has a score of 80.57, by far the highest of any *Idol* contestant. She is also aspirational to her fans, because she cultivates her celebrity. Underwood first played the celebrity dating game by being linked romantically to Dallas Cowboys quarterback Tony Romo and *Gossip Girl* actor Chace Crawford, and in 2010 she married Ottawa Senators hockey player Mike Fisher. She is entirely inoffensive and, despite marrying a Canadian, is apple-pie all-American with her blonde hair and blue eyes—that makes her the ideal brand spokeswoman for companies like Vitaminwater and Olay. Plus, she knows the importance of hitting the road. Underwood has played more than three hundred shows since her

Idol win. Each performance brings in about $350,000 to be split between Underwood and the concert promoter.[7]

The Cash Cow is a performer with high sales in a low-growth market. After starting out a Star, Kelly Clarkson was a Cash Cow in 2011, nearly nine years after her *Idol* win. It's a terrible title but not a bad market position. Over the course of her nine-year career, Clarkson has sold 10.5 million albums. Though she consistently performs well on the charts and continues to sell, the pop audience has changed since her 2002 win. It keeps getting younger. By 2010, artists like Justin Bieber, Ke$ha, Miley Cyrus, and Lady Gaga were cutting significantly into Clarkson's fan base of tweens and teenagers. Additionally, the entire rock market—of which Clarkson (and pop generally) is a part—declined by 16 percent in 2010. And unlike Underwood, Clarkson simply doesn't have the kind of celebrity personality that excites the tabloids and endears her to the public, which makes her less sought after by brands. This could be a personal preference. Clarkson claims that fame has never been her goal. "I could give a crap about being a star," Clarkson told *Elle* magazine in 2007. "I've always just wanted to sing and write." Yet her ability to consistently generate platinum albums and rally people to buy concert tickets makes her a Cash Cow and therefore a valuable asset for Sony. She consistently performs well for her label and requires little handholding or capital investment. Both Clarkson and Underwood have remained with divisions of Sony—Kelly with RCA and Underwood with country label Arista Nashville.

What do these two artists, by far the biggest superstars *Idol* has produced, have in common? They're women, they're easy on the eyes, and they won the competition at a young age (Clarkson was 20, Underwood was 21). It could be a coincidence, or it could be that American consumers of celebrity respond best to pretty, young, aspirational women.

In 2009, Season Eight runner-up, Adam Lambert, eclipsed that year's winner, Kris Allen, from the very start and has since been the quintessential Problem Child for 19 and Sony. The eyeliner-wearing glam rocker recalled a punk aesthetic while belting out poppy dance anthems like Madonna and Lady Gaga. After finishing in second place, Lambert spoke frankly to *Rolling Stone* magazine about his homosexuality and history of drug use.[8] His confessional attitude proved to be publicity gold. The article rebranded the twenty-seven-year-old in a way *Idol* contestants have rarely branded themselves—as an "other"—and his outrageous confessions catapulted him to a higher circle of fame than Allen, who possessed boyish good looks and a phenomenal voice but was also married, sweet tempered, and frankly, boring. But Lambert's edginess was both an asset and a liability. In 2009, the market was looking for the "other," but Lambert was a loose cannon, and that could hurt potential sales. If the *Idol* Machine picked him up, he could be trouble from the start—yet with the potential for a high payout.

Mere hours after Lambert's admission hit the media maelstrom on a Wednesday morning, the singer signed a deal for his solo record debut with RCA Records, a division of Sony. Lambert made headlines again at the American Music Awards ceremony later that year by performing a racy dance sequence complete with simulated oral sex and a gay kiss live onstage. The stunt boosted Lambert's name recognition but ultimately proved costly to the *Idol* franchise, as crisis managers felt the need to put some distance between the family-friendly brand and Lambert's raunchy performance. His first album, *For Your Entertainment*, sold less than a million copies.

Still, the market in 2011 was hungry for edginess, as evidenced by the stratospheric rise of Lady Gaga and her outrageous dance anthems, ambiguous sexuality, and pro-gay messages. So while Lambert's market share was low, the market for "the other" was growing. "The gay thing these days is a brand in itself, and his appeal to the tween market that drives the sales for *Idol* products these days will be huge. The biggest trend for tweens isn't to be in the crowd these days, it's to stand out in it. That is what Lambert has done by branding himself this way," explained brand futurist Martin Lindstrom, author of *Buyology* and a market-trend analyst.

So Lambert was a Problem Child. He had potential, but his brand needed constant nurturing and policing to survive. Problem Children can become Stars or Dogs. They have the potential for high growth but they require significant investments of time and money and a lot of nurturing. At the time of this writing, it is still unclear which way Lambert will go.

The Rise and Fall of Taylor Hicks

Take a look at the *Idol* contestants next time they take the stage together during the show's Hollywood Week. Think about the music you and your friends listen to. Think about who looks like a star. That seems to matter when it comes to future long-term album sales. When America votes, however, it doesn't think about these things. People vote with their hearts and not their wallets. That's what makes America so special.

What made Simon Cowell so special as a judge and a record executive was that something like a BCG matrix consistently occupied his mind. He could tell who would make him money and who wouldn't. Driving him mad was the fact that America liked to vote off the moneymakers (sometimes, it has been theorized, just to spite Cowell). Insiders have speculated that is one of the reasons Cowell parted ways with *American Idol* in 2010 to launch an American version of his British hit, *The X Factor*, a near *Idol* clone with one important difference: The judges mentor the contestants and help shape their narrative arcs and musical repertoire. It is designed to be a more foolproof system, one that eliminates the Dogs through expert manipulation of the process. *The X Factor* is meant to prevent a Taylor Hicks.

Hicks auditioned for *American Idol* in Las Vegas on October 10, 2005. He came out of the audition with the approval of judges Randy Jackson and Paula Abdul but not Simon Cowell, who warned early on that Hicks would never make it to the final round.

But make it he did, and at twenty-nine Hicks became the oldest *Idol* winner and one of the oldest contestants ever to make it into the top ten. His narrative, like Clarkson's, was heavy on the empathy. Viewers sympathized with his story of growing up in a broken home in suburban Alabama, teaching himself to play harmonica at sixteen and guitar at nineteen. By the time he was twenty, Hicks's hair was almost entirely gray. That was endearing. He was charming on screen, singing crowd-pleasers like Stevie Wonder's "Living for the City" and Queen's "Crazy Little Thing Called Love," and he cultivated a devoted voting block who nicknamed themselves "The Soul Patrol." But though the judges agreed that Hicks was talented and they enjoyed his bluesy renditions, they weren't as certain that he would fare well in the broader marketplace.

"You could tell watching that finale that Simon was slowly dying on the inside and wanted Katharine McPhee to win," said *Billboard* magazine's *Idol* reporter Ann Donahue. "Taylor was good at this one thing he did, and he was very appealing because he was the first Idol who didn't look like he was twenty-two, and that resonated with an older crowd. That crowd was so excited about voting. But they wouldn't be as excited about buying albums."

McPhee was young (twenty-one years old), pretty, and talented. She had the qualities that turned Clarkson and Underwood into stars. Yet it was Hicks who won on the night more people voted for *Idol* than for the president of the United States.

After his first album sold only 704,000 copies—the lowest of any *Idol* winner up to that point—Arista (a division of Sony), 19 Entertainment, and Hicks broke up in 2006. It remains unclear whether he was dumped by the management company or opted to bail when he realized they wouldn't be allocating him the attention and investment needed to nurture his nascent brand.

What is clear is that Hicks had been labeled a Dog. A Dog has low market share in a low-growth market. Hicks's genre of bluesy rock had little potential for radio airplay and was difficult to market. There was no growth to be had. His first album only proved his critics right when it sold fewer copies than any previous *Idol* winner's. Kris Allen and Lee DeWyze would later have debut albums with much worse sales than Hicks's (around 326,000 and 133,000 respectively), and they, too, have since been labeled Dogs. What do all these canines have in common? They're men, they're not obviously pop singers, and they're a little older.

At the time of the split, Hicks didn't have his own publicist. It was up to him to craft the narrative of the split, and he hadn't a clue how to do it without the *Idol* Machine. With few other options available, the gray-haired crooner wrote on his MySpace page:

> To all my fans and The Soul Patrol, I want to take a moment to talk about the recent news that my label and I have mutually parted ways. The important thing for all of you to remember is that I've been a working musician my whole life. This is turning

the page on a new chapter of my career. Artistic freedom and control is an exciting prospect. The things that are most important to me is [sic] creating my art, performing it, and my fans. With the momentum that all of you have created over the years, Taylor Hicks is not going to stop anytime soon. . . . Sit tight, because the best is yet to come!

Hicks still claims that his parting with Sony and 19 was mutual. Others claim that the *Idol* Machine made it clear the relationship would never work out. Hicks said he wanted more autonomy and the chance to build his own branded empire. (Artists signed as part of the *Idol* contract lose control over their albums and their image.) The record label and management team want to make money and believe they know how to do it best. In many cases, as evidenced by a near century of successes, they do. Hicks believed that in his case, however, they did not. He says he wanted out as much as they did.

"I wanted to get back into songwriting, and I wanted to organically meet my fans and develop an album. I wanted to write my own records, and I didn't want to be told how to do it," Hicks told me. The label and 19 wanted him poppier. Pop sells. But Hicks was a crooning rocker, and he insisted that he stick with that identity, even though the label maintained there was no market for his sound.

At that point Hicks saw his only option as implementing a direct-to-consumer marketing plan to create demand for his brand. More than thirty million people had voted for him to win over Katharine McPhee. Now he just had to find a way to get in their face and motivate them to buy his product.

Finding himself without the *Idol* Machine, Hicks had to dig into his own pockets to start a label and produce an album, titled *The Distance*, himself.

"I knew how broke people in this business can be, and it scared me. You just don't have all the financial backing that a major label has, and basically what you have to do is look within your bank account and see how you can take your record directly to the fans," Hicks said. "The scary thing about the record business is that you come off a show like *Idol* and the *Idol* fans buy your record, and the second record it is up to you." Second-album attrition following *Idol* is the norm, regardless of whether the *Idol* Machine sticks with you or not.

But what was missing without the *Idol* Machine, besides the copious amounts of cash, was the Machine's vast network of contacts, including radio DJs, TV and film synergies, and concert promoters, that help an artist market, distribute, and sell himself or herself.

To reach the consumer directly, Hicks hit the road. He had to build up his base and cater to the fan profile that had voted for him on *American Idol*. That audience was a little older (mid-thirties and up) and spread out across the country, mostly in landlocked states. Lacking the money to propel his own tour, Hicks signed a deal to join the national tour of the Broadway production of *Grease* in the role of Teen Angel.

The Teen Angel part is small, nearly a cameo, but Hicks's name was put at the top of the marquee. Over eighteen months the show toured in forty-eight states, and Hicks was able to use *Grease* to market himself directly to consumers. Lacking the intermediary support of a major-label distributor, he also needed a way to sell his music directly to his fans. So Hicks struck a deal with the show's producers. Following each performance of *Grease*, Hicks did his own miniature concert, performing a song off *The Distance*. Following that, Hicks personally sold the album and his merchandise in the lobby.

"You have to go back to the fan base on the road. You have to be tangible to them," Hicks said. "If you're not tangible to them, you become obscure."

So night after night Hicks performed the role of Teen Angel and night after night he shook hands and hugged fans, posed for their pictures, signed their albums, and kissed their babies. During the few nights he had off, Hicks put in personal appearances at local sporting events and casinos, commanding $10,000 an appearance, which he planned to invest back into this own label, Modern Whomp Records, after the tour.

Over the course of the eighteen-month tour, Hicks told me, he sold— by hand—100,000 copies of *The Distance*. He came in direct contact with more than two million fans and says he grossed around $3.5 million, about half what an episode of *Idol* makes in a half hour but still, to put it in perspective, more than three times the average annual income of a CEO at an S&P 500 company. It isn't superstar money but it all belonged to Hicks, and he didn't have to pay large percentages (up to 50 percent) to 19 Entertainment for the Machine.

In June 2010, Hicks finally got off the road, several million dollars richer and with a fan base he hoped would embrace his next project.

"Now I own my own label. I own my own masters [recordings]. If I get just one hit off the next album, I own the rights to that hit, and in the music business that is huge," Hicks said.

He traveled back to Los Angeles for the tenth season finale of *American Idol*, a showdown between the hippie earth mother Crystal Bowersox and homely paint salesman Lee DeWyze, a singer who reminded many in the audience of Hicks and whose debut album would ultimately sell fewer copies than Hicks's debut did.

At one point Hicks stood behind the *Idol* studio staring at the trailers for the various artists who would be performing on the show, some of them former Idols like himself. He couldn't help but think about how much money was being wasted that night.

"Each of those trailers had eight people standing around them and four wardrobe racks of clothes. There I was with just my one publicist," Hicks said. "I was thinking to myself, 'Wow! Someone must be getting rich. I hope it's the artists, but I'll bet it's not.'"

Conclusion

American Idol has failed to live up to its promise to create superstars, the likes of Underwood and Clarkson, each season. Artists Jennifer Hudson and Chris Daughtry have both had successful careers post-*Idol*. But neither was the winner. Hudson came in seventh place in 2006 during the third season and Daughtry in fourth place in the fifth season. Daughtry's albums consistently sell well— the first sold 4.8 million copies, the second 1.2 million, and Hudson, though her albums have been less successful (833,000 and 326,000 copies sold), won an Academy Award in 2007.

The vast majority of former Idols are not superstars or even on the public radar for long. They find careers in musical theater or return to civilian life. Starting with *Idol*'s tenth season in January 2011, 19 Entertainment hoped to start making real stars again. The development, distribution, and marketing of *Idol* contestants was taken away from Sony and given to Universal Music Group's Interscope Geffen A&M, in hopes that a different label could breathe new life into the franchise.

When this book went to print, Hicks was still on his own. Going forward, he planned to keep it simple, keep his team small, and strike his own deals. He had created a small resurgence of his brand on the strength of his own hard work and willpower. Eventually the industry and America started paying attention to him again, and there were whisperings within the Hollywood Industrial Complex that Hicks wasn't over just yet. In April 2011, Hicks did a cameo on *Late Night with Jimmy Fallon*, singing with Comedy Central talk show host Stephen Colbert. Six years after his *Idol* win, industry watchers want to talk about commercial and television opportunities for Hicks.

American Idol gave Hicks his start and helped create his brand. But if Hicks becomes a Star, it will be all on his own.

---

1   In 2004, 122,267,553 people voted in the presidential election. George W. Bush won with 62,040,610 votes.

2   Carter, Bill. "For Fox's Rivals, 'American Idol' Remains a 'Schoolyard Bully.'" *The New York Times*, 20 February 2007.

3   Pomerantz, Dorothy. "TV's Biggest Moneymakers." *Forbes*, 16 March 2011.

4   Herrera, Monica. "Can 'American Idol' Be Saved?" Billboard.com, 21 May 2010.

5   Different seasons have had varying numbers of contestants competing in the semifinal and final rounds.

6   "'Idol' Contestants—No Schtupping the Judges." TMZ. AOL News, 13 May 2010.

7   "Carrie Underwood Is Top Earning Idol." *Forbes*, 21 May 2009.

8   Grigoriadis, Vanessa. "Adam Lambert: Wild Idol." *Rolling Stone*, 25 June 2009.

10

David Arquette and Celebrity-Charity Synergy: Fame Will Feed the Poor

Charities and celebrities have long created alliances to their mutual benefit. Celebrities give charities exposure; charities give celebrities empathy. Being connected to the right celebrity helps a charity raise more money. Being connected to the right charity makes a celebrity more likable, and likability equals bankability.

Standing before a crowd of Hollywood heavy hitters gathered at celebrity manager Eric Kranzler's house in 2009, David Arquette clinked his glass with a nervous hand. The Golden Globe Awards were happening later in the week, and some of the room's frenetic energy could be attributed to award-season jitters and calorie-restricted diets. But Arquette's nervousness was not about the awards—he was not nominated—but about getting his words exactly right on this night. He was going to give a speech about the domestic hunger-relief charity Feeding America and, unbeknownst to him, herald in a sea change in the way the organization raised money.

"That's when I knew David was the right guy for us," Phil Zepeda, Feeding America's senior vice president of communications, later told me about that night at Kranzler's house. "Here was this good guy who emotes so much passion and brings along other people with him. Here is a guy who can make people step up for a cause." Zepeda had recruited

Arquette to help him rally celebrity support for the cause of hunger relief, and after this star-studded night he felt the flush of vindication. This was the moment when Zepeda knew celebrities would change the future of his organization.

Arquette, an actor best known for his role in the *Scream* horror movie franchise and as the husband of sitcom actress Courteney Cox, is shy in intimate settings, but when he stood to speak to this crowd, which included his wife, her friend Jennifer Aniston, and the actors Leonardo DiCaprio and Jason Bateman, the room became eerily quiet. Arquette stammered a little. When he tripped over words, everyone in the room laughed along with him. He then told them about Feeding America, a charity with which he had recently begun working.

This evening marked a pivotal moment for the charity. Unlike AIDS or catastrophes in Africa, the problem of hunger in a wealthy country like the United States has always been hard to get donors to rally around. The nonprofit was in a struggle to rebrand itself and to make the cause something the average American wanted to support. Convincing a room of power players with vast influence and the ability to command media coverage could change the game for the charity.

In addition to carving out celebrity relationships, Feeding America had recently changed its name from America's Second Harvest, to make the cause more attractive and aspirational to donors. To make the organization even more appealing, they wanted to create an Entertainment Council of high-profile individuals who would act as ambassadors of the charity. They needed a celebrity to lead it, someone who could give them access to other celebrities and galvanize the Hollywood community to in turn galvanize the whole country. The trouble was finding the right celebrity.

The name that consistently comes up in any discussion of celebrity and do-gooderism is Bono, the lead singer of the rock band U2, who has been championing AIDS charities in Africa since 1999 and routinely campaigns to raise awareness of the pandemic through consumer-targeted fundraising campaigns like ONE and (RED), a brand-licensing program where proceeds from sales of, for example, Gap T-shirts or iPods are used to fight the spread of disease. Bono was the forerunner of the business model for the modern celebrity-charity alliance.

There are three tiers of alliances between celebrities and charities:

Tier 1: Celebrities who donate their time, attending charity galas and fundraisers, so that wealthy donors can gawk at them like they're animals in a zoo while photographers take pictures and video that will get the organization media coverage.

Tier 2: Celebrities who commit to a more formal alliance with a charity. This is a kind of brand marriage between the celebrity and the charity, in which celebrities consistently donate their time and their celebrity to a single organization.

Tier 3: Celebrities who form their own charities.

In the past decade, philanthropy has acquired a patina of sexiness, and part of this newly acquired appeal comes from charities partnering with celebrity brands in a strategic alliance beneficial to both parties. The Hollywood Industrial Complex behind a celebrity knows their brand needs to be likable in order to succeed commercially. Charities can help soften Hollywood's biggest jerks. In return for perceived good works, a celebrity garners the goodwill of the American public and generates positive publicity for their personal brand. Who doesn't like someone who plays with kids with cancer, gives shoes to the homeless, or volunteers at a soup kitchen?

The incentives for nonprofits are different but related. Partnering with a celebrity heightens an organization's visibility and its ability to attract both individual and corporate donors in an increasingly competitive giving marketplace. Put simply, celebrities help people determine how they want to spend their money, even when it comes to charity.

Defending the benefits of actress Angelina Jolie's charitable efforts with the United Nations High Commissioner for Refugees (UNHCR), the *New York Times* editorial writer and humanitarian crusader Nicholas Kristof summed up why celebrities and charities need one another: "One of the perennial problems for humanitarian crises is that no one pays attention, and so these crises never get resources. That's partly a problem of the news media, especially television, and partly a problem of politicians who just aren't interested in distant problems that don't have quick-fix solutions," Kristof wrote in 2008. "But celebrities carry a spotlight with them, and if they can use some of that glow to highlight the needs of Darfur, Congo or Chad, that saves lives." [1]

A History of Celebrity-Charity Strategic Alliances

Over the past century, the celebrity-charity alliance has evolved into an institutionalized cobranding relationship that operates like a business partnership, with players on both sides working to maximize the gain and minimize the risk to their respective parties.

Such alliances have their beginnings in World War II, when the United States Army and the Screen Actors Guild cooperated to launch USO Camp Shows, Inc., whose task it was to keep the men and women of the armed forces entertained. During the peak of the war's action in 1945, USO Camp Shows presented seven hundred shows a day—a total of more than 300,000 performances overseas and on the home front—to an audience totaling more than 173 million. Participating celebrities included Judy Garland, Frank Sinatra, Fred Astaire, Humphrey Bogart, and Lauren Bacall.

Another notable early celebrity-charity relationship was the entertainer Danny Kaye's work with UNICEF. The son of Russian-Jewish immigrants in Brooklyn, Kaye was fond of the underdog and difficult causes. His involvement with the children's charity began with a disastrous 1953 flight from London to New York. When his plane's engine caught on fire, the pilot made a forced landing in Ireland, and on the next flight out to New York Kaye was seated next to UNICEF executive director Maurice Pate, who confided in Kaye that one of his organization's major hurdles was name recognition.

Shaky from a near-death experience and feeling altruistic, Kaye said he was eager to help, and the result was a documentary, *Assignment Children*, underwritten by Paramount Pictures with proceeds going to UNICEF. It documented Kaye's tour of UNICEF projects in Myanmar, India, Indonesia, Korea, Thailand, and Japan. Over the next thirty-three years Kaye traveled the world making speeches and giving performances on the organization's behalf. He once promoted the nonprofit's Trick-or-Treat campaign by flying his own plane around the country to enlist child volunteers.

But up until the 1980s, celebrity charity work remained a pet project. Then the era of excess witnessed the rich and famous doing charity work like it was pure Colombian cocaine. Elizabeth Taylor arguably became the first modern celeb activist when she positioned herself as the world's leading AIDS crusader, following the death of her friend Rock Hudson. It was the first time that a major celebrity stood up in public to fight for AIDS relief.

The cause of famine relief was also making headlines. Nineteen eighty-five saw the singer Harry Belafonte organize a supergroup of musicians that included Michael Jackson, Bruce Springsteen, Stevie Wonder, Lionel Richie, Paul Simon, Tina Turner, Willie Nelson, Bob Dylan, Diana Ross, Steve Perry, and Smokey Robinson, to record the song "We Are the World" to raise money for aid to Ethiopia. It became a number one hit and raised $10.8 million in just four months for the cause.

Later that year, rock stars Bob Geldof and Midge Ure organized a multivenue relief concert—Live Aid—to raise more funds to fight famine in Ethiopia. The lineup included Sting, Elton John, U2, Run-DMC, the Pretenders, Billy Joel, Madonna, and Bob Dylan. Bruce Springsteen was invited to play but declined because he didn't realize what a big deal the show was going to be.

Activism had become a party. If you weren't invited, you were no longer part of the "it" crowd.

Since the turn of the millennium, the celebrity-charity alliance, like most things in Hollywood, has become further institutionalized as part of a celebrity's business portfolio. Today, creating a charitable image is integral to building the celebrity brand.

The Business Behind Today's Celebrity-Charity Alliance

When a client comes in to meet with the team of agents at United Talent Agency (UTA) in Los Angeles to talk branding, development, television, movies, and books for the first time, Rene Jones is also in the room. She represents philanthropy. Jones is the founding director of the UTA Foundation, the private, nonprofit charitable arm of the firm. Every talent agency worth its salt has a Rene Jones, whose job is to pair celebrities with charities, create campaigns, and champion the celebrity do-gooder image.

This matchmaking process is almost as intimate as a meeting with a dating counselor. "What I learned early on is that the best thing to do is sit down with a person and talk about where they are from and what is meaningful to them. It's always better when we find a fit for somebody that is organic and it is something they can grow with and learn and get their hands dirty," Jones said.

Jones asks questions like: What issue means the most to you? What makes you angry? What would you get out of bed for at five thirty on a cold morning? She gives them a stack of reading on various charitable organizations.

Jones helps them decide whether they can only handle going to another rubber-chicken dinner and having their picture taken or are passionate enough about anything to forge a long-term relationship.

For the celebrity who wants to take philanthropy to Tier 3, there is Trevor Neilson and the Global Philanthropy Group. The former director of public affairs and special projects for the Bill & Melinda Gates Foundation, Neilson is the man celebrities recruit when they want to become very involved. He has been behind campaigns and foundations created for Demi Moore and Ashton Kutcher, Madonna, Angelina Jolie and Brad Pitt, and U2.

Charities have also staffed up to support the celeb-charity alliance. Most of the larger charities and nonprofits (those with annual gifting in the eight-figure range) employ a dedicated coordinator of celebrity affairs, whose job it is to meet with the agency foundations and select the right celebrities for their cause. For example, UNICEF has an international team of Goodwill Ambassadors that includes celebrities from around the globe. The Red Cross formalized its National Celebrity Cabinet in 2002 in order to organize and leverage its celebrity relationships, and in 2008

David Arquette would help Phil Zepeda and Feeding America create their Entertainment Council.

Risks

As in all dealings with celebrities, there are risks to a charity partnering with someone famous. Sometimes the star factor can overwhelm a cause. Celebrity demands can also drive up the cost of publicity events if organizers aren't careful to say upfront that they will not foot the bill for all transportation, hair, makeup, and accommodations for a celebrity plus entourage.

Sometimes celebrities simply behave badly with little warning at all.

In 2007 the Academy Award–nominated actor Ralph Fiennes flew from Australia to India in his role as a UNICEF ambassador. During the flight he was accused of having sex in a bathroom with a Qantas flight attendant. The flight attendant in question, Lisa Robertson, later admitted the tryst and was fired from the airline. UNICEF swept the issue under the rug and kept Fiennes on as an ambassador, but not before spending considerable resources dealing with the media fallout.[2]

"Charities become starstruck too, and sometimes they are just so grateful to a celebrity that they aren't thinking critically about their brand," Jill Zimmerman, vice president of the nonprofit consultancy the Alford Group explained to me.

Naomi Campbell famously upset the group People for the Ethical Treatment of Animals (PETA). She posed for a 1994 ad campaign for PETA that featured the tagline "We'd rather go naked than wear fur." But then, in 1997, she strutted down a Milan catwalk dripping in fur. Her representative at the Elite model agency helpfully pointed out that she had only signed up for the one anti-fur campaign.

"There is nothing worse than someone who may be well-intentioned but is out of their element," UTA's Rene Jones said. "It's not just a matter of jumping on the red carpet with some talking points."

Even the most well-intentioned of celebs, those who go the Tier 3 route and start their own charities, often bungle their finances or leave management in the hands of practical strangers in far-flung areas of the globe, people with little experience with handling millions of dollars in donations.

In January 2010, the performer Wyclef Jean and his charity Yéle Haiti came under fire after receiving millions of dollars in donations following the devastating Haitian earthquake. It came to light that Yéle Haiti had paid Jean and his business partner at least $410,000 for rent, production services, and Jean's appearance at his own benefit concert.[3]

In 2011, Madonna sued the director of her foundation, Raising Malawi, to recover $3.8 million in squandered donations meant to build a school in the impoverished African country. The project never broke ground, there was no title to the land, and there was a lack of accountability from the team in Malawi and the management team in the United States. In the past decade, consumer watchdogs have focused more heavily on helping consumers weigh the risks associated with celebrity when choosing where to donate their money.

"We try to get a message across to the public that they have to use their head and do some research and due diligence when they're donating to a charity and not just act because that charity has at its helm a celebrity," Ken Berger, President of Charity Navigator, the nation's largest charity watchdog, told me. "Celebrities have tremendous influence. They can be role models or role disasters."

An unintended consequence of these celebrity-charity alliances is that time and money are spent policing them, to ensure that the consumer doesn't get hurt. The Better Business Bureau's Wise Giving Alliance also tries to do the watching for consumers. They keep a careful eye on celebrity participation in nonprofits on behalf of the average donor, who may be suckered into a cause orbit by a glamorous spokesperson.

"We try to help charities understand that being involved with celebrities is a double-edged sword. You can take your good name and attach it to a celebrity who will give you mileage in terms of public exposure, until something bad happens with a celebrity and then you're defending your actions with that celebrity," said Wise Giving Alliance CEO Art Taylor.

Taylor encourages nonprofits to hold a conversation among board members at the highest level, so everyone is well aware of the possible risks of getting involved with a celebrity. That conversation is generally awkward. Zepeda and the board of Feeding America had that risk conversation with David Arquette before they made the decision to forge ahead with the Entertainment Council. They raised the question of whether they could fire a celebrity volunteer who misbehaved. Zepeda said "Hell, yes!" The board's official stance was that, should one of their celebrities become involved in unsavory behavior, they would make an announcement that this person was no longer connected to the organization and try to create distance between it and the offending star.

"We hold them to the same standard we would hold any volunteer. If any volunteer were to violate our trust in any way, we would have to take action," Zepeda told me. "We can't treat a celebrity any different."

Unfortunately, their talk would prove useful when dealing with Arquette down the line.

Rewards

With the high risks come high rewards.

Individuals and institutions donated $303.75 billion to charities in 2009. Considering that giving contracted along with everything else during the economic downturn, that's a sizable chunk of change.

Exhibit A: Contributions by Donor in Billions, Expressed as Percentages

Figures courtesy of Giving USA

■ Individuals: $227.41
■ Corporations: $14.10
■ Foundations: $38.44
■ Bequests: $23.8

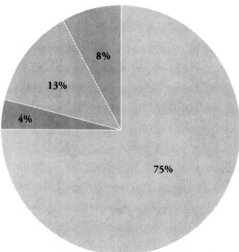

Exhibit B: Contributions by Recipient in Billions, Expressed as Percentages

Figures courtesy of Giving USA

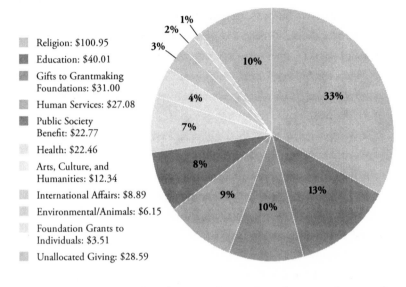

- Religion: $100.95
- Education: $40.01
- Gifts to Grantmaking Foundations: $31.00
- Human Services: $27.08
- Public Society Benefit: $22.77
- Health: $22.46
- Arts, Culture, and Humanities: $12.34
- International Affairs: $8.89
- Environmental/Animals: $6.15
- Foundation Grants to Individuals: $3.51
- Unallocated Giving: $28.59

Competition for this cash is fierce, as the number of registered nonprofits has grown at an eye-opening rate in recent years. "In 1996 there were 1.1 million nonprofits in the United States. In 2006, there were nearly 1.5 million. That's a 36 percent increase while donations are on the decline," explained the Alford Group consultant Jill Zimmerman.

Celebrities give nonprofits a competitive advantage when it comes to stimulating more donations. And as the concept of lifestyle marketing has evolved into celebrity lifestyle marketing, charities have found it beneficial to position themselves not as mere aid organizations but as a lifestyle choice. Who better to sell that savoir faire than a celebrity spokesperson?

David Arquette and Feeding America

Feeding America's goal is to provide food to the one in six Americans they say are affected by food insecurity. From their food banks they distribute food (everything from industrial-sized bags of rice to canned goods donated by an elementary school) to approximately 61,000 local charitable agencies that provide food directly to individuals and families in need.

In 2007, when Phil Zepeda was making plans to rebrand America's Second Harvest as Feeding America, he knew he wanted to raise public awareness of his organization's mission and that launching a celebrity initiative would be integral. Zepeda, having come from the Red Cross, where he worked as the organization's manager for online giving, borrowed aspects of his plan from that organization.

"When we created the Entertainment Council we knew that we were somewhat stealing from the Red Cross, but we knew they wouldn't mind," Zepeda laughed.

To start, Zepeda knew he couldn't roll out a celebrity campaign on his own, so he brought in the consulting firm Sunshine Sachs, headed by former New York mayor David Dinkins's chief of staff Ken Sunshine and his younger partner Shawn Sachs. Sunshine Sachs is a full-service publicity firm that is unique in that its client roster includes politicians, celebrities, and nonprofits, so they can easily provide synergies between these disparate groups. The Sunshine Sachs celebrity roster included Leonardo DiCaprio, Ben Affleck, Justin Timberlake, Nick Lachey, Lance Bass, Jon Bon Jovi, and Barbra Streisand.

Zepeda and Sunshine Sachs together crafted the "Going Home for Hunger" campaign as their initial entry into the world of celebrity. Sunshine clients Nick Lachey and Ben Affleck went home to Cincinnati and Boston respectively and volunteered at the local food bank. Sunshine Sachs installed a photographer and a cameraman with each celebrity and then opened the stunts to the general media as Lachey and Affleck gave their reflections on the events. They issued a press release and hired photographers to snap pictures that were disseminated to weekly magazines like *Us Weekly* and *People*.

"It got us some strong recognition," Zepeda remembered—so strong that during the holiday season the online DVD rental company Netflix signed on as a corporate cosponsor to send four celebrities back to their hometowns. Now Kevin Bacon, Adrian Grenier, Teri Hatcher, and Morgan Freeman were spreading the word about hunger, and someone else was underwriting the costs. The phones at America's Second Harvest began ringing with calls from managers, agents, and publicists, all eager to get their clients good press by associating them with the organization.

The name change to Feeding America was finalized in September 2008, and the celebrity going-home campaigns went so well that in November of 2008 Zepeda was ready to assign someone as chairman of the Entertainment Council. He wanted a "Connector," someone in the entertainment community who would roll up their sleeves and do the outreach, tell their famous friends, "I'm working with Feeding America. You should too." During a coffee date, Rene Jones of UTA got wind that Feeding America was looking to partner with a celebrity. She called Zepeda and threw out the name David Arquette.

Zepeda thought Arquette was maybe a little off the beaten path, but he was willing to listen to what Jones was proposing. "If David does this, he's going to commit himself 120 percent," Jones promised Zepeda.

David Arquette comes from a family of actors. His siblings, Rosanna, Alexis, Richmond, and Patricia, are all in the entertainment industry. During the 1990s, Arquette had a number of bit roles on television shows like *Blossom* and *Beverly Hills, 90210* and in movies like *Buffy the Vampire Slayer*. His most famous part to date was playing the lovably bumbling police officer Dewey Riley in the *Scream* horror movie franchise. In 1999, he married the famous television actress Courteney Cox, who had starred as Monica on the beloved American sitcom *Friends*. The marriage was a merger that made him abundantly more famous. When a D-level celebrity marries an A-level, he or she is immediately bumped up to at least the B level. In 2000, Arquette pursued a stint as a professional wrestler with World Championship Wrestling (WCW), eventually winning the WCW World Heavyweight Championship.

More than just an actor and the husband of a very famous woman, Arquette is also a Connector who, because of his web of family and friends, is at the center of a powerful group of celebrity brands.

After Jones talked to Zepeda and proposed that Arquette start working with the nonprofit, Zepeda reached out to the actor. Arquette told Zepeda that he wanted to get a feel for the organization and how they worked before committing himself. In fact he wanted to get some volunteer miles under his belt without cameras around. This insistence on starting slow and starting anonymously was just one of the ways in which

Arquette was an anomaly from the start. Unlike the celebrities in the first batch of Feeding America alliances, he didn't want press or attention.

The actor began volunteering at St. Joseph Center's food pantry in 2008 on a weekly basis and under cover of darkness. The press never got wind of his activities—proving that celebrities can be anonymous when they choose to be. When he was unable to go to the pantry because of a schedule conflict, he signed a friend in to work his shift. Zepeda was impressed.

Arquette was officially named the chairman of Feeding America's Entertainment Council in the fall of 2008, right after the name change, and was instrumental in recruiting the council's first members, among them chef Mario Batali, television host Rachael Ray, actor Matt Damon, actor and producer Tyler Perry, and country music artist Phil Vassar.

The members of the Entertainment Council agreed to lend their names and likenesses to the nonprofit, to throw fundraisers, and to testify before Congress on hunger issues—a Tier 2 alliance.

Arquette's job was to act as the official celebrity face of the organization. That meant he would interact with the media as frequently as Feeding America's CEO.

But Arquette did more than that. He consistently talked Feeding America up to his family, friends, and business acquaintances, bringing his wife, Courteney Cox, into the fold along with their close friends Ben Harper and Laura Dern and the godmother of his and Cox's daughter, Coco—Jennifer Aniston.

Zepeda realized just how invaluable Arquette was to their mission of enlisting celebrities to help disseminate Feeding America's message when Arquette organized the party at the agent Eric Kranzler's house.

"We didn't call anyone. We were just at the start of our new brand launch," Zepeda said. "So we get in this room and my eyes were popping out of their sockets. I was so starstruck my wife won't even let me talk about it anymore."

In another instance of Feeding America leveraging Arquette as a Connector, the charity announced an auction with the Clothes Off Our Back Foundation and promised to auction off cereal bowls signed by celebrities. Arquette packed boxes of bowls in his car and went door-to-door with a stack of Sharpie pens, getting his friends to sign bowls in the days before the event.

In January 2009, Arquette helped organize a presidential inaugural ball, which Feeding America hosted in partnership with the Recording Industry Association of America and at which the popular singer Rihanna performed. "That ball really welcomed us to the scene of big players in the nonprofit world. . . . It put us in the same arena as a St. Jude or the Elizabeth Glaser organization," Zepeda told me.

Feeding America measured the success of its brand relaunch and its celebrity campaigns by how much public awareness of the organization grew in the three years following the relaunch.[4] Prior to the change of name and the arrival of celebrities on board, 8 percent of the population had some familiarity with America's Second Harvest. By June 2009, after the name-change, 16 percent of the population had some familiarity with the brand, and by June 2010, 23 percent of the general population were familiar with it. Feeding America had 5.1 billion media impressions in 2009, with half of those being tracked to celebrity involvement with the organization.

The rebrand and celebrity synergies certainly bolstered the nonprofit's bottom line. In 2009, Feeding America's fundraising grew 34 percent to $75 million, and food donated or salvaged increased by 22 percent to 2.6 billion pounds. In 2010, Feeding America raised nearly $100 million, a 33 percent jump over the previous year, and the organization distributed nearly 3 billion pounds of food, a 15 percent increase over the year before. The organization's A-list partnerships landed it coverage in *People* and on *Entertainment Tonight*.[5]

"I knew he was a good guy. Now I know he is a great guy. We would never have gotten to where we have made it today without David Arquette," Zepeda told me during the summer of 2010. "There are a lot of pitfalls of working with celebrities—imagine if we had chosen someone like Tiger Woods or Mel Gibson to represent us."

David Arquette would never be a Tiger Woods or a Mel Gibson, but in the fall of 2010 his personal life did begin affecting his ability to be the public face of Feeding America. Arquette split from his wife and entered rehab for alcohol abuse. He also gave a series of erratic and emotional interviews to the radio host Howard Stern about his and Cox's sex life.

Before Arquette's personal crises could affect the charity, Zepeda says, he voluntarily stepped down as chair of the Entertainment Council that fall, citing a busy schedule. Remember the organization's plan for dealing with difficult celebrities: They would create distance between themselves and the offending star. When I asked Zepeda in the spring of 2011 what Arquette's involvement was, he simply told me that David was taking a break but was still involved with Feeding America.

By then, Feeding America had hired a dedicated celebrity coordinator, former television producer, music executive, and celebrity booker Audrey Onyeike, to lead their entertainment industry initiatives. Back in the day, Onyeike had been Whitney Houston's publicist, at the time of *The Bodyguard*, before the scandals and the drugs.

Onyeike told the story of the Arquette split more bluntly than Zepeda: "He had a meltdown and we had to say, 'We had a nice run with you, David, but we need to back off a little bit.' It's a delicate dance and it is ongoing."

Conclusion

The inroads into the celebrity realm that Arquette paved for the charity have continued to pay off. Feeding America set the new standard for celebrity-charity partnerships. Among its other initiatives is a partnership with General Mills and the NBC weight-loss competition, *The Biggest Loser*. For every pound that contestants lose, General Mills donates a pound of food to a Feeding America food bank. The deal is regarded as a boon for all involved. Feeding America gets exposure and food, General Mills gets exposure, and *The Biggest Loser* becomes not just another exploitative weight-loss show but an exemplar of altruism.

Feeding America also partnered with the singer Beyoncé and General Mills to deliver 3.5 million meals to local food banks, and the effort was promoted during each stop of Beyoncé's 2009 tour. Matt Damon, Ben Affleck, Taye Diggs, and Ana Ortiz worked on a series of public-service announcements highlighting hunger for the organization in 2010, and in the spring of 2011, radio host Nick Cannon—husband of singer Mariah Carey—teamed up with Feeding America for the *Stamp Out Hunger* campaign.

Cannon was a great fit because he had a history of going to food banks as a kid, and the timing of the collaboration maximized the alliance's exposure. It was no accident that Cannon's involvement coincided with his very famous wife's very famous pregnancy (with twins, no less). In crafting the campaign, Feeding America realized that Cannon was going to be getting a lot of attention in May 2011, the month Carey was due to deliver.

It is Onyeike's job to exploit those opportunities. "I'm looking out for the next big thing and big person and trying to grab them before everyone else wants them," she explained.

Despite the bumps in the road, Feeding America is proud of having found a way to make hunger relief sexy. If sexy is what is needed to make sure more Americans don't go to bed hungry every night, then Zepeda and his team will keep the sexy coming, and the celebrities on board.

[1] Kristof, Nicholas. "Angelina Jolie and Darfur." *The New York Times*, 20 October 2008.

[2] Knowsley, Jo. "Air Stewardess: Secrets of My Five-Mile High Sex Romp with Ralph Fiennes." *Daily Mail,* 17 February 2007.

[3] "Wyclef Jean's Funny Money." The Smoking Gun. Turner Sports and Entertainment, 14 January 2010.

[4] Feeding America measures aided awareness, which is whether a person expresses familiarity with a brand after they hear or see the name.

[5] York, Emily Bryson. "How Feeding America Became the Go-to Cause for Marketers; Rebranding Catapults Charity onto Partners' and Celebrities' A-List." *Advertising Age,* 3 May 2010.

11

Lindsay Lohan and Charlie Sheen: The Importance of Brand Consistency

Brand consistency is the hallmark of a successful product. Consumers need to know what they are spending their hard-earned money on. When brands act erratically, consumers become confused and wary. By 2011, Lindsay Lohan had become an untenable brand. She wasn't unbankable or uninsurable; she was inconsistent and that is what caused her value to plummet. Charlie Sheen was a worse offender of humanity, morality, and the legal system than Lohan ever was; yet following his 2011 offenses Sheen was famously "winning."

It is an understatement to say that 2010 was a terrible, no-good, very bad year for Lindsay Lohan. She was erased from promotional materials accompanying the Nintendo DS video game of *Mean Girls*, the movie that just a few years earlier had solidified her stardom. Why? Marketers were afraid moms would see Lohan's face and pass. She was fired in pre-production from the biopic of porn star Linda Lovelace, by the one director still willing to take a chance on her. On top of these relatively minor indignities, Lohan was jailed, rehabbed, jailed, then rehabbed once again.

In just six years, Lohan had gone from being an asset on a project to being a liability. The press has always claimed her sloppy and seemingly drug-addled behavior makes her unbankable and uninsurable. Neither of those claims is accurate. The dirty secret of Hollywood brand management is that no one is unbankable or uninsurable; there is always money and there are always projects for a celebrity brand that is likable and consistent. Lohan had become unlikable and inconsistent. That's why no one wanted to work with her.

The story of Lohan's rise and fall is a cautionary tale for a generation of young starlets about bad decisions and poor crisis management. As Lohan moved from one side of the balance sheet to the other, from Cash Cow to train wreck, she destroyed hundreds of millions of dollars in potential brand value. But that value destruction was not the result of her self-destruction, it was the result of a seeming inability to remain consistent. She didn't follow the bad-girl narrative, a good-girl narrative, or an uplifting redemption narrative. She couldn't even stick to a lesbian narrative for the better part of a year.

Lohan's early kid-movie successes, followed by her faltering transition into the young adult market, and subsequent decline in value form an interesting object lesson in the importance of brand consistency in the Hollywood system and elsewhere.

Brand Creation and Lindsay Lohan

Lindsay Lohan began generating value at an age when most children are learning to use the toilet. Her parents signed a contract with Ford Models when she was three years old, and her red hair, freckles, and all-American adorableness landed her high-profile gigs with companies like Calvin Klein and Abercrombie Kids. At age eleven Lohan made her motion picture debut in Disney's 1998 remake of *The Parent Trap*, playing the dual role of twin girls trying to reunite their divorced parents. The film made $92 million at the global box office, and the young Lohan entranced film critics.[1] *Los Angeles Times* critic Kenneth Turan praised her preternatural poise, going so far as to refer to her as "the soul" of the film.[2]

Lohan scored a lead role opposite Jamie Lee Curtis in the wacky comedy *Freaky Friday* in 2003 at age sixteen. Film critic Roger Ebert praised the young actress for having "that sort of Jodie Foster seriousness and intent focus beneath her teenage persona."[3] Younger audiences liked her too. *Freaky Friday* earned Lohan a Breakthrough Performance award at the MTV Movie

Awards, and the film generated $160 million at the global box office.[4] As she approached her eighteenth birthday, Lohan signed on for *Mean Girls*, her first film outside the Disney family. The snarky comedy, written by *Saturday Night Live* alumna Tina Fey, became both a critical and commercial success, generating $129 million in worldwide box office receipts.[5]

Following *Mean Girls*, Lohan returned to the screen—and Disney—with *Herbie: Fully Loaded*, which earned $144 million.[6] *Herbie* was a critical failure but it represents the monetary high-point of Lohan's career and the peak of her brand value as a plucky and wholesome all-American starlet. Lohan took *Herbie*—a bad movie with a weak script—and through her star-power, talent, and brand strength transformed it into a hit.[7] The return on the studio's investment of $8 million for Lohan's salary was 300 percent.

Post-*Herbie*, Lohan had a decision to make—stay in Hollywood or head to college. For a celebrity, four years away from Hollywood is like two decades in regular-person years. The threat of lost income alone looms large, but the potential to lose momentum and an adoring audience looms larger. I interviewed Lohan in 2005 at a crowded party for the fashion house Fendi in midtown Manhattan hosted by designer Karl Lagerfeld. It took nearly an hour for her embattled publicist Leslie Sloane Zelnick to corral her client for a two-minute interview. I asked Lohan about possibly returning to the East for school. A distracted Lohan said she was considering a stint at New York University (NYU). "I'm a New York girl, and it's easy to get to London and L.A. from here," she said breathlessly, before flitting off in search of another glass of champagne, paparazzi trailing behind her.

When the paparazzi maelstrom consistently erupted around Lohan following the filming of *Herbie*, Disney executive Nina Jacobson sat Lohan down and said, "This is the moment in your career where you either become Kristy McNichol or Jodie Foster."[8] Kristy McNichol was a successful child actress in the 1970s whose erratic behavior cost her a lucrative career. Jodie Foster is a two-time Academy Award–winning actress and director who also began her career as a seventies child star.

There is plenty of supporting evidence that college does not actually hurt a young actress's career. Foster famously attended Yale University and returned to win two Oscars. Women contemporary with Lohan who chose college include Natalie Portman (Harvard), Claire Danes (Yale), Julia Stiles and Anna Paquin (Columbia), and Anne Hathaway, who attended Vassar for several semesters before transferring to NYU's Gallatin School of Individualized Study. *Harry Potter* star Emma Watson enrolled at Brown University in 2009, evidently with no fear that doing so would jeopardize her position as the highest-grossing lead actress of the past decade. At just nineteen, Watson secured $15 million for each of the *Potter* series finale's two parts (putting her 2009 earnings at $30 million) and was the top-earning woman on the *Vanity Fair* magazine earnings list for 2009, a list that included actresses twice her age.[9]

Portman and Stiles each secured spots in multimillion-dollar franchises, *Star Wars* and *Bourne* respectively. Paquin landed a role on the critically acclaimed HBO drama, *True Blood*, and Hathaway became one of the most in-demand actresses in the business. All of these educated ladies prove that talented young actresses don't have to be penalized when they go away to college.

Exhibit A: Lohan Box Office Returns in Comparison to Her Contemporaries

Figures courtesy of BoxOfficeMojo.com

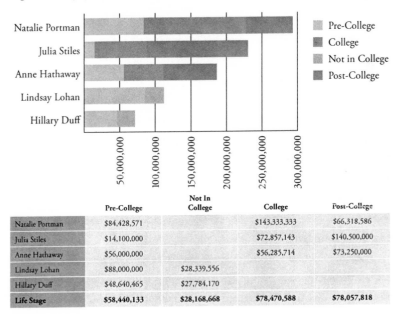

	Pre-College	Not In College	College	Post-College
Natalie Portman	$84,428,571		$143,333,333	$66,318,586
Julia Stiles	$14,100,000		$72,857,143	$140,500,000
Anne Hathaway	$56,000,000		$56,285,714	$73,250,000
Lindsay Lohan	$88,000,000	$28,339,556		
Hillary Duff	$48,640,465	$27,784,170		
Life Stage	$58,440,133	$28,168,668	$78,470,588	$78,057,818

An argument can also be made that attending college gives an actress an edge in the scrum for Academy Awards. Of the thirty-nine women nominated for the Best Actress Academy Award since 2000, twenty-five had some schooling beyond high school. The opportunity cost is low and college could have helped solidify Lohan's identity and given her something to fall back on if being famous did not pan out.

But Lohan decided not to matriculate at NYU or anywhere else. She was an impressionable teenager with poor parental guidance and the world was her oyster. So in 2006 Lohan partied hard with the likes of Paris Hilton, Nicole Richie, Tara Reid, Mischa Barton, and Britney Spears. She stayed out late, left her underwear at home, and was frequently photographed in a state of disarray. In November 2006, the *New York Post* published a picture of Spears, Lohan, and Hilton all piled in the front seat of Hilton's car, with the headline: "Bimbo summit." The accompanying article did not do Lohan's fledgling brand any favors. Inside it read: "3 Bimbos of the Apocalypse: No clue, no cares, no underwear."

Partying with these notorious bad girls put Lohan at a remove from the American consumer who had paid seven dollars (matinee prices) to see her films and made her a millionaire before she was old enough to vote.

Paris Hilton could get away with this kind of behavior, to an extent, because she created her brand by dancing on tables at nightclubs. Britney Spears got her start as a teenage Lolita inviting listeners to "Hit me, baby, one more time," and the only reason Tara Reid remained famous after her *American Pie* debut was that she was believed to be drunk all the time. (Although note that once Reid shed her apple-cheeked *Pie* persona, her projects dried up as well.) Lohan, however, had been the earnest A-student who didn't drink and didn't know how foxy she was. America didn't like this new, more vulgar version of Lohan, and that was clear in the box office totals for her next project, *Georgia Rule*. It was the first instance of Lohan's brand inconsistency.

On paper, *Georgia Rule* looked like the opportunity of a lifetime. Lohan would be starring opposite living Hollywood legend Jane Fonda, who after a long absence had made a triumphant return to the big screen with 2005's *Monster-in-Law*, a film that co-starred pop-singer turned-actress Jennifer Lopez and grossed $154.7 million.[10] There was no reason why Fonda's next film, in which she was again paired with a popular and attractive young woman, shouldn't deliver similar returns. In addition to Fonda and Lohan, the film also starred *Desperate Housewives* star Felicity Huffman and was directed by Garry Marshall, the creator of *Happy Days* and director of *Pretty Woman* and *The Princess Diaries*. It should have been a home run for Lohan.

From the start there were problems on set. A film can lose as much as $400,000 a day for each day that one of its major stars is absent from the set, and Lohan kept calling in sick after long nights of partying. In a stern letter threatening legal action against the star, James G. Robinson, CEO of Morgan Creek Productions, wrote: "We are well aware that your ongoing all night heavy partying is the real reason for your so called 'exhaustion'. We refuse to accept bogus excuses for your behavior.

"To date, your actions on *Georgia Rule* have been discourteous, irresponsible and unprofessional. You have acted like a spoiled child and in so doing have alienated many of your co-workers and endangered the quality of this picture."

Earlier in the week Lohan had been rushed from the set to a Los Angeles hospital after she "got overheated and dehydrated" from filming in 105-degree weather, according to her publicist, Sloane Zelnick. She received a vitamin B12 shot and was hydrated and released that same day. But no one was buying the dehydration story. Robinson's letter continued: "Moreover, your actions have resulted in hundreds of thousands of dollars in damage. We will not tolerate these actions any further.

"If you do not honor your production commitments, including your scheduled call time for tomorrow, and any call times thereafter, we will hold you personally accountable. This means that in addition to pursuing full monetary damages, we will take such other action as we deem necessary to preserve the integrity of the *Georgia Rule* Production as well as Morgan Creek's financial interests."[11]

The missive became public when it was leaked by a Morgan Creek employee who hoped that public humiliation might whip the young star into shape. The consumer of celebrity information was now well aware that Lohan was behaving like a professional jerk.

Georgia Rule did get made and was released on May 11, 2007. Lohan had been paid in the ballpark of $5 million to star in the film, which had an overall budget of $30 million. It received middling reviews and grossed only $24 million in worldwide box office returns.[12] Lohan not only no longer added value to a project. She destroyed it. Consumers were obviously confused about what they were buying when presented with a Lohan film.

A movie entitled *Poor Things*, in which Lohan was slated to appear opposite veteran actress Shirley MacLaine, was simply scrapped by studio executives unwilling to take the risk on the self-destructing young actress. Her fees for *Poor Things* would have remained in the $5 million ballpark, and Lohan had become expensive to insure. Hollywood insurance policies work by establishing the value of a celebrity to a project, estimating how much value will be lost if the celebrity cannot perform, and taking out a policy against that circumstance. The premium paid depends on the celebrity's worth and the risk. Lohan's worth was decreasing, but her risk was high. To be hired again, Lohan would need to post her salary as bond, or pay for her own insurance. Even on an independent film, that would run between $1 million and $2 million. Doable, surely, but worth it? All relevant parties decided that it wasn't.

Lohan's Continued Inconsistencies

Rehab is the celebrity equivalent of children being sent to their rooms. They are supposed to emerge properly humbled, having atoned for their sins. The actor Mel Gibson went to rehab to bolster his image after a DUI arrest when he made the mistake of not only driving drunk but also outing himself as an anti-Semite who believed Jews were bent on world domination. This might have been a career-ender in an industry dominated by Jewish executives, but Gibson went to rehab, repented, and made an on-screen comeback in the 2010 thriller *Edge of Darkness*.

In celebrity-world, rehab can cure anything, not just a disdain for the chosen people. Mel again found himself in hot water in 2010, when he was charged with assaulting his girlfriend, the mother of his youngest child. Still, because Mel was a consistent offender of humanity, work didn't dry up, and he appeared in the Jodie Foster flick, *The Beaver*, the next year. Former *Grey's Anatomy* star Isaiah Washington even popped into rehab for calling a homosexual costar a faggot, and professional golfer Tiger Woods began his 2010 personal redemption tour with a four-month stint of inpatient treatment for sex addiction.

Rehab looked like a sensible option for the Lohan brand.

The process started before *Georgia Rule* reached screens. On January 18, 2007, Lohan checked herself into the Wonderland Center rehabilitation facility for a thirty-day stay. In May, she checked into Promises Treatment Centers, where she remained for forty-five days. Less than two weeks after leaving Promises, Lohan refused a field sobriety test. She was taken to a local police station, where her blood alcohol level was found to be above the legal limit and where police discovered a vial of cocaine in her pocket. In August, Lohan entered the Cirque Lodge rehabilitation center in the picturesque Rocky Mountains of Utah in hopes that her third stint in rehab would do the trick.

But the erosion of her brand value continued. She was even an inconsistent rehabber, unable to commit to any sort of redemption narrative.

On August 23, 2007, Lohan pleaded guilty to cocaine use and driving under the influence. She was sentenced to one day in jail and ten days of community service, ordered to pay fines and complete an alcohol education program, and placed on three years' probation. "It is clear to me that my life has become completely unmanageable because I am addicted to alcohol and drugs," Lohan said. On November 15, Lohan served only eighty-four minutes in jail. Jail sentences for minor crimes are often cut short by Los Angeles sheriffs, who manage the county jails, because of overcrowding. After her conviction for driving under the influence, Nicole Richie spent one hour and twenty minutes in jail on a four-day sentence. Paris Hilton had earlier been sentenced to forty-five days on a driving violation and was released after three days. She was only sent back after an outcry over preferential treatment.

Lohan seemed properly chastised by her stint in jail. She didn't sell her story to anyone and managed to stay out of the press for a month. This looked like it could be the start of a comeback, if only she could stay out of the spotlight for a while. She couldn't commit to that either, and weeks after rehab she called in to a Las Vegas radio station to try to win tickets to a Hannah Montana concert for a friend's niece. It was a flimsy excuse for a woman whose publicist could have gotten her the tickets with one phone call. She was simply craving attention.

Lohan's inability to commit to treatment and a redemption narrative erased all of the modest gains from rehab. Fans don't like being taken for fools. Fool me once, shame on you; fool me twice and I'm going to buy a ticket for somebody else's movie.

Following an extended stay at the Betty Ford Center later the same year, she was seen partying at clubs and kissing anonymous men. She was hot and cold, good and bad, clean and wasted. No one knew which Lindsay they would get on a particular day. Her behavior was so self-destructive and erratic that at the end of 2007, while I was working as a reporter at the *New York Daily News*, my editors instructed me to pre-write Lohan's obituary, in case she died over a weekend or while I was on vacation.

Back in 2008, cleaning up wasn't Lohan's only path to brand redemption. Two additional narratives make a fallen celeb likeable to the American consumer of celebrity: romance and babies. But coupling-up didn't mean that Lohan had to meet a nice man, settle down, and start having those babies. In a progressive, increasingly gay-friendly culture, she had options. By 2008, Lohan was regularly seen being affectionate with rock 'n' roll heiress Samantha Ronson, an up-and-coming DJ on the celebrity party scene. Tabloids were careful with the budding romance, reluctant to "out" the starlet, but Lohan cleared up the rumors when she wrote a letter to the *New York Post*'s Page Six gossip column affirming her affection for Ronson. "I care for her very much and she's a wonderful girl," Lohan wrote. "She loves me, as I do her."[13] In an interview with

Harper's Bazaar magazine Lohan said, "I think it's pretty obvious who I'm seeing. . . . I think it's no shock to anyone that it's been going on for quite some time."[14] Gossips gave the couple the obligatory schmushed nickname "Rohan," and photographs of Lohan hopping into Ronson's DJ booth, all the while sipping water and Red Bull and other nonalcoholic beverages, ginned up the best press that Lohan had enjoyed since *Herbie*.

Going gay seemed like a good strategy for Lohan. If she could only stick with it.

But just as Lohan dropped the ball with rehab, her inability to commit to the gay lifestyle turned fans off. Lohan proclaimed her love for Ronson but was loath to describe herself as a lesbian or even as bisexual, and she frequently said that if things fizzled with Ronson—as they did in late 2009—she would go back to dating men. She was a sexuality flip-flopper.

A February 2008 attempt to resuscitate public interest with an artsy restaging of the photographer Bert Stern's famous "Last Sitting" session with Marilyn Monroe proved to be another disappointment. Hollywood nudity is difficult to do right. Public perception of the nudity discriminates along the lines of motivation and need. Serious actresses like Kate Winslet and Julianne Moore, who are widely perceived as enjoying their pick of high-profile projects, can bare all in the name of art and are often applauded for their willingness to do so. For a celebrity skirting a professional meltdown, however, the decision to pose nude is more often regarded as an act of last-ditch-effort desperation.

Stern and Lohan's shoot for *New York* magazine was at the Hotel Bel-Air, the photos duplicating the 1962 originals down to the lighting, bleached white wig, and the subject's willingness to be photographed in little more than a chiffon scarf. Talking about the Marilyn shots, Lohan said, "Here is a woman who is giving herself to the public. She's saying, 'Look, you've taken a lot from me, so why don't I give it to you myself.' She's taking control back.'"[15]

The shoot was a boon for *New York*, whose web traffic increased a stunning 2,000 percent on the day the pictures were posted. NYmag.com recorded a total of more than forty million page views that Monday and Tuesday, more than thirty-four million of which came from the Lohan portfolio.[16] That kind of traffic is worth approximately half a million dollars to a website like *New York*'s.

But Lohan only received more negative blowback. Few people in the industry or outside it believed her confident assertions about resuming control. She was called "desperate" and a "skank." One critic commented that the only thing Lohan and Monroe had in common was that they appeared intoxicated.

Lohan didn't even make money on the pictures. *New York* paid Stern a standard photographer's fee and Lohan nothing.

What Lohan and her management hadn't considered was that posing nude rarely translates into a bankable brand revival.

Likability Is the Key to Value

Value in Hollywood doesn't come from the selling of actual celebrities. Value is determined by how much money the project an individual is attached to can generate. A singer's value is quantified by album sales. If a person is a spokesperson for Maybelline mascara, then value is determined by how many tubes of eyelash enhancer are purchased. If that project is a movie, then the celebrity's value is determined by how well the movie does at the box office.

When a movie studio makes an initial investment in an actor by paying their salary, the actor is committed not only over the course of the filming but until the movie arrives in theaters. There is no secondary market. If the studio desires to exit the contract at some point in the process, it can't resell the actor or actress to the next highest bidder. The costs are sunk. So considerable effort is put into picking the right individual, one who will move the maximum amount of product.

The producers and banks that put up the financing for movies and television shows rely heavily on Q scores when figuring out which personalities to invest in. Q scores are the invention of Steve Levitt, president of Marketing Evaluations and a man who has been quantifying popularity since he graduated from Hofstra University more than forty years ago. In essence, Q scores are a measure of how likely a celebrity is to win over the American consumer.

Levitt runs a twelve-person team out of his Manhasset, Long Island, office; their job is to attach numerical figures to performers and products so that movie studios, television networks, and consumer brands looking to license a celebrity image have a way of knowing whose bright white smile will bring the best return on their investment. Rarely is a multimillion-dollar decision on an actor or actress made without a look at their Q score.

Twice a year, Marketing Evaluations evaluates more than 1,800 personalities, shows, and images. After all these years, the data that can make or break a celebrity's year is still compiled just as it was in the 1960s, with a pencil and a survey mailed out to a consumer panel. More than 100,000 American consumers, ranging in age from six to 106, are surveyed to establish the Q scores. They are given a list of personalities and brands, along with brief descriptions of each one. First they are asked whether they are familiar with a particular brand or personality. This answer is taken as a measure of "brand awareness" and affects how seriously an executive who's buying this information will take the next two scores: the celebrity's positive Q and negative Q. The positive Q is a quotient of how many people who were familiar with a celebrity feel positively toward them. The negative Q indicates how many people feel negatively. These scores are designed to be interpreted in tandem. An aspiring celebrity may be relatively unknown, and thus have a low score on measures of brand awareness, but if they have a high positive Q, they could be a good investment if exposed to a wider audience.

A person who is widely recognized but has a negative Q score is obviously a bad investment. Just how bad depends on the gap between their positive and negative Qs.

One of the reasons Lohan had difficulty getting work after 2007, and why in 2010 she was dropped from the Lovelace biopic, is that her Q scores were some of the worst Levitt has seen over his entire forty-year career.

Exhibit B: Lindsay Lohan's Q Scores 2004-2010

Provided by Marketing Evaluations

	Familiarity	Positive Q	Negative Q
2004	20%	19	20
2005	53%	13	33
2006	72%	13	37
2007	74%	11	43
2008	80%	11	51
2009	79%	9	55
2010	84%	9	52

In 2004, Lohan had a brand awareness of only 20 percent. Her positive Q was a 19 and her negative was a 20. As a Disney child star with low awareness among adults, she was at this point still considered a good investment, albeit one who needed extra attention in order to best position her brand.

By 2005, when her excessive partying and un-Disneylike behavior were being serialized in entertainment magazines, Lohan's brand awareness shot up to 53 percent and with it her negative Q, up to a 33. Her positive Q, meanwhile, dropped to 13. By 2006, her brand awareness was 72 percent—almost three out of four people recognized her face and her name. But her positive Q was only a 13, while her negative was a 37. "That's just a terrible relationship. You had three times as many people feeling negative about her as you did feeling positive," Levitt told me.

The highest possible Q score is 100, but that's rare. The average positive score is an 18. The highest ever was for Bill Cosby, who had a 71 in 1985–6. To place Lohan's scores in perspective, her college-attending contemporary Emma Watson, beloved due to her role of Hermione in the *Harry Potter* franchise, had a positive Q of 22.

With each of Lohan's inconsistent brand decisions, the gap between her positive and negative Q scores widened. After her arrests and subsequent rehabilitations, Lohan's Q again fell in 2007. With 74 percent brand awareness, she had a positive rating of 11 and a negative rating of 43. Her failed relationship with Ronson, as well as her nude photo-shoot in *New*

York magazine, increased her awareness score to 80 percent in 2008, while her positive rating remained an 11. Her negative rating, however, shot up to a 52. By any objective standard of accounting, Lohan was getting more famous and more unlikable. By 2010, 84 percent of those polled were familiar with Lohan. And yet her positive rating reached a new low of 9, her negative rating remaining at 52. More than five times as many people disliked Lohan as liked her.

"Michael Jackson had Qs in that range for a long time," Levitt explained. Almost as an afterthought he added, "His stats only went up after he died."

Lohan wasn't unbankable because her insurance premiums were too high or because she represented a risk to production schedules. Lohan was unbankable because she was unlikable and inconsistent in her behavior.

A film project is presold to markets in the United States and internationally before it is even made, and the producer takes those presale figures to a bank to obtain loans. The value of any one of the package's assets—be it an actor or a director—goes up or down based largely on public opinion and the intangible buzz surrounding that person. The banks and the movie studios are essentially placing a bet. When negative buzz about someone gets so bad as to turn people off from seeing a movie, then their value and bankability are eroded. Lohan's Q scores marked her as box office poison.

In 2009, Lohan took on another narrative when she signed on as an artistic advisor with French fashion house Emanuel Ungaro, which hired Lohan to inject a young sensibility into its brand. At least, that was its party line. In truth, Ungaro wanted to piggyback on her name recognition with the younger American market. The publicity of having Lohan aboard was what Ungaro CEO Mounir Moufarrige was after.

"Fashion is becoming boring," Moufarrige said. "Celebrities, everybody talks about. They move right, there's paparazzi. They move left, there's paparazzi. So what, she crashed her car? I crashed my car ten times." The collaboration was a failure, and Moufarrige resigned from Ungaro two months after Lohan's debut collection was panned by fashion critics. Lohan and the design firm quietly parted ways before her viral ability to deplete value could further infect the company. The next two years brought more arrests, more rehab, and more failed projects.

In 2010, Lohan was the top choice to play the complicated porn star Linda Lovelace in the biopic *Inferno*. She was struggling with low likability, but like Moufarrige, the producers believed that Lohan's name lent an edge and a certain cachet to their small independent film. From May 2010, when it was officially announced that she would star in the film, until November of that year, *Inferno* received millions of media mentions because of its connection to Lohan. But once the *Inferno* brand was in consumers' minds, they no longer needed the troubled actress. In November, after Lohan went to yet another rehab facility, the film's makers announced they were dropping the starlet from the project.

"We have stuck by Lindsay very patiently for a long time, with a lot of love and support," director Matthew Wilder said. "Ultimately, the impossibility of insuring her, and some other issues, have made it impossible for us to go forward." A similar situation arose in the spring of 2011, when producers of a John Gotti biopic floated Lohan's name—in a starring role—to the press and then retracted it. Lohan was officially signed to the film in April, but as of this writing it remained to be seen if Lohan would see the project through or if the producers wanted her for a temporary bump in media attention.

A consumer wouldn't buy peanut butter if one day it was salty and sweet and the next day it was sour. Lohan couldn't commit to being a bad girl, and she was unable to save herself and commit to being good. She was increasingly vulnerable. Her inconsistencies and her inability to exploit the system as well as it exploited her virtually ensured her career nosedive.

What Charlie Sheen Can Teach Lindsay Lohan About Brand Value

Charlie Sheen has never been a model citizen. His character on *Two and a Half Men* was based on his real-life indiscretions. Sheen has been arrested on domestic violence charges and is an admitted (and proud) cocaine addict, a promiscuous connoisseur of porn stars and prostitutes, and thrice divorced. And in 2011 he was the highest-paid actor on television, commanding a salary of nearly $2 million per episode for playing the same jerk he was in real life.

Sheen was finally fired from the CBS sitcom after he publicly insulted the show's producer and creator, Chuck Lorre. The insults came amid a series of network interviews and Internet rants, each one more bizarre than the last, in which Sheen claimed he was a warlock with tiger blood and Adonis DNA. He glorified a household in which he was serviced by two women young enough to be his daughters, kissing both of them on-air during an interview with ABC. He chain-smoked and cursed. He claimed he was clean in terms of drugs, but no one believed him. The fact that he appeared to be on a never-ending bender only made the entire performance more surreal and more lucrative.

Sheen is proof that drug use and egregiously bad behavior don't kill a career in Hollywood as long as you're consistent about it. He is peanut butter that always tastes sour, and America found that consistency delicious. Soon after his split from CBS, the entertainment conglomerate Live Nation created a licensing package for Sheen to put Tiger Blood and other catchphrases like "Duh, Winning" on T-shirts, mugs, bumper stickers, and other mall stand gag gifts.

The actor has consistently failed up. Following his public meltdown and firing from *Two and a Half Men*, the deals began rolling in. Sheen was offered a television show with Mark Cuban's HDNet network. He sold out live tour dates across the country in record time. Sheen didn't use the social media site Twitter before the incident with CBS, but when he finally embraced the medium, he gained an unprecedented three million followers in two weeks. Sheen just kept winning. He may have been making bad decisions in his personal life, but in his professional life those decisions built his brand, because they were consistent.

Brand consistency didn't work for Charlie Sheen just because he is male and men are expected to behave worse than women. It also worked for the supermodel Kate Moss, who has notoriously partied hard and abused drugs. In 2005, London's *Daily Mail* newspaper ran a photo spread of Moss snorting what they claimed was cocaine. She quickly issued an apology but never gave any indication that she'd made any lifestyle changes. In

2007, Moss came in second on the *Forbes* top-earning models list, making $9 million for the year.

Conclusion

Lindsay Lohan's rise to fame and subsequent fall from grace is a lesson in poor decision-making by a team of people who should have known better and who ultimately contributed to the downfall of a highly talented young woman. Lohan's path to punch line could have been diverted. While many of Lohan's actions can be blamed on her and her alone, it is naive to believe that an eighteen-year-old couldn't have been helped by serious-minded adults strong enough to urge her to make savvier choices and keep her on a consistent path.

Going forward, the more reckless Lohan is, the fewer movie offers she will receive and the more of a discount investors in Lohan will demand. Conversely, if Lohan operates consistently, movie offers will come in and the discount rate will go down. If Lohan can commit to the three Rs of the serious comeback narrative—rehab, redemption, romance—she might have a shot at winning America's heart—and wallet—again.

A comeback will require that Lohan no longer make her own decisions. Just as Jamie Spears, the pop singer Britney Spears's father, took over as conservator of Spears's estate when she had her very public meltdown, someone might need to step in and help Lindsay Lohan manage the internal machine, publicity, and marketing of brand Lohan and help her stick to a single script. Maybe it should be Charlie Sheen.

Worst-case scenario is that her brand value, like Michael Jackson's, has nowhere to go but up in the afterlife.

---

[1] *The Parent Trap* (1998). Box Office Mojo. IMDb.com. Retrieved 2010-3-10.

[2] Turan, Kenneth. "Happily Trapped." *Los Angeles Times*, 29 July 1998.

[3] Ebert, Roger. "*Freaky Friday*. Movie Review." *Chicago Sun-Times*, 6 August 2003.

[4] *Freaky Friday* (2003). Box Office Mojo. IMDb.com. Retrieved 2010-3-10.

[5] *Mean Girls* (2004). Box Office Mojo. IMDb.com. Retrieved 2010-3-10.

6   *Herbie Fully Loaded* (2005). Box Office Mojo. IMDb.com. Retrieved 2010-3-10.

7   *Herbie* had a production budget of $50 million and generated nearly three times that at the box office. Any movie that makes money can be considered a hit. This was a definite commercial success.

8   Waxman, Sharon. "For Lohan, a Mix of Sympathy and Scorn." *The New York Times*, 31 May 2007.

9   Newcomb, Peter. "Hollywood's Top 40." *Vanity Fair*, March 2010.

10 *Monster-in-Law* (2005). Box Office Mojo. IMDb.com. Retrieved 2010-3-10. For a romantic comedy with a budget of $43 million, it was a huge success.

11 "Lindsay Lohan Blasted for Heavy Partying." *People*, 28 July 2006.

12 *Georgia Rule* (2007). Box Office Mojo. IMDb.com. Retrieved 2010-3-10.

13 Froelich, Paula. "Lindsay Dad: Sam's 'Hideous.'" *New York Post*, 24 September 2008.

14 Heyman, Marshall. "Lindsay Lohan: Myth vs. Reality." *Harper's Bazaar*, March 2008.

15 Fortini, Amanda. "Lindsay Lohan as Marilyn Monroe in 'The Last Sitting.'" *New York*, 18 February 2008.

16 Hau, Louis. "Cashing in on Nude Lindsay Photos." *Forbes*, 27 February 2008.

12

Michael Jackson and Elvis Presley:
The Afterlife of Fame

If you've toured Graceland, tasted Cherry Garcia ice cream, or plopped a kid in front of a Baby Einstein DVD, you've bought what the dead are selling. Just because a celebrity has left this world behind doesn't mean they stop generating value and income for those still here. In fact, some celebs become more profitable after they die. Michael Jackson is one example of a postmortem Cash Cow. Death gave his brand the reinvention that would have been impossible in life; digitization and globalization could make him the most valuable dead celebrity of all time.

On July 7, 2009, Michael Jackson pulled off the greatest performance of his career—in a solid bronze casket.

The carefully orchestrated circus that was the King of Pop's memorial service at the 20,000-seat Staples Center in Los Angeles allowed family and friends to mourn the untimely death of a loved one. It was also an opportunity to turn a man castigated in life into a national hero.

The reclamation script was pitch-perfect. Jackson's brothers sat in the front row of the massive auditorium, each wearing a single white sequined glove. Mariah Carey, Stevie Wonder, Lionel Richie, Jennifer Hudson, Usher, Jermaine Jackson, and Shaheen Jafargholi all sang Jackson's songs, while John Mayer played guitar. Berry Gordy, Brooke Shields, and

Smokey Robinson gave eulogies, while Queen Latifah read "We Had Him," a poem written specially for the occasion by bestselling author and poet Maya Angelou. The crowd gave the Reverend Al Sharpton a standing ovation as he tearfully addressed Jackson's three children: "Wasn't nothing strange about your daddy. It was strange what your daddy had to deal with."

It would have been much too much for anyone but Michael Jackson, but it worked. Funeral coverage dominated cable news for two days. The social networking site Facebook reported six thousand Jackson-related status updates a minute; they came in faster than reports about Barack Obama's inauguration months earlier. The funeral spectacular marked the start of the singer's comeback and the creation of a postmortem brand.

Executives within the dead celebrity business refer to the high-net-worth deceased as "delebs," and today these executives preside over an industry that is valued at more than $800 million a year and growing. The attraction of this segment of the celebrity market is obvious: The dead are the easiest clients to manage. Not only do they not meddle in their business affairs, they won't get caught with their pants down, drunk-driving, or making a racist remark to TMZ. And in an industry where vast sums are made in merchandise licensing and symbiotic partnerships, dead celebrities have just as much earning power as the living and sometimes more.

For some deceased musicians like John Lennon or Michael Jackson, the revenue produced by their music catalogs makes up the bulk of their earnings. Approximately 60 percent of a musician's postmortem revenues comes from catalog sales. But an estate actively working to maximize merchandising opportunities will derive the second-largest share of its revenues from licensing, receiving a cut of sales from items like an Elvis Presley–themed cruise in the Bahamas, a Marilyn Monroe lace decoupage wall clock, or Steve McQueen suede leather driving shoes.

Exhibit A: Top-Earning Dead Celebrities 2006-2009

Figures courtesy of Forbes

2006

1. Kurt Cobain - $50 million
2. Elvis Presley - $42 million
3. Charles M. Schulz - $35 million
4. John Lennon - $24 million
5. Albert Einstein - $20 million
6. Andy Warhol - $19 million
7. Dr. Seuss - $10 million
8. Ray Charles - $10 million
9. Marilyn Monroe - $8 million
10. Johnny Cash - $8 million

2007

1. Elvis Presley - $49 million
2. John Lennon - $44 million
3. Charles M. Schulz - $35 million
4. George Harrison - $22 million
5. Albert Einstein - $18 million
6. Andy Warhol - $15 million
7. Dr. Seuss - $13 million
8. Tupac Shakur - $9 million
9. Marilyn Monroe - $7 million
10. Steve McQueen - $6 million

2008

1. Elvis Presley - $52 million
2. Charles M. Schulz - $33 million
3. Heath Ledger - $20 million
4. Albert Einstein - $18 million
5. Aaron Spelling - $15 million
6. Dr. Seuss - $12 million
7. John Lennon - $9 million

8. Andy Warhol - $9 million
9. Marilyn Monroe - $6.5 million
10. Steve McQueen - $6 million

2009

1. Yves Saint Laurent - $350 million
2. Rodgers and Hammerstein - $235 million
3. Michael Jackson - $90 million
4. Elvis Presley - $55 million
5. J.R.R. Tolkien - $50 million
6. Charles M. Schulz - $35 million
7. John Lennon - $15 million
8. Dr. Seuss - $15 million
9. Albert Einstein - $10 million
10. Michael Crichton - $9 million

When Michael Jackson passed away from an overdose of the powerful anesthetic Propofol at the age of fifty, he was more than $400 million in debt, some of which was accruing interest at incredibly high rates. He had been dogged for years by scandal, including charges of child sexual abuse, though a Santa Barbara County jury had found him innocent in 2005. He was the defendant in lawsuits pending in several states and foreign countries, and sixty-five creditors' claims were filed against him. Jackson had plans to embark on an ambitious series of concerts that would, he and his handlers hoped, both redeem his image and restore his bank accounts. Close friends feared that Jackson wouldn't be able to complete the concerts, which would have left the singer on the hook to the concert promoter for another $40 million, according to court papers. Jackson was not able to complete those concerts before he died.

Before his body was cold, the movers and shakers in the singer's life started hustling. From the time he passed away to the end of summer 2009, the Jackson estate grossed $100 million.[1] By the end of 2010, they had pulled in $310 million. John G. Branca, Jackson's longtime lawyer, was named as a coexecutor of the estate along with John McClain, a music executive and Jackson family friend. Branca had been the principal architect of Jackson's financial empire on and off for the two decades before his death. His clients have included the Beach Boys, the Doors, Aerosmith, and the Rolling Stones. He also represented the Elvis Presley estate for a time, but he says his world changed in 1980 when he was introduced to a twenty-one-year-old Michael Jackson. Interviewed in August of 2009, months after his client died, Branca was pleased with the results of his recent deal-making. "Clearly that's a new record for estates that likely will not be broken."

Deciding what model to adopt for the Jackson posthumous estate management did not take long. No one had done it better dead than Elvis Presley. "When you look at what the Presley estate has done, you see the opportunities," Branca said. "I quite frankly think this will be a bigger estate," not least because Branca saw that the Jackson brand had immediate opportunities in two areas Presley couldn't capitalize on during his early deleb years: the global market and the digital market. Jackson had a huge and young international fan base, including many consumers of digital media like video games, ringtones, and apps.

Elvis Presley made $55 million in 2009, thirty-two years after his death. That's more than most living celebrities make. Managed well Michael Jackson could pull in three times that amount every year for the next three decades.

The First Deleb

The King of Rock and Roll died at his Memphis home, Graceland, on August 16, 1977. His nine-year-old daughter, Lisa Marie, was left as the sole heir to the estate. Because her father's will held her inheritance in trust until her twenty-fifth birthday—February 1, 1993—Elvis's ex-wife, Priscilla Presley, managed things on behalf of her daughter. Graceland was the physical representation of Presley's legacy and a touchstone for his surviving family members, but also a bit of a financial albatross. The white-columned mansion on 13,588-acre grounds cost more than half a million dollars a year in maintenance and taxes, and Presley had not died with much cash.

"He didn't really have a lot of money, maybe $1 million in checking and $100,000 in savings, but to keep up a place like that and pay the taxes there was just no way," Presley's childhood friend Jerry Schilling, the eventual creative affairs director of Elvis Presley Enterprises (EPE) and author of *Me and a Guy Named Elvis* told me. The decision to open Graceland to the public and turn it into a tourist attraction was inspired by the necessity of raising funds just to maintain the property. Priscilla Presley formed a board of trustees for the estate and made keeping the property for her daughter her primary goal. She was the one who made the tough decision to open Graceland to the public. "It was against all odds," Schilling recalled. "The feedback in Memphis was that it would last six months."

But Priscilla had done several years of homework, even visiting William Randolph Hearst's castle in San Simeon, California, to get a first-hand look at the estate's business model. She hired a CEO, Jack Soden, to oversee the project, raised money from private investors, and according to Schilling, who was in close consultation with Priscilla during this process, Graceland was in the black six months after opening.

The estate opened for tours on June 7, 1982. Today it is one of the most popular tourist attractions in the world, seen by 566,000 people a year. The focal point of the business is the guided mansion tour, which at twenty-eight dollars a head includes a walk through the historic residence as well as an extensive display of Elvis's gold records and career mementos. In conjunction with the nearby Heartbreak Hotel, a boutique hotel catering to Graceland visitors, an automobile museum housing Presley's cars, several restaurants, and a wedding chapel, the property brings in approximately $27 million in revenue a year.

Presley's estate was immediately turned into a corporation. On the team of Elvis Presley Enterprises were CEO Jack Soden, Priscilla Presley, several attorneys, and Schilling, who had also managed the Beach Boys and Jerry Lee Lewis and would later serve as Lisa Marie Presley's first manager. (Schilling would also later give Branca his first job as an attorney, working with the Beach Boys.) EPE managed Graceland, the rights to Presley's intellectual property, and all licensing of his image for merchandising.

For two decades the Presley estate was the gold standard for deleb management. Then around the turn of the century the deleb industry began to evolve. The pool of celebrities, living and dead, had grown astronomically with the rise of cable TV, reality TV, and the Internet. The new ease of global distribution gave all celebrities the opportunity to become worldwide brands. The combination of increased competition for consumer attention, coupled with the expanding global market, made EPE realize that they needed a partner to grow the Presley business and reach a young, international audience, as well as to police unauthorized use of the King's likeness in far-flung areas of the globe like India and China.

In 2004, Robert F. X. Sillerman, a New York music entrepreneur who founded the music and sports promotion company SFX Entertainment, purchased 85 percent of EPE and Graceland for around $100 million, and added it to the portfolio of his company, CKX, which also owns 19 Entertainment, the entertainment behemoth that includes not only the *American Idol* TV show in the United States but local adaptations of the *Idol* format that air in more than a hundred countries.[2]

The deal relieved Lisa Marie Presley of $25 million in debt and allotted her a cash payment of $53 million. Presley's daughter continued to own Graceland but Sillerman and CKX controlled all the rights to the museum. The entire Elvis estate made around $45 million the year Sillerman purchased it, and he thought it could make more. His plan was to push for more aggressive marketing to make Elvis an even bigger earner.[3] Three years later, in 2007, the estate made $49 million. They were solid gains but they still needed to ensure Presley's fame didn't die with his original baby-boomer fan base, and that meant introducing Presley to an audience that wasn't yet born when the King passed away.

Exhibit B: CKX Year-End Revenue in Millions for 2008 and 2009
Figures courtesy of CKX

	2008	2009	Change
19 Entertainment	$229.2	$263.5	15.0%
Elvis Presley Business	$54.9	$60.6	10.4%
Muhammad Ali Business	$4.0	$4.2	5.1%

The CKX strategy by 2007 was to cull unprofitable licensing deals and search for more lucrative ones, such as those signed with American Greetings (whose products included gold-plated Christmas ornaments for the boomers and ecards for the younger generation) and Hershey's (who created a peanut butter and banana creme cup to mark the thirtieth anniversary of Presley's death). A limited-edition Elvis shoe from the young fashion designer Ed Hardy and an Elvis-branded debit card issued by Visa also made the cut. The company's new strategy was to cut back on the overall number of licenses by about 20 percent to keep the King's good name from being tarnished by an overabundance of tacky products. Starting from a base of more than three hundred, they pared it down to 247 in 122 countries.

CKX synergy drove another attempt to market Presley to younger fans. In 2007, using a technology called rotoscoping, Elvis Presley was seen performing a duet on *American Idol* with singer Celine Dion. In February 2010, CKX and EPE launched their grandest initiative yet, the world premiere of *Viva ELVIS* by Cirque du Soleil in Las Vegas. Out promoting this tribute to the life and music of Elvis Presley was none other than *American Idol* host—and household name amongst the tween crowd—Ryan Seacrest.

Today the Presley revenue stream consists of three components: intellectual property, including the licensing of the name, image, likeness, and trademarks associated with Presley, as well as royalties from motion pictures, television specials, and recorded music; the operation of the Graceland museum and related attractions, like the Heartbreak Hotel; and lastly, the relationship with Cirque du Soleil. CKX realizes its business model depends on maintaining the Elvis mythology. The company offers a caveat to investors in the annual report that, "although we believe that Elvis Presley fans will continue to visit Graceland and purchase Elvis Presley–related merchandise, any tarnishing of the public images of Elvis Presley could materially negatively impact our business and results of operations." And as the life, times, and artistic contributions of Elvis Presley fade further into the past, his brand value and earning power may decline if CKX doesn't continue to innovate.

Selling the Dead

Elvis Presley Enterprises pioneered a business model for selling a dead celebrity. When EPE first came together in the late 1970s, they couldn't have imagined the kinds of revenue opportunities that would exist thirty years later. Today there are few limitations on how a deceased celebrity can be packaged and sold. Things that would have seemed gauche in life become possible in death, because the deleb's image is a pastiche and a conduit for nostalgia. For example, Frank Sinatra's estate signed a deal with Warner Music Group in 2008 to explore a restaurant chain and an Ol' Blue Eyes–themed casino. A California company produces a red wine called Marilyn Merlot. Fred Astaire's widow allowed her late husband's elegant dance moves to be used to sell Dirt Devil cordless Broom Vacs in a 1997 Super Bowl halftime ad, and during the 2010 recession Steve McQueen appeared in a series of advertisements for the Swiss bank UBS that were meant to restore consumer confidence. Very little is off-limits.

Product licensing deals are pretty straightforward. Say someone wanted to manufacture cereal bowls with Presley's picture on them. They would approach CKX and pitch the idea: "We have this great idea for cereal bowls with Elvis's face at the bottom. We think it will really inspire Grandma to get all of her vitamins by plowing through to the bottom of her cream of wheat each day." CKX would then consider the deal and judge whether it could erode the integrity of the brand or if it simply feels unsavory. If CKX green-lights the project, the management company receives an advance payment from the bowl manufacturer and then a portion of the sales from each bowl sold. It also receives a quarterly reporting of sales of said bowls.

That these opportunities to exploit every deleb's image exist today is in part the result of intense lobbying efforts. Until the early 1980s, a celebrity's right to control or profit from their name or likeness died along with them, and their heirs had very little say in how the celeb's image was used. Two celebrity managers, Mark Roesler and Roger Richman, working independently in Indiana and California respectively, began publicly and vociferously arguing to change the laws, so that it would become possible to pass along rights of publicity in the same way that a house or china set is passed along. In turn, a manager—a lawyer like them—would get a percentage of the new revenue opportunities. They created a new niche business.

In 1984, Richman flew to Sacramento with the sons of John Wayne, Harpo Marx, and Abbott and Costello, and the grandson of W. C. Fields, to press California state legislators for protection of the images of deceased celebrities. Richman was ever the pitchman addressing the politicians. He showed his disgust with deleb exploitation by providing a vial of Elvis Presley's sweat—being sold with the tagline "His many years of perspiration can now be your inspiration"—and pointed to snippets of Marilyn Monroe's alleged last bedsheet being sold attached to a greeting card featuring a Monroe look-alike posing as her corpse.

The result was the 1985 passage of the California Celebrities Rights Act, which forbids the use of a celebrity's image, including a name, voice, signature, photograph, or likeness, without the permission of the family, for fifty years after the figure's death.[4] This act allows only the family and their hired agents to exploit the dead.

Far from Richman and Hollywood, Mark Roesler was working in the 1970s as a roofer to put himself through business and law school in the middle of the country. After he graduated, he began doing legal work for the company that owned the copyrights for Norman Rockwell, and he discovered that he liked working on the periphery of fame. When the Elvis Presley estate needed a business agent as they prepared to open Graceland to the public, Roesler was in the right place at the right time and landed the job. His brush with the rich and well known, even if they were long buried, inspired him to become a Hollywood agent.

"I realized, being from Indiana and the only experience I had was putting on roofs, to break into the agent business with celebrities would be a bit hard," Roesler told me. "But when I got involved with the Elvis estate, I started raising questions about why aren't other celebrities protected like Elvis?" Roesler soon realized that he didn't have to go to Hollywood to start working as an agent after all. He had grown up five miles from where film star James Dean grew up and was buried in Marion and Fairmount, Indiana.

Roesler visited with the Dean family and learned they had no idea they could own the rights to Dean's image, nor did they know that their famous ancestor's image was being used illegally all over the world. With the rise of Internet networks and search technology, it became easier for Roesler to crack down on illegal usage and to gauge the demand for Dean's image and likeness in order to determine an estimate of what the family might make.

"No one understood what they were missing back then," Roesler said. "It also wasn't a business model that could generate revenue. No one took the time to build it into a business." Several years later, Roesler fought a legal battle against Warner Bros., when they claimed ownership of the merchandising and endorsement rights to James Dean, who was under contract to them when he passed away. Roesler argued that Dean's family legally possessed those rights, and in 1992 the courts agreed. In 1993, Roesler took director Spike Lee to task on behalf of Malcolm X's widow, Betty Shabazz, for using "X" in merchandise promoting his biopic of her deceased husband.[5] And in 1994, Roesler lobbied for the creation of Indiana's Right of Publicity statute, which would protect the family's right to the image and likeness of a famous personality for a hundred years— fifty more than Richman's legislation granted—and give Roesler the ability to operate his business out of Indiana.

Once the laws had changed to give an estate control over the image and name of a deceased individual, a market naturally emerged. Roesler created the firm CMG Worldwide, headquartered in Indianapolis and with an office in Los Angeles (not the other way around, as most people assumed). Richman created the Roger Richman Agency. Both operated the way agencies like Creative Artists Agency and United Talent Agency did for living celebrities.

The market was so lucrative that by 2005 even Bill Gates wanted in. His photo archive, Corbis, purchased the Roger Richman Agency to create GreenLight. The first thing GreenLight did was cull deceased celebrities who weren't moneymakers from Richman's stable. They cut the list by about two-thirds.

Exhibit C: Roger Richman Agency Client List 2005 (Pre-GreenLight)

Clara Bow	William Powell	Leonard Bernstein
Nigel Bruce	Basil Rathbone	Maria Callas
James Cagney	Edward G. Robinson	Maurice Chevalier
W. C. Fields	Rod Serling	Bobby Darin
John Ford	Gloria Swanson	Harry James
John Garfield	Rudolph Valentino	Al Jolson
Betty Grable	Rudy Vallee	Ethel Merman
Susan Hayward	Jack Webb	Nelson Riddle
Boris Karloff	Johnny Weissmuller	Artie Shaw
Bert Lahr	Mae West	Isaac Asimov
Burt Lancaster	George Burns &	Andrew Carnegie
Gypsy Rose Lee	Gracie Allen	Albert Einstein
Vivien Leigh	Jack Benny	Sigmund Freud
Ida Lupino	Jimmy Durante	Buckminster Fuller
Walter Matthau	Emmett Kelly	The Wright Brothers
Steve McQueen	Marx Brothers	Mark Foo
Mary Pickford	George Balanchine	Goose Tatum

"To be frank, most of them weren't generating much revenue. That didn't mean they didn't have name recognition, but it meant they weren't global enough in stature. We originally cut the roster to ten folks who we believed really had potential and pushed them out globally," GreenLight vice president David Reeder told me.

Exhibit D: Corbis GreenLight Client Roster 2010

Albert Einstein	Andy Warhol	Thomas Edison
Bruce Lee	Mae West	Buzz Aldrin
Steve McQueen	The Wright Brothers	Maria Callas
Johnny Cash		

Richman may not have been as discerning as GreenLight in choosing who he represented, but he was a bulldog for his clients. He once threatened an ad agency for daring to use an image of Albert Einstein—his head half-shaved—in an ad promoting remedies for hair loss, without permission.

Today GreenLight and CMG are the two major players in the deleb industry.

"We have eyes all over the world," Reeder said. GreenLight prides itself on the quality of its client roster, and looks down on its competitor, Roesler's CMG, because of its focus on the quantity of dead celebrities they represent. With fewer clients, Reeder believes it is easier to go out and be proactive both offensively (landing new deals for clients) and defensively (making sure that a client's image is not being used by someone who has not paid to use it).

GreenLight's eclectic clientele includes the Wright Brothers, opera star Maria Callas, and actor Steve McQueen, who has had a couple of breakout years selling Ford Mustangs and watches and is very popular in Japan. They once brokered a deal for a Mexican city to use the image of Bruce Lee for a public-works water project.

"You can imagine how unsophisticated heirs are about how to value a person in the market. That's our job, to understand the market, the value of the personality, and to price that opportunity," Reeder said. "Oftentimes, when we're taking on new properties, we hear about deals the estate did before we came in and we know they underpriced."

Albert Einstein, not surprisingly, survived the cull of Richman's client list after the GreenLight acquisition. Einstein's beneficiary is the Hebrew University of Jerusalem, and since the late nineties he has earned them millions from Baby Einstein videos and Nike commercials.

Signing the Dead as Clients

When your client is no longer of this world, how do you market to them? How do you convince them to choose you over your competition? Obviously the heirs are CMG and GreenLight's target audience. But sometimes the savvy pre-dead celebrity catches their attention. Deleb new-business acquisition focuses on three categories of potential clients:

1. Deceased celebrities.

2. Celebrities who are still living but whose heyday has passed. They want help extracting maximum value from their formerly famous image.

3. Living and thriving celebrities who want to plan their postmortem estate management. This third category is the trickiest and most awkward to approach, but GreenLight's David Reeder thinks it will get easier in time, as the deleb business model becomes further institutionalized in the Hollywood Industrial Complex.

"If I were a living celebrity like George Clooney, this is something I would be taking note of. If you know you have commercial value today, then the last thing you want to happen is to have your estate put you in things after you die that you never would have done while you were alive," Reeder told me. "Maybe George Clooney doesn't want to be in a bunch of cigarette and liquor ads when he dies." Overcoming a potential client's hesitation to talk about their own death can be difficult, but Reeder stresses that postmortem image management is a valuable and necessary part of estate planning.

Then there's category number two, the formerly famous; they're not dead, but their career is. For example, CMG first became involved with former pin-up Bettie Page in the early 1990s, after Roesler got a call from his friend, *Playboy* magazine founder, Hugh Hefner.

Hefner told Roesler that a good friend of his needed some help. He explained that she was a woman who had pioneered the sexual revolution but was currently locked away in a mental institution. Roesler was confused. He didn't know who Bettie Page was. So Hefner sent a box of "Bettie things" to Roesler's Indianapolis office. There were some sex toys and bondage instruments, things the administrative assistants—all good members of their local garden clubs—were downright shocked and a little upset by. Roesler didn't think it was something he should get involved in, but he could not bring himself to say no to Hugh Hefner.

Roesler met with Page, and they made a plan to shift the focus of her image away from the nudity and onto how she changed attitudes toward "deviant" sexuality and feminism.

After Page passed away in 2008, Roesler and CMG brokered deals for three Bettie Page–themed stores that sold vintage and retro clothing combining a mid-century aesthetic with mild *Playboy*-style titillation. Page's image was used to sell a line of Bettie Page lingerie and nylon stockings for the company Secrets in Lace, and she appeared in television and online ads. From 2005 to 2010, Page was working more than she had in the previous twenty-five years, and she was dead for two of them.

For CMG and GreenLight, managing the dead is more lucrative than managing the living. The agent or manager who makes deals on behalf of a living celebrity typically takes a cut of between 10 and 15 percent. Firms that work on behalf of delebs have a cut of all deals in the ballpark of 35 percent for the agency and 65 percent for the estate.

Death Becomes Them

Death can also solve profit-draining image problems.

According to Steven Levitt of Marketing Evaluations (the firm that calculates the Q score measuring a personality's overall likability), celebrities like Presley, Johnny Cash, and Jackson become more valuable to marketers in death.

Levitt created Dead Q in response to the licensing and rights revolution happening around dead celebrities at the turn of the century, and has since watched the trend toward an increase in positive feelings for a celebrity after their death—a veritable death bump.

"Once a celebrity passes away, the public is more apt to focus on their talents and the good in their life than the bad," Levitt explained. Presley's positive Q score was at 25 before he died and in 2009 reached 34. Johnny Cash's positive Q rose from 19 to 35 following his death.

The death bump happened for Jackson as well. In February 2006, Michael Jackson's positive Q score was a 9 and his negative was a 67. According to Levitt, that was a historical low within the entire celebrity population. But by November 2009, five months after his death, Jackson's positive Q had skyrocketed to a 34 and his negative Q had dropped to a 27. It was an unprecedented turnaround, played to the sound of dinging cash registers. With likability comes marketability.

Jackson's longtime friend and lawyer John Branca had a plan in place to proceed to business as usual just a week after the singer died—before those elaborate funeral plans were even finalized. Jackson's will and trust granted his mother, Katherine, guardianship of Michael's three children and 40 percent of his estate for the remainder of her life. His children would receive a combined 40 percent of the estate and whatever remained in Katherine's trust upon her death. The remaining 20 percent would go to charities benefiting children.

The will also named Branca as coexecutor of the estate and hence responsible for generating money for the estate. Thankfully Branca had a knack for making money where no money had been made before. It was he who found the financing for Jackson's 1982 hit *Thriller*. At a time when music videos typically cost around $50,000 to make, the young and impetuous Jackson was letting his creativity run wild, driving costs for the video to around $1 million, with no clue how to pay for it. In a move that would eerily foreshadow a deal for movie rights sold after Jackson's death, Branca suggested making a separate video filmed by somebody else about the making of the *Thriller* video. He pitched the idea to MTV and Showtime and returned with $1.2 million in financing. The *Making of Thriller* video sold more than a million copies. Album sales spiked by fourteen million, bringing the grand total to more than forty million and making it one of the most successful albums of all time.[6]

The pair were inseparable for many years. Jackson was the best man at Branca's first wedding, at which the Reverend Little Richard presided. But they parted ways several times over the years, as various family members and managers quibbled over the level of Branca's influence in Jackson's affairs. The call to reunite for the last time came less than a month before the singer's death and was made by Jackson's newly rehired manager, Frank DiLeo, who told Branca that Jackson wanted his input once again. Branca met with Jackson on June 17, 2009, at the Forum in Inglewood, where the King of Pop was rehearsing for his big comeback. "We hugged each other," Branca said. "He said, 'John, you're back.' It was very emotional. I showed him the agenda." It was exactly what Jackson wanted, Branca said, including a concert movie, books, and merchandising deals.[7]

Branca and coexecutor McClain knew that refurbishing the tarnished Jackson brand would first require refocusing attention on his talent. It started with the memorial service and continued with a documentary-style film cobbled together from rehearsal tapes for his London comeback, *This Is It.* It was backstage raw footage similar to that used for the *Thriller* documentary. The film made $72 million at the domestic box office and nearly $189 million overseas.[8]

"People came away from that movie with a completely different view of Michael," Branca said. "Rather than being this out-of-control eccentric, they saw him as the ultimate artist, the ultimate perfectionist, but at the same time respectful of other people."[9]

Jackson's three children, who prior to his death had been hidden from the world, also played an integral part in rehabilitating his brand once they were brought into the spotlight. Prince Michael, Paris, and Blanket proved themselves to be well behaved, unnervingly polite, and utterly enamored of their father in the year following his death.

The offers just rolled in.

In March of 2010, Sony Music Entertainment announced a seven-year distribution deal for as many as ten new Jackson projects—including unreleased recordings, DVDs, and even video games—valued at around $250 million. The estate claimed to have around sixty unreleased recordings of Jackson's that could be packaged into two or three albums. The real moneymaker, however, would be the video games. In January 2011, the world was introduced to *Michael Jackson The Experience,* created by Ubisoft for the Wii, a fully interactive video game in which players learned Michael's signature dance moves. It was soon rated the number one video game on Amazon and by April had sold more than three million copies before the company launched the game on the Xbox 360 and PlayStation 3. Taking the Jackson brand fully digital, the games were integrated with Facebook, so players could auto-update their pages on the social network with progress, pictures, and other achievements from their playtime.[10]

Delebs do eventually go cold. While Jackson's estate enjoyed large returns immediately following his death, they cannot expect to maintain that rate of return, in the hundreds of millions, on a yearly basis without a lot of hustle. Branca and his team were lucky to have a merchandising and licensing plan already in the works when their client passed away, so that they could hit the ground running that summer. Jackson nostalgia fueled the sale of thirty-one million albums in the first year after his death alone.

"The prices are highest up to two years after the celebrity has passed," longtime celebrity autograph and memorabilia dealer Todd Mueller told me. The same holds true for partnerships and licenses. When the rush of initial curiosity and emotion expires, the real work of brand value extraction begins. In addition to the major deals, the film deal and Sony, on the buy-side there was a serious market for Jackson licensing for twelve months after his death. Matt Delzell is an account director at Davie Brown Entertainment, a marketing firm that helps brands like AT&T, State Farm, and Frito-Lay pair up with celebrities for licensing or promotions. Starting in June 2009, Delzell told me, clients were clamoring to work with Jackson.

"Michael Jackson is so sustainable because he is such a global icon and a global opportunity," Delzell said. "And today, with the technology available, musical artists will be able to record new songs with him. Elvis didn't have that when it was two, three, or five years after his death, when his music was still very much in people's minds."

So will Michael Jackson ultimately be a bigger moneymaker in the coming decades than Elvis Presley? The fan bases are equally strong. The major revenue streams are similar: image and likeness licensing deals; intellectual property deals, including album sales, films, and TV programs; video games; and the wild cards, like Graceland or Cirque du Soleil.

But the multimedia opportunities today far surpass what was available when Presley died, and it is these advances in technology—such as the video games mentioned above—that will likely allow the Jackson estate to surpass the Presley estate in value.

The Jackson estate will need to gin up a wild card, some kind of mother ship for Jackson's image. The Presley estate has Graceland, which not only generates income from visits and sales of memorabilia but also helps keep the Presley legend tangible for generations who never experienced the singer in life. The Jackson estate anchor could be a physical presence like Graceland or some form of digital multimedia monument. It will probably be something the likes of which we have never seen before, just as the singer was during his life.

Jackson's near mythical Neverland Ranch, named for the place in *Peter Pan* where children never grow up, will never be the physical touchstone that Graceland is. To save the property from foreclosure, majority control was taken over by Colony Capital LLC (an international investment firm with stakes in French professional soccer team Paris Saint-Germain and Raffles Hotels and Resorts) in 2008, though at the time of Jackson's death the estate still owned an undisclosed partial stake in the ranch.

Where Graceland is near to metropolitan Memphis and very accessible, Neverland Ranch is a two- to three-hour drive from Los Angeles on a good day. Visitors take a winding mountain road to reach the estate, which is surrounded by neighbors who are none too keen on sharing their seclusion with a theme park. Even though it contains two railroads and various amusement rides, like the Pirate Ship, the Octopus, and the Wave Swinger, in today's amusement park market it not only comes across as dated but also as a little sad, like a long-abandoned boardwalk. Being the site where many of Jackson's accusers claim that he mistreated them, the place is still haunted by the ghosts of scandals past. Still, the idea of Neverland is worth more than the actual property. By 2011, the estate was in talks to license the Neverland name and concept out to a third party, with the possibility of creating an interactive theme park in a place like Las Vegas or Dubai. If Neverland can be recreated as a franchise opportunity, it could be a venture several times more lucrative than Graceland, by virtue of being exportable around the globe.

Conclusion

In October 2010, *Forbes* magazine compiled its macabre annual list of dead-celebrity earners. Michael Jackson blew Elvis Presley out of the water with earnings of $275 million. That was more than that made by Lady Gaga, Jay-Z, Beyoncé, and Madonna combined.[11] And Jackson had added $35 million to that figure by the end of the year.

"Six months before Michael Jackson died you couldn't give away an apparel license. There was too much baggage associated with Jackson," CMG's

Roesler said more than a year after Jackson's death. Minimizing the resurfacing of that baggage will be paramount to maintaining revenue for the estate.

Others are even more optimistic that the massive baggage doesn't matter anymore. "The Jackson estate has all the necessary tools to go on forever," former Elvis Presley Enterprises executive Schilling told me. "People ask me all the time, 'Why Elvis? Why is he still out there thirty years later?' First of all it's because of his talent and his career when he was alive. And after that you need a strong organization."

Going forward, it may be prudent for Branca and the Jackson management team to sniff out a willing partner like CKX, who can take advantage of synergies with other clients, or else hire a CMG or GreenLight to handle the continued exploitation of Jackson's rights. It took years to perfect the postmortem Presley brand. Jackson's estate is estimated to reach the billion-dollar mark less than five years after his death.

Managed properly, the Jackson legacy will be a hugely profitable endeavor for all players who (legally) ride the King of Pop's sequined coattails, and it will be the new model for how celebrities make money in the afterlife.

[1]   Arango, Tim. "Jackson Earnings Grow by Millions After Death." *The New York Times*, 12 August 2009.

[2]   Elvis Presley Official Web Site, 21 July 2010.

[3]   "Lisa Marie Presley Selling Elvis Estate." Associated Press, 16 December 2004.

[4]   Glionna, John M. "The Late, Great (and Profitable)." *Los Angeles Times*, 6 October 1997.

[5]   Horovitz, Bruce. "When X Equals $: Spike Lee's New Film Creates an Instant Icon." *Los Angeles Times*, 3 November 1992.

[6]   Daly, Michael. "Michael Jackson Turned to Old Friend and Entertainment Lawyer John Branca in Times of Trouble." *New York Daily News*, 2 July 2009.

[7]   Deutsch, Linda. "MJ Estate Executor Branca Was Close Friend, Architect of Extraordinary Wealth." Associated Press, 15 August 2009.

[8]   *This Is It* (2009). Box Office Mojo. IMDb.com. Retrieved 2010-7-20.

[9]   Sisario, Ben. "A Year Later, Jackson Estate Is Prospering." *The New York Times*, 22 June 2010.

[10]   Lee, Chris. "Michael Jackson Estate, Sony Music Entertainment Strike Distribution Deal." *Los Angeles Times*, 16 March 2010.

[11]   Greenburg, Zach O'Malley. "The Rich Afterlife of Michael Jackson." *Forbes*, 25 October 2010.

Acknowledgments

This book wouldn't have happened if my wonderful and amazing Jane Friedman hadn't recognized that a former gossip columnist could and should write something serious about the business of celebrity.

I want to thank Brendan Cahill and Mary Sorrick for taking a three-page outline to twelve chapters, my editor Megan Hustad for making my words sing, Nicole Passage for reading it one hundred times, and Libby Jordan and Lisa Weinert for being my biggest cheerleaders throughout this process.

Thanks to George Rush, Joanna Molloy, Ben Widdicombe, Colleen Curtis, and Chris Rovzar for turning me from a green journalism school graduate into a stealthy reporter, especially Joanna Molloy for telling me to always follow the money.

And to the many friends who read dozens of drafts: Sara Chadwick Jackie Cascarano, Christine Ryan, Benny Castaldo, Denise Warner, and Evan Meagher. And finally to my parents, John and Tracey Piazza, who I think finally understand what I have been doing this past decade.

cover design by Milan Bozic
interior design by Danielle Young

paperback ISBN 978-1-4532-5819-4
hardcover ISBN 978-1-4532-0555-6

Published in 2011 by Open Road Integrated Media
180 Varick Street
New York, NY 10014
www.openroadmedia.com

BY: _____

CPSIA information can be obtained at www.ICGtesting.com
Printed in the USA
BVOW040349200412

288120BV00002B/2/P